FOREIGN INTRIGUE

FOREIGN INTRIGUE

THE MAKING AND UNMAKING OF A FOREIGN SERVICE OFFICER

Eric Kocher

NEW HORIZON PRESS
Far Hills, New Jersey

Library of Congress Catalog Card Number: 90-52985

Eric Kocher
  Foreign Intrigue

ISBN: 088282-054-0
New Horizon Press

To Peggy.

To all the Kochers everywhere.

and

To the Creative Writing Group of Great Neck, New York.

CONTENTS

PART III—THE UNMAKING OF A FOREIGN SERVICE OFFICER

PREFACE

When I think back over my Foreign Service career, it is easy to remember major events—not only the pleasant ones, but, sometimes, even more vividly, the ugly ones that many psychologists tell us we are more likely to forget. Whatever the nature of the event, however, I remember it imperfectly, with its edges undefined and often in shadow.

I kept no journal or diary during those years, so there remained no written word to capture the details and nuances of exactly what transpired. I did sometimes consult those individuals who were still alive in my search for accuracy, but, unfortunately, many of them are now dead, their personal memories lost to me forever. Although, for the sake of privacy, I have changed some names, still, I have certainly held to the original tone and mood of each event included in this book, even if I cannot vouch for the precise details of chronology of some events and the exact words used in each conversation. My apologies to those whose words I try to reconstruct but who might have phrased them better.

What you will find in the following pages is the truth as I remember it.

PROLOGUE

I emerged from the revolving door into the sunlight and stopped. I took a last look back. Behind me in the lobby of the State Department building stood an American flag with its stars and stripes, and, beside it, the Secretary of State flag with its stars and eagle, one claw holding an olive branch and the other holding arrows. Even then, in the intensely bright light, the lobby, as seen through the glass of the entryway, seemed murky and cast in gloom.

In my hand was a piece of paper I had just been given by the Retirement Branch of the Department of State. The paper officially informed me that I was retired as of that day, July 1, 1968. It also informed me that I would be getting a disability pension—rather hefty, and tax-exempt at that. Still, I was restless, dissatisfied, and I had no reason for being either: I might be through with the Foreign Service, but I certainly wasn't through working. In fact, I had already accepted an offer from Columbia University to become associate dean of its School of International Affairs. Peggy, my wife, and I were already caught up in the struggle to find an apartment in New York for the fall.

I felt the paper in my hand again. It was the last tangible vestige of my career in Foreign Service, and made me suddenly and sharply aware of the absence of two other traditional tokens of leave-taking.

I was missing another piece of paper given routinely

to retirees, a certificate signed by the Secretary of State and presented in an elegant calligraphic hand, for "loyal and meritorious service to the United States Government." Since I had not been given this certificate, the implication was clear: I had obviously failed to perform loyal and meritorious service to the United States Government. A year earlier the implication would have enraged me; now it only brought a wry smile to my face.

I was also missing the alcoholic high that I often brought with me from the small receptions usually thrown for high-ranking retiring officers. Today my head was completely clear because there had been no reception.

Exactly what was "loyal and meritorious." The phrase lingered in my mind. Does an officer's contribution have to be recognized by the Department before it becomes "loyal and meritorious?" Since the certificate is awarded uniformly to all retirees who have not embarrassed the Department, does it then become a meaningless pat on the back? And if so, how can its denial or absence be a slap in the face?

These and other thoughts continued to haunt me as I walked away from the Department into the hot sun of July, my certificate of retirement still clutched in my hand.

PART ONE

THE MAKING OF A FOREIGN SERVICE OFFICER

ONE

All's Well That Begins Well: The Early Years

I was already half-way through my career when my friend Rob McClintock summarized his years in the service for me, "If you're not paranoid in the Foreign Service, you must be crazy." Rob had been ambassador to Cambodia when the unstable Prince Sihanouk was its ruler, and ambassador to Lebanon in the 1950's when the country was in turmoil. He, if anyone, knew what he was talking about. I remember a picture of him, riding through Beirut in the back seat of a long convertible, top down, American flag waving, his white poodle and swagger stick on the seat beside him, being chauffeured to an important meeting through streets filled with hostile mobs. You have to be crazy to carry off something like that. But his flair for drama and incongruity quieted the astonished rioters, and he made the front page of *The New York Times* the next day. Any rationally thinking person would have been relegated to the obituary page.

"Rob," I said admiringly, "Craziness must have been one reason why I entered the service."

It was clear to anyone that a career, whose prerequisites included a full day of written, oral, and psychological testing, plus endless security checks, and whose lifestyle ordinarily prevented the successful candidate from leading a normal family life, must have special attractions. Foreign

travel, adventure, new people, new languages and new
countries were some of the attractions.

Like thousands of others, I entered the Service for
these obvious reasons. But, as I listened to Rob, I realized I
too had always cherished a bit of the irrational, of the un-
predictable. I didn't adopt a white poodle or a swagger
stick, but I did make many misguided efforts to solve insoluble problems. I have always enjoyed a little craziness in
my life, and I was not disappointed in all my twenty two
years in the Service.

As it turned out, these were not my only reasons for
entering the Service.

My earliest international memory—in fact, my earliest
memory of any kind—is of a tramcar screeching and swaying along the savannah past Queens Royal College in Trinidad. In those pre-World War I days, Trinidad was part of
the British West Indies. My father, a German, had, in the
best Horatio Alger tradition, left southern Germany to seek
his fortune. His father, a brewer in the Kocher River area
of Wurttemberg, wanted him to become a minister, a prospect my father distinctly wanted to avoid. Instead of looking for work in other parts of Germany, he opted to go
abroad. Perhaps "international" was also in his blood.

For whatever reason, he worked in Belgium for several years until he was advised by a doctor to seek a
warmer climate, as he suffered from chronic sinusitis. He
soon indentured himself to a Trinidad cocoa plantation
owner. Like many wise young men, he married the boss's
daughter, and, eventually, became a partner in the cocoa
business. My mother had been born in the United States,
but her parents were also German.

My second earliest memory has to do with *Coolie
Hosein*, the annual Trinidad festival of the native coolies,
when poverty and illness are forgotten for one glorious
evening of revelry. I can see myself—a small boy trembling
with excitement and terror, clinging to a column of our

house, from behind which I could watch the revelers flowing into our garden. Dressed as fantastic dragons and huge devouring birds, the natives danced closer to me to the deafening beat of the drums. As if in a nightmare, I was hypnotized, unable to move, talk or cry out. Suddenly, a huge, fantastic bird in red and purple feathers danced around the column, stretching out his claws to touch me. Released from the spell, I fled screaming into the house, there to be solaced by our old cook, who was always there when I needed comforting. On that day of *Coolie Hosein,* she was unusually sad, her eyes filled with tears. As always when tears replaced her smile, she came to me with a small tin cup and begged me to urinate in it. Laughingly, I did so. She took the cup and drank the liquid, a soft smile spreading over her face. The urine had done its work. It had washed away her sadness—at least for a while. Even today, when I see a tin cup, I think back affectionately to our devoted old cook and the curious way in which she would drown her sorrows.

My next memory fades to World War I. I was four or five and completely unaware of battles, of what they were or that they were even taking place. What I did know, however, was that my father had been thrown into a prisoner-of-war camp because, as I found out later, Germany and England were at war and all Germans and their families instantly and automatically became enemy aliens.

I visited my father twice a week and, as I remember, the camp was not unpleasant. He was living with about 40 other POWs in a small wooden barracks and was apparently well fed. Because of his abundant common sense and genial disposition, he was chosen by his fellow prisoners to be their leader in all negotiations with the British concerning camp matters.

I can picture myself—the same small boy, this time in a large white sailor hat that protected me from the burning sun—on a visit to the camp. According to my sister, the whole family was allowed to enter the camp compound. She and I would climb on my father's knee, while mother and my older brother sat next to him. Dad would point out the little garden he was cultivating, flowers or vegetables I cannot remember which, but it was only when he talked of them that the sad dispirited look on his face gave way to lively satisfaction.

My oldest brother Paul and my mother remember the hostility with which we were treated by the British, but I remember no incident with my few British playmates that indicated my world was changing.

As I grew older, my memories accumulated rapidly. In 1919, when I was six years old and the war was over, my father was finally released, after four years of internment. His interests in the cocoa business, which had been confiscated by the British at the beginning of the war, were never returned, and the family was urged—perhaps even forced—to leave Trinidad. We had one close relative at that time, my grandmother on my mother's side, who lived in Brooklyn. With her consent, we decided to move in with her until my father could establish himself in business.

I remember the eagerness of the whole family to move to America. Not only would my parents be able to escape the hostility they still felt in Trinidad, but even then America emitted an aura of glamor and moneyed well-being which intrigued and excited me. Its unknown quality also made me apprehensive, and that particular combination of excitement and fear became a recurring theme through much of my life.

Immediately upon arrival in America, my father applied for United States citizenship. I remember the passion in his usually gentle voice when he soon thereafter urged his children to become citizens of any country where we might eventually be working. Otherwise, he warned, we, too, might spend years in a prisoner-of-war camp.

In school, both prep and college, I majored in French and Spanish language and literature. I learned to read and write them as skillfully as I read and write English. I never questioned my competence in language until I went on my first European trip—a gift of my grandmother after I graduated from Princeton in 1932—and found to my dismay that I could read everything and say nothing.

On my first night in Paris I bought a map and visited on foot many of the major sightseeing attractions on the left and right banks, arriving back at my hotel at dawn. This was living at its most glamorous, a night I hold precious as my first glorious introduction to international living. But despite my excitement, I was angry. Why couldn't I speak the damn language? Here I was in Montmartre, the very center of Parisian night life, mingling with the painted filles de joie roaming the streets, and failing miserably to communicate with them.

In my naive schoolboy fashion I wanted desperately to ask them—for sociological reasons, of course—why they were whores, what actual traumas and family disasters had brought them to the oldest of professions. I used gestures, smiles, grimaces, and in return I received smiles, gestures, and endless undecipherable phrases. The evening, though not without its attractions, left me dissatisfied and resentful toward all the language teachers who had taught me over the years but who had failed to teach me to communicate with foreigners. Frustration, then, was another motivation for my international career.

When I graduated from college, the country was mired in economic depression. There were few, if any, jobs for the inexperienced. My father, accordingly, sent me to Harvard Business School to earn an MBA. It was an expense he could ill afford, but he claimed the degree would be useful in the business career I would undoubtedly enter. I had no interest in business, but I did not resist. I also have no doubt that if I had gone to my father with a proposal for any other career, he would have supported me in my choice. Alas—I had no choice! I knew little of the working world, and, apart from a few obvious professions such as doctor and lawyer, I knew nothing about careers.

At that time, I was only nineteen. The reason for my early graduation—and my naiveté—was that in school I had stuck to my books. I had participated in no extracurricular activities. I had literally spent all my time, except for a daily swim, in the library or in my room, studying. I seldom read the papers and knew little of events outside the school.

I was also bored at Harvard. I spent two years with no goal other than good grades. None of my studies interested me. Again I indulged in no extracurricular activities. I stayed glued to my books, finding the courses difficult and ending my first year having failed marketing. It was my first flunk in all my years of school and the thought mortified me. I should have suspected then that business was not my forté, that I should look elsewhere for a career, but fortunately I did not drop out. The MBA, though I never used the substance of its courses in any of my future careers, was instrumental in landing me a job in 1934.

The economic depression was still ravaging the country, and even with my MBA I found no openings in New York. My father suggested I go to Washington. There, with his New Deal, Roosevelt was opening up new government agencies almost every month. Jobs were available. This was a difficult suggestion for my father to make: an ardent Republican, he was sending his son into a nest of Democrats.

"Go to Washington," he said sadly. "Even with the Democrats. But you'll come back to New York in a year or two."

I went to Washington. It would be seven years before I would return, just before World War II.

In Washington, my two jobs in the New Deal had no direct relationship to anything international, but they contributed in an odd way to my leanings toward an international lifestyle, at that time still largely undefined and only vaguely felt. I first worked at the Federal Housing Administration. It was a night job, eight in the evening to two in the morning. I was assigned to a calculating machine in an enormous room filled with perhaps seventy or eighty similar machines. The clattering was like a Walpurgis night. I partially escaped into a more seductive world by imagining the surrounding din was actually modern dissonant music, which then led my mind to thoughts of symphonies and opera houses and from there to Asia, Africa, Europe, everywhere.

I soon got a promotion and found myself wrestling with the problem of correlating rents with a number of toilets and rooms in Detroit, a deadly kind of statistics and an equally deadly job. My only consolation was that I was at least earning a salary which, for the first time, enabled me to support myself.

Later, as one of the first employees in the newly organized Social Security Administration, I found myself with the fancy title of Associate Social Science Analyst, and then Associate Economist. I worked on forms and developed procedures which processed claims of applicants for benefits. The higher I got on the promotional ladder, it seemed, the drearier the work and the more pretentious the title.

I realized that forms and procedures were essential to the success of a vast organization. I also realized that some individuals found that kind of work rewarding, but I knew I wasn't among them. However, I was reluctant to throw over a job that offered me a reasonably good living, especially while America was still struggling through its most severe depression. On every street corner unemployed fathers were selling apples for a living, and "Brother, Can You Spare A Dime?" had become the plaintive hit song of the time.

It was confusing for me to feel boredom in Washington during the 1930's. Roosevelt's New Deal had ushered in a surge of enormous high morale—of heightened spirit and dedication—but, alas, I felt this only vicariously. What I did feel was tremendous envy for all those who so joyously embraced a working day of ten or twelve hours without even a thought of overtime or extra compensation. A new and revolutionary thought began to present itself to me: work did not need to be the burden that my father felt when he started working in New York. Unconsciously and early on I must have absorbed his feelings of powerlessness and obligation. He had been forced, by the misfortunes of war, to nail himself to a job that gave him no satisfaction in order to provide for his family. In my mind, sacrifice and

work had became inseparable. What was true for him
would be true for me. I could not morally collect a pay
check until I had paid for it with burden and boredom.

And so, ultimately faced with the evidence that all
around me in Washington people seemed to be having fun,
that the more the New Dealers worked, the more replen-
ished with energy they seemed to become, I chose to look
inward. What career would excite and render me wholly
alive? I yearned for something to involve me emotionally. I
instinctively thought "international" without even knowing
how it applied to me or how it could be applied.

Thus, my Washington experience, which so far
amounted to five years of stupefying work, indirectly and
in mysterious ways led eventually to international work.
Negative stimuli can be just as productive as positive ones
in sorting out a career and advancing toward a goal.

There were a few bright lights in my otherwise glum
Washington landscape. The brightest perhaps was Pauline
Frederick, who was working at the North American Newspaper Alliance before becoming NBC correspondent to the
United Nations. We became good friends, and she twice
invited me to the annual press ball at the White House and
introduced me to Eleanor and Franklin Roosevelt, the Presidential couple I most admire in recent history. Both evenings were memorable.

It was about this time that I finally became aware of
the Foreign Service. Actually, I knew more about the Foreign Legion than the Foreign Service. After all, the bold
gentlemen of the Foreign Legion had been glorified in
"Beau Geste" and numerous other films riding heroically
through desert outposts, their capes swirling in the wind.
All I knew about the Foreign Service was that it was somehow part of the Department of State, which I passed every
day on my way to work. State was then housed in an aristo-
cratic old building next to the White House. It was reputed
to be filled with cookie pushers and men in striped pants or

tuxedos always rushing to a series of endless parties, there
to be served by waiters in white uniforms, offering exquisite canapes and caviar from silver platters.

Odd, the metamorphosis of my cocktail party experiences. First, an unattainable vision, then to the glamor of
actual achievement, and, finally, to revulsion after years of
too many, too frequent.

Passing the State Department building every day set
something stirring inside me, if only a feeling of "Why not
me?" But it was no easy gestation. Only years later, in the
Army, would the feeling become an urge. At the moment, I
was still too deaf to hear the call.

After five years in the Civil Service, I left Washington
in desperation to study playwriting at Yale, certainly as desperate to escape as to write plays. I had loved the theatre
for many years, and, with the complete assurance of youth,
I felt convinced I could write a play to rescue Tallulah
Bankhead, my favorite star at the time, from the mediocre
plays she kept appearing in year after year. It seemed at the
time a perfectly logical assumption.

A lot of things seemed likely in 1939. It was likely
there would be a war; it was likely I would be in it; and,
unless I took a fast dive into playwriting, it was likely I
might never have another chance to do so.

I smiled as I signed up for Yale, realizing that after
graduation I would have gone to all three major Ivy League
schools: Princeton, Harvard, and Yale. There was something embarrassing about that heavy triumverate; it's ne-
cessity seemed to suggest immaturity and ignorance about
my future, but I doubt that I saw it that way at the time. As
one of my puzzled friends suggested at the time, "Why are
you going to so many colleges? Are you so dumb you can't
learn anything?"

Whereas in Washington it had been difficult to meet
anyone not working in government, at Yale it was similarly
difficult to meet anyone not obsessed with the theatre. In
fact, so absorbed were these students in the theatre that no
one was interested in politics and very rarely could you
find anyone even remotely aware of an imminent war.

After my first year at Yale, I went to Provincetown on Cape Cod for the summer to write a play for Tallulah, although she did not know it. It appeared that half of the artistically-inclined refugees pouring in from Europe were summering there because of its reputation as the bohemian capital of the East: Hans Hoffman, Anais Nin, Lilli Palmer, Lisette Model, and, most particularly, Valeska Gert, the great dancer-singer-mime from Germany.

The daughter of a Berlin butcher, Valeska left home at an early age and soon stripped herself of her bourgeois background. In pre-war Berlin she had become a reigning star of cabarets and night clubs with her own coterie of groupies who visibly adored her for her rebellion against all things bourgeois. Valeska dressed to shock. Her black hair was closely cropped like a man's crewcut. With her red lips, blunt nose, and red, loose-flowing pajamas she purposely resembled a clown. She swished her hips on the street, provoking stares, curiosity, and sometimes unease, the combination of which she loved and aimed to promote. Many people assumed she must be a prostitute, although sexually speaking, Valeska was one of the purest people I knew. She never drank or smoked and was convinced that stimulation should come from within. "It's inside and you just pull it out when you need it," she advised. To my knowledge, she never had a lover, either male or female, in either Provincetown or New York. In the milieu in which she moved, abstinence was an anomaly.

Valeska was determined to start a night club, and when she heard about my business background she decided I should be her manager. It was a wild idea, of course. What did I know about running a night club? About running anything? Two years earlier I would have run the other way, but the decision to escape Washington had given me a new kind of self-assurance. I no longer felt compelled to submit to self-destructive situations if I didn't want to. I had a choice, and I realized I was eager to embrace the bizarre. I was ready to try new ventures, new ideas. I agreed to work with Valeska until I had to go back to Yale in the fall, and so, in an empty shack near the beach, we

started a small night club that proved moderately successful.

In general, I gravitated naturally toward Valeska and
the other refugees, who were much more interesting than
the Americans I met in Provincetown. Then one day I met
Tennessee Williams, coyly dodging the waves along the
beach.

The night he showed me a copy of his first major play,
"Battle of Angels" was unforgettable. The precipitate closing of the play in Boston some months earlier had left him
despondent and financially bankrupt. I read it and knew
immediately that he had enormous talent. In the next few
months, I helped him with meals whenever I was paid
from my two legitimate jobs, one collecting bills for a local
doctor and the other valet-parking for the Lobster House.

Many evenings Anais Nin would sit with me on the
curb while I waited for the next car to park. She wore
gypsy clothes and loose, flying hair, and sexuality seemed
to be her specialty. We would discuss its relationship to the
spirit, then she would compare the sexuality of European
men with that of American men, the latter clearly losing
her personal vote.

What with these diversions, jobs and the night club, I
never did finish my play for Tallulah.

When I graduated from Yale the following year, I
helped Valeska start a night club in New York's Greenwich
Village. She called it the Beggar Bar. I introduced Tennessee to Valeska and she gave him a job as a waiter. Every
weekend, Tennessee, who wrote his name 10/c, would wait
tables and read his poetry to the clientele. Julie Hayden,
who would later play in his "Glass Menagerie," but who on
those evenings looked like any other star-struck groupie,
was often in the audience.

Tennessee did well as a waiter, but Valeska, despite her
broad view of life and people, was miserly and small when
it came to money. At the end of one Saturday evening when
Tennessee handed over the cash he had collected, Valeska
suspiciously demanded, "Where's the rest?"

"That's all," he said. The tips, of course, he would keep for himself.

Valeska demanded to see the money he was withholding; her voice was angry and accusing. Tennessee listened to her tirade without a murmur, and, finally, in a sudden gesture of rage, he dug deeply into his pocket, produced a handful of coins and flung them at her face. They landed on her cheeks and fell to the floor. She looked at him in silent amazement, the first time I have ever seen Valeska at a loss for words. Still voiceless, Tennessee turned and rushed out. He never saw her again. But his memories of that night must have softened, for in his *Memoirs* he refers to her as "the incomparable Valeska Gert."

That winter was memorable in another respect. I met my future wife.

I had signed up for a playwriting course held jointly by Theresa Helburn and John Gassner at the Dramatic Workshop of the New School. Terry Helburn's niece, Peggy, was working with her at the Theatre Guild. On the nights that Terry taught the seminar, Peggy would also be there. I liked the way she looked.

One night it came time to discuss the play I had submitted for discussion by the group. Copies had been distributed in advance, and all members of the seminar were expected to read it before class. I got many reviews of the play, from nonsensical to perceptive, but the one that impressed me most was Peggy's. I could tell she had read the play closely. She knew names and motivations and plot. Her notice was by no means a rave, but she had sensitivity to the play's problems as well as constructive suggestions for its improvement. A few minutes after she had finished her critique, I decided to get to know her.

We had only one date—a subway ride taking her home from school—before I was inducted into the army. But we corresponded during the war while I was overseas. Peggy went from stage manager of the original *Oklahoma!* into the WASPS (Women's Air Force Service Pilots), towing gliders and targets in the Air Force Training Command in Texas.

The last time I saw Valeska was at Camp Kilmer in 1942. I had been inducted and was waiting for a troop ship to take me and thousands of other GIs across the Atlantic. Two days earlier, I had written Valeska in Provincetown telling her I would be leaving shortly for Europe. I was in my tent after breakfast packing up for the move when I was hastily summoned by the commanding officer. Perplexed, I went to his office and was told that a strange, sinister woman outside demanded to see me. When I heard it was Valeska, I rushed to greet her. She was dressed in green pajamas. With her beach shoes and German accent, she had aroused more than a little suspicion. Was she a German spy? What did she want of me?

I told the lieutenant questioning me that Valeska was a great night club performer and I was her impresario. His eyes opened with surprise when he heard the word "impresario." I could see the erotic thoughts bouncing around in his eyes. He questioned me sharply: "What did you do as— whatever you said." I told him how I had organized the publicity for her in the Beggar Bar. I could see he was patently let down. Then he let the news drop. The whole unit was moving in another hour to Louisiana.

"Louisiana!" I was shocked.

"Camp Claiborne—basic training."

"But I thought—someone said—Europe—troop ship to Europe."

"What a dumb bastard!" he roared. "Eating everything that comes out of the rumor mill."

I saw Valeska for several minutes with the lieutenant hovering in the background. She said she had gotten my letter and decided to leave Provincetown immediately, hoping to get to me in time for a personal goodbye. Without changing her clothes she had jumped on the next bus to New York and from there had taken another bus to Kilmer. She had arrived at midnight, the night before, and, of course, had found no empty rooms in the local inns and rooming houses.

"Where did you sleep, for God's sake?" I said.

"In the meadow," she replied as naturally as if she slept in a meadow every night.

With any other woman I might have worried. We said an affectionate goodbye in front of the startled lieutenant. When Valeska left to return to Provincetown for an engagement at her night club that evening, I didn't have the heart to tell her I was only going as far as Louisiana.

I later heard that during the war Valeska continued the Beggar Bar with enormous success for some time. She wrote me that one night a couple of soldiers refused to pay their bar bills, and she had to confiscate their ID cards as security. They in turn shouted it was illegal to take their cards and threatened to turn her over to the Military Police. She shouted back, "Give me my money!" The GIs appealed to the MPs who stormed through the Beggar Bar and retrieved the two cards. Stopping in front of the two mattresses on the floor, the ones I had installed for Valeska to provide added sitting space for the audience for her performances, the police immediately accused her of operating a brothel. She laughed at their accusations, and explained the mattresses were actually the front row of the theatre she and I had created. She added that it was the easiest way to let the audience in the back rows of benches see the stage. The MPs were not impressed. They closed the place.

After that Valeska performed wherever she could. At the end of the war she returned to Germany and started two new night clubs, one called the Witches' Kitchen, the other the Pig's Stall. I could tell she had not changed. I visited her twice in Germany before she died in 1980. She was indeed "incomparable."

TWO

The War Years

After being a nightclub impresario and playwright manque, my army career was, if anything, a non sequitur. Certainly the beginning was not auspicious.

I began as a private who, for six months, dug latrines in Louisiana as part of my basic training. Then I got a promotion to technical sergeant. "Why," I wondered? "Were my latrines dug better than anyone else's?"

With that question still unanswered, I received the rating of a draftsman and was sent to an engineering regiment. Anyone who knows me is cognizant of my complete incompetence with technical matters. However, my job, in the crazy, but charming, way of the Army, turned out to have nothing to do with engineering. Nor did my draftsman rating have anything to do with drafting. I ended up as an administrative assistant to a colonel, helping him with personnel and budget matters.

In two weeks, the colonel and I were on our way to England, bunkered in the hold of a troop ship with blacked out portholes. Most of the hold's several hundred occupants, including myself, had taken to sleeping with gas masks on in order to filter the assorted stenches emanating from too many bodies in too little room.

In England, we arrived at Bristol and took a train to destination unknown. Hundreds of GIs stuffed every seat and corridor of the train. All of us spent many hours trying

to guess where we were going. One group guessed Scot-
land, another group Wales, everyone hoped London. By occasional glimpses of the sun, we presumed we were going
north and east.

The train eventually stopped at a small station toward
the end of the afternoon. When we saw the sign on the
platform, we howled in laughter. It announced *Moreton-
on-the-Lugg*, a name I shall cherish forever. It somehow
seemed absolutely appropriate for a bunch of bedraggled
GIs on a crazy blind journey.

We trudged with full pack and gear for about five
miles and arrived toward the evening of that hot August
day at the magnificent grounds of an English manor. I remember the greeting from the very gracious but overly ar-
ticulate lady of the manor. Flushed with patriotism, she
thanked us effusively for coming to save England and liber-
ate Europe. Her thanks unfortunately developed into a full-
blown speech involving little tales of English history and
the meaning and implications of patriotism. At first appre-
ciative of her heart-felt greetings, we stood rigidly at attention. But as the talk continued for forty minutes, we started
shifting from leg to leg. Our packs were relentlessly heavy
in the heat, and we squirmed as their weight seemed to
increase in direct proportion to the weight of the lady's
words. As she finished her speech with a ringing declaration of British-American unity, we sank gratefully onto the
grass in exhaustion.

For security reasons we were not allowed to divulge
our location in our letters back home. My best friend,
Ralph, red-haired, imaginative, and witty, sensed an irresistible challenge. How could he manage to inform his
friends that we were in Herefordshire without arousing the
suspicions of the rather dull lieutenant who censored our
mail? It didn't take Ralph long to find his approach, since
Herefordshire was named after Hereford cattle, reddish in
color with white points.

Immediately he set to work writing more letters than
he had written in weeks, in each of which he complained of

an invasion into his tent by reddish cattle with white throats, feet and bellies.

His complaints were so insistent that the censor tried to be helpful. "I haven't seen more than one or two cows," he said. "But I know what a nuisance they can be—leaving plops all over the place. I hope there aren't any in your tent."

"Oh no, Lieutenant," Ralph said. "They wouldn't do that."

"You never can tell. If they do, perhaps I can get the engineers to use some chemical to keep them away."

Ralph looked at him with cow-like eyes of appreciation. "Oh, Lieutenant, thank you. I really appreciate your help." He gave the lieutenant a smart salute. We learned later that Ralph's ploy worked brilliantly.

Our stay in the area of Moreton-on-the-Lugg was my first introduction to living abroad. I was enthralled by off-duty visits to the lovely quaint village with its tea house and pub. In our tents at night, my GI friends and I passionately discussed the British monarchy. Would it survive the war? In our superior wisdom we were convinced that the days of royalty were at an end. After each European war royal families had dropped by the wayside. Obviously it was now Britain's turn.

We shared wonderful moments of camaraderie with the British soldiers at the pub. Toward the end of an evening, we'd raise our mugs and toast both Yanks and British. Inevitably one of the British soldiers would yell: "And what's wrong with the Yanks?" As if waiting for the signal, the Yanks would yell in unison: "They're overpaid—over-sexed—and over here!" The evening would end with yells and cheers, and many of the Yanks were only too eager to act out what they were supposed to be.

After two months in Moreton-on-the-Lugg, we abandoned the airfield we were building, presumably because the location was undesirable. We moved on to Cheltenham where, in the mud and darkness of November, we started constructing a warehouse which, in turn, after several weeks, was likewise abandoned before completion. I began to wonder why we were leaving a trail of half-finished projects behind us in England, a perversity whose most tangible result appeared to be using up whatever precious food supplies from America might better have been given to the British in return for devastating their countryside. When I was told we were winning the war, I could only presume that the Nazis were outsnafuing the Americans.

Before long, I got a direct commission to second lieutenant and left the regiment for an assignment in London. I worked in ETA headquarters where, in a small office by myself, I helped in the planning of *OVERLORD*, that wonderfully-titled plan for the invasion of France. My task was to figure out how to fit vehicles, tanks and jeeps on the landing craft being built for the cross channel invasion. I was given the dimensions of the various craft together with the exact measurements of each tank, truck, and jeep. Then I fitted as many vehicles as possible into the theoretical boats.

The exercise reminded me of the same mindless tasks I had labored over in Washington, only this time all my mathematical calculations were done by hand, thank heavens, without the accompaniment of clattering machines. More importantly, I understood the significance of what I was doing.

Each day, at the end of work, I would throw my papers into a pouch and send them by messenger to a general in Bristol. My figures, after being checked, were used in the initial invasion. Somewhere along the way I was awarded a Bronze Star for my "outstanding achievement." I accepted it gratefully, but the award, which I had previously considered an honor, diminished vastly in my esteem, as I realized that fitting vehicles into craft was an exercise any schoolboy could have performed with honors.

Since the army gave me an allowance of a pound a day for a room, I scoured the Chelsea area around Sloan Square for a rooming house. In the process I came upon Veronica, a young air raid warden, handsome yet also pretty, half English, half Italian, with the best qualities of each. I grew very fond of her, perhaps I was even in love.

But I am a slow starter in everything, including love, and I certainly wasn't aware that our first meeting was unusual in any way. It was pleasant enough, but there were no thunderclaps accompanied by rolling drums and strobe lighting. Rather, it was the accumulation of small things— the sum of which became far superior to the parts. We shared little meetings, little events, visited the London sights on my day off, took walks along the Thames. I sat with her at her air raid warden post as often as I could and accompanied her on her rounds checking blackout precautions on her block. Then we would sit and gaze up at the skies.

London was a paradox. On the one hand, it offered beauty and serenity with its history on every street corner. But often, death rained from the skies and made couples such as Veronica and myself fearful of whether we had any future. It was in a London zoo that I learned to face one of my own fears.

For years I had been terrified of snakes, even the thought of them made me shiver. On one of my off days I visited the London Zoo, which contained several boa constrictors. I offered the keeper of the snakes a pound if he would let me handle one of them. I was surprised—and dismayed—at how quickly he agreed. He opened the cage, grabbed a boa in his huge hands and invited me to touch it. Sweating, my heart racing, I reached over and slowly touched the boa. I was shocked. Instead of slime and wetness, I was touching a dry and cool surface. The snake may have been drugged or, more likely, sated to the point of lethargy on a lunch of piglet or goat, for it was passive in the hands of the keeper. Suddenly he pushed the snake into my arms and I found myself holding it and rubbing my hand over its back, as if I were caressing a pet. Ever since, I have had no fear of snakes.

Eventually, Veronica steered me to a lovely Edwardian mansion whose landlady was the wife of E. P. Clift, a well-known theatre producer. I took a room there and had occasion to talk at length with Clift about the London theatre scene. Before leaving the United States, I had seen Thorn-

ton Wilder's "The Skin of Our Teeth" and carried enthusiastic memories of the play with me to London. I asked Clift if
he knew of it. When he said he didn't, I tried to find a copy
in London, but the printed script had not yet crossed the
Atlantic. I wrote a friend in New York and, a few weeks
later, a copy arrived in the mail. I gave it to Clift to read.

Wilder's play presents the indomitability of the human
family despite catastrophes throughout the ages. One scene
occurs in the age of the dinosaurs and one of them makes a
stage appearance.

Clift promptly returned the script to me with a superior, almost contemptuous, smile. "A dinosaur on stage!
Well, well," he tittered in a silly way, "But, my dear boy,
how can I get Olivier or Richardson or Gielgud or Vivien
Leigh to play with a . . . dinosaur?"

I was cheered after the war, on my return to America,
to read that "Skin" was being produced in England to great
acclaim, by another producer. The star, of course, was
Vivien Leigh.

After struggling with landing craft, tanks and vehicle
dimensions during the day, it was a welcomed relaxation
to be able to spend most of my evenings in the London
theatre. I looked up Valeska's husband, Robin Anderson,
who was John Gielgud's stage manager in "Love for Love."
Through Robin I met many of London's theatre notables,
including Gielgud, Noel Coward and two of his ingenues
from "Present Laughter," and Dame Edith Evans, who
turned out to be as much of a delight in person as she was
in "The Importance of Being Earnest."

One evening, Veronica and I met Laurence Olivier and
Vivien Leigh at the Churchill Club, where they were giving
a brilliant talk about England to American officers. Olivier
and Leigh were the golden couple of the English theatre,
occupying much the same position as the Lunts in America.

London was marvelous in many ways. Even though
we were in the midst of fighting a war, I could not help my
feelings of excitement and pleasure. It was a time when the
two main pursuits of my life, theatre and internationalism,

began coming together, and the strength of their combined powers made me euphoric. I wrote a melodrama, with an international setting, for Flora Robson. I sent it to her and, soon thereafter, had it returned with a lovely note of appreciation. Playwrighting provided an emotional bang, but a financial bust.

As Robert Anderson, the playwright, said in later years, "You can make a killing out of the theatre—but not a living." As the unlikelihood of making either a killing or a living became clearer, my enchanted London days and evenings ran out. I was transferred to Bristol just before the invasion, and knew I would soon be in France.

I said good-bye to Veronica with sadness. We had grown very close during our year together. The summer before, we had vacationed at an old inn in Devon. I remember with emotion the long walks we took on the lonely moors, and even the frigid rain that one day drove us, drenched, but exhilarated, into the shelter of a small cave buried in the hillside.

We wrote regularly after I left for France and, subsequently, Belgium, until one week there was no letter from her. The second week there was still no letter. Somehow I had to contact her. I had taken German lessons in London in preparation for the invasion, so, with some concern, I wrote my tutor and asked him to find out how Veronica was.

Weeks later he sent me a letter. It stated that a German V-2 rocket had struck Veronica's block, destroying her home and killing her and her mother. Ironically, she should have been at her post, but, since she had been on duty the night before, her supervisor had allowed her to stay at home and sleep.

I was appalled at myself. Veronica was dead and I had never told her I loved her. Perhaps because I was not sure I was in love. Perhaps, caught up in the scenario of a soldier who might not return, it never occurred to me that I would be the one to survive.

After the invasion, I bivouacked for a while in an apple orchard in Normandy. Later, with the liberation of

Paris and northern France, I became town major in Reims. Although only a captain by then, I was the ranking American officer in the city. As such, I negotiated with the mayor for billets to house American troops, as well as for French labor to help us unload ammunition trucks, trains and the like. During the many weeks of our negotiations I made rapid progress in improving my conversational French, and before long I was able to dispense with the services of an interpreter.

Each morning at ten I appeared at the office of the mayor, a jolly, fat little man. Each day, before we began our business, he would open a bottle of champagne and propose the same toast: *"à la Belle France et également à la Belle Amerique."* By the time our first agenda item was disposed of, the bottle was empty and another had promptly appeared.

From ten in the morning until late in the afternoon I sailed along on champagne. I learned to hate champagne. To this day I still refuse it, to the astonishment of many American hostesses.

Since Reims is the champagne capital of France, it was inevitable that sooner or later I would meet the owners of several brands of champagne, including Goulet and Heidsieck. Because of the difficulty of traveling within France during the war, the young Heidsieck heir had not been able to get to Paris for many months to see his mistress, and, knowing I could travel, he begged me to take a message and a small gift to Henriette. I was delighted to oblige. Several days later I had an occasion to be in Paris and went to her apartment. Henriette turned out to be most personable—possessing the most unlikely combination of glamour and fat and was easily twice the age of young Heidsieck.

When she opened the door, she was wearing a painter's smock and had just completed a portrait. She showed me through her studio, then introduced me to her husband. They invited me to dinner, then to the Comédie Française to see Paul Claudel's "Souliers de Satin."

I saw Henriette several times and kept up a lively

friendship with her. She and her husband led quite independent lives. They both had lovers, yet enjoyed each other between romantic attachments. It all seemed so comfortable, so right, I wondered why Americans didn't try the same life-style. I was pleasantly surprised at this thought. I had started to lose my naivete at Provincetown two years earlier, and it seemed that I was now fast finishing the job.

That winter I spent in Namur, Belgium. The unit I was attached to was ADSEC COM ZONE. Most people assumed it meant Advanced Section Combat Zone, but it actually stood for Advanced Section Communication Zone, a clarification I often avoided in the hopes of impressing my friends back home.

In Namur, an industrial town in the coal mining area, we were quartered in an old hotel. I was walking one day with five other officers on the broken sidewalks and crooked cobblestone streets when we were openly solicited by a young girl. Since I was the only one who knew French, I acted as interpreter.

The girl's name was Francine. Her home had been bombed, and her family had all been killed by the Germans, or so she said. She needed food and shelter. It was not the first time we were solicited and regaled with tales of disaster. But this time the story rang true. Perhaps it was her haunted eyes—and the smile that seemed close to tears. Or perhaps her chubby face reminded me of the valiant prostitute in de Maupassant's story "Boule de Suif," (Ball of Fat). We hired, or it might be kinder to say adopted, Francine. We rented a room for her in our hotel, fed her with stolen PX food, and enjoyed frequent visitation rights.

When we were about to leave Namur she wept with all six of us. She made us promise to come back, but of course we never did.

Towards the end of the war I was sent to Munich. I had been assigned to General Patton's Third Army, and papers were in the works to promote me to major. It would be weeks before I was demobilized and free to choose a career which at that time remained an undefined "international" vision. I spent many hours considering the possibilities in government, business, banking, foundations, non-profit organizations, and the newly established United Nations organization.

Meanwhile I would have time to look up old relatives in Germany. One of my father's sisters was in Plochingen in Württemberg, and I visited her to see if family relations, damaged by the war, could be patched up. She embraced me at the door of her small house as emotionally as she had embraced Hitler and Hitlerism. She had been one of the early followers of the Führer and had written passionate letters praising him to my father in America, who in turn wrote equally passionate letters denouncing him. Soon there were no more letters on either side. Now Aunt Emma was beaten; she was consumed by a personal desperation at losing the war and direct betrayal by her idol. She never recovered from the love affair, and in another year she died.

Before returning to Munich I visited the small cemetery of Plochingen and looked at the aging gravestones. As my father had told me, there were more Kochers than any other family in the cemetery. I experienced an odd, rather mystical feeling to be with so many ancestors from past centuries, their presence marked on decaying stones covered with moss and grass.

Flowing through Munich was the Isar River with its lovely, emerald-green water. On nice days that summer the river bank was filled with Germans sunning, swimming, picnicking. I joined in the swimming only to find myself a few hundred yards downstream swimming into a sewer which poured out human waste. Quickly I swam back to the bank. I went to talk to the Germans about the sewage, but I received only shrugs in reply. I wondered if the feces flowing into the river came from war damage of a treatment plant—or if defeat had produced such apathy among the Germans that it led them to accept all vicissitudes of life.

I talked to a former soldier in the German army who turned out to be an Austrian farmer. He said he had never been a Hitler lover; as a peace-loving Austrian, he had been forced to sign up. Now, delighted that the war was over, he looked forward to return to his farm in Austria. He was grateful for the arrival of the Americans and even more grateful when I offered him cigarettes and chocolate.

Encouraged by his friendly reception, I talked to many other Germans. Almost without exception, they claimed to be haters of Hitler, saying they were forced to support the monster, and were delighted at the arrival of the much-beloved Americans. I suspected most of them were ridiculous liars, saying what they thought the Americans wanted to hear. Dissatisfied, I continued to look for what I must have been subconsciously seeking, an unrepentant German, if one really existed.

One lovely sunny afternoon, I spotted a young blond German officer in uniform sitting by himself along the bank of the river. He sat a hundred or more yards away from any of the other Germans. I hesitated before approaching him, for I realized he was maimed, half of one foot shot off and replaced by a prosthetic device. I greeted him and smiled awkwardly. He looked at me, and his face expressed undiluted hatred. Then he stumbled to his feet in a rage and hobbled away. Embarrassed, I watched him pass from sight, and I respected his honest reaction.

I visited Dachau a week or two after it was taken over by the Americans. Expecting to find the camp emptied, I was shattered to find a half dozen human skeletons tottering around on the grounds. I was not prepared for the horror I saw; my stomach started churning as if it was trying to absorb a body punch. The American colonel in charge told me these were the last humans remaining in the camp, and even then he was waiting for an ambulance to take them to the American hospital.

The same day I visited Berchtesgarden and the Eagle's Nest, Hitler's retreat high in the mountains. A magnificent lodge perched on the edge of a cliff, it had views of unparalleled grandeur on all sides. I felt I had passed from hell to heaven in a few hours, from the degradation and horror of Strauss' Salome caressing the disembodied head of John the Baptist to the lofty emotionalism of Wagner, both extremes of the German temperament.

Again I wondered what could be done with the wretched lives and shattered cities after the war. There must be some contribution I could make—not necessarily toward a world without war, which even then I thought an unrealistic prospect, but at least toward the reconstruction of the human chaos and wreckage which surrounded me.

THREE

The UNRRA Years

There were thousands of displaced persons in Germany. It was impossible to travel between two towns and not encounter long columns of people dragging their ragged possessions on carts and makeshift vehicles along the highways. Some were former slave labor of the Nazis, some collaborators, some had just escaped the furnaces in time. All were dazed and homeless, without direction, in search of new homes and lost relatives.

It was the job of the United Nations Relief and Rehabilitation Administration (UNRRA) to round up these miserable people and care for them until they could be resettled. UNRRA housed them temporarily in camps and barracks, fed them, treated their medical problems, even gave the illiterates an interim education.

I had intended to return to the States immediately upon discharge. Now, after experiencing these endless columns of hopeless people, I decided to stay on in Europe to work with UNRRA. It was a field in which I had no experience or training, but, with the idealism of youth and abetted by the general euphoria accompanying the end of the war, I gained a kind of crazy assurance that I could be useful.

So far I had spent over three years in Europe. Each year the pull toward international work had become more powerful. However, I also felt a wild counter-pull. I would

like to return to America. What was Peggy like; had she
changed? We were writing regularly, but it wasn't enough. I
was eager to see her again. I was getting letters from other
friends and family. Births, weddings, deaths, the whole cycle of life was rolling on inexorably across the Atlantic and
I was no longer part of it. This feeling of loss made me
moody at times. Only gradually, as I learned to regard
America as a small unit in a global community, could I
come comfortably to terms with international living.

The same day I was discharged from the Army in
Paris, I applied for a job with UNRRA. In a few days I was
heading for their headquarters in Holland where I was appointed director of three displaced persons camps: a Jewish camp, a Polish camp, and a Yugoslavian camp, each
housing perhaps 200 people. These camps were all located
in Austria. The DPs, we were told, had been rounded up by
the Army.

After a brief training period in Holland, I set out for
Austria with a team of ten members in a weapons carrier.
The UNRRA team, one of the first post-war examples of a
truly international effort, was my first experience working
with individuals of different nationalities. With me were a
Dutch assistant director, a Brazilian welfare officer, an
American welfare officer, a Dutch secretary, a French
nurse, a Belgian doctor, an American supply officer, a Belgian assistant supply officer, and a French cook. Later, in
Austria, we picked up a Yugoslavian interpreter. I was delighted to have such a varied group, and I was eager to see
what I could do with it.

On our trip to the camp our main physical obstacle
was crossing rivers. Many bridges had been bombed and
not yet repaired. Often we would be driving along a beautiful two-lane highway that would end abruptly at a body of
water. We could see the continuation of our beautiful highway on the other side of the water, maybe thirty or forty
feet away. Old road maps were no longer useful. Sometimes we relied on rumors. Where we expected to find a
bridge, we often found only remnants of bent pieces of
metal in the water below. Sometimes we took a small ferry,

if there was one; other times we reconnoitered along dirt roads parallel to the river until we came to an improvised bridge strong enough to support us. Each detour was a frustration, each delay an annoyance and the team members, eager to arrive in Austria, were daily growing more curious about the people we were sent to help.

After a week or ten days on the road, living on C-rations and whatever other food we could scrounge from American Army units, we arrived in Braunau am Inn in Austria. It was ironic, and probably ill advised, to locate three displaced persons camps in the suburbs of Hitler's birthplace. Even though the memorials to Hitler had been torn down, the Nazis' presence seemed to hang over the town.

On arrival, we called on the *Bezirkhauptmann,* the ranking Austrian official of the region. A pleasant and efficient administrator, he was helpful to us in many ways during our year in the area. He confiscated two old BMWs for the use of the team and provided us with Austrian labor and supplies to help us run the camps. Until our arrival, he and his office had been feeding and administering all the DPs. Now he was grateful to relinquish to us the responsibility for the camps and their inhabitants.

The DPs were all casualties of the war, yet they seldom fraternized. Language barriers did not keep them apart, for there existed a *lingua franca,* a pidgin-German known by many who had worked willingly or unwillingly for the Nazis. The separateness of the groups went deeper than language. The Jews were suspicious of the Poles for their anti-Semitic history and looked down on the Yugoslavians as illiterate peasants. The Poles and Yugoslavians in turn were jealous of the Jews who lived in houses with running water and plumbing and in the individual apartments constructed by the Nazis for the skilled labor used in a nearby aluminum plant. The Poles and Yugoslavians lived in primitive wooden barracks.

In addition, the Yugoslavians complained that our UNRRA team was lavishing more time and attention on the Jewish camp than on the other two. I explained that the

Jews, physically weak from deprivation and scarred from years of brutalization and abuse, needed more attention. In comparison the Poles and Yugoslavians were healthy and sound. Besides, I continued, the Polish and Yugoslavian DPs had elected their own popular leaders who were already administering the camps efficiently. Both camps had schools for their youngsters. All UNRRA could do for them now was try to accelerate their repatriation. Each DP would soon be asked to fill out an application, listing addresses of all known living relatives, and would be given a choice of three countries for possible resettlement.

What I did not tell the Yugoslavian and Polish leaders was that the Jews were disunited. They had held several elections for a camp leader, but no candidate was able to win a majority of the votes. Basic to their disagreement were strongly-held political and religious beliefs. The Socialists were contemptuous of the Orthodox for their outmoded and rigid behavior, while the Orthodox in turn accused the Socialists of being "ungodly Communists." Both factions staged frequent screaming matches. Their emotionalism threatened to tear the camp apart. I was miserable, not knowing how to handle dissensions based on factors I had never experienced.

Finally I asked representatives of both sides to come to my office for a discussion. At the meeting I emphasized that the lack of leadership among the Jews prevented us from helping them. I offered their failure to agree on a school curriculum for their children as a case in point: Ten and twelve-year-old kids were running around the camp aimlessly instead of learning to read and write while the two factions battled it out. Aracy, our Brazilian welfare officer, who had years of experience in education, needed the cooperation of both sides to work up a curriculum. We warned that every week lost without a school would deprive the children of skills badly needed in the post-war world.

The Socialists yelled at the Orthodox to return to the sixteenth century and the Orthodox yelled back accusing the Socialists of conspiring with the devil. Eventually, someone suggested that I become the leader of the Jewish camp. I dodged this neatly by pointing out that as supervisor of three camps in the area it would be unseemly for me to be the leader of any one camp. After whispering together, representatives of both sides proposed that I choose their leader. Against my better judgment, but desperate to end the leadership dispute, I suggested that Gelbartowitz, a Polish moderate Socialist, who had barely gotten the largest number of votes in the last election, would make an effective leader. Reading the darkening Orthodox faces and sensing an impending storm, I quickly added that the leader should have an Orthodox Deputy. Both suggestions were eventually accepted, but not before another crossfire of accusations erupted from both sides.

Before Gelbartowitz became leader of the Jewish camp he came to me with a request: "Help me practice my English." He wanted to go to Canada or to the United States. A Polish Jew, he chose to be in the Jewish camp and not the Polish camp with those "goddam anti-Semites." Intelligent and friendly, he could be verbally abusive when crossed.

Immediately after our meeting we established a school. Aracy, the Brazilian welfare officer, was put in charge. She combined the strength and endurance of her South American Indian background with the warmth and intensity of the Latin. She had a constructive suggestion for every problem and, with her wonderful mixture of humor, firmness, high spirits, and an unconquerable belief in the DPs, she became the single most popular member of the team. She located a former teacher among the Jews and made him school principal. She also found an Orthodox Jew who, though he had no experience in education, was willing to learn as deputy to the Socialist principal. Together, this threesome planned a school curriculum and went about requisitioning the books from UNRRA Headquarters in Vienna.

A mere two days after they began this cooperative effort, long before the books arrived, the school opened. It was with enormous satisfaction that Aracy, the two princi-

pals, and I greeted the youngsters. I had just shaken the
hand of Moses, a determined six-year-old who told me with
assurance he was going to America when my secretary interrupted. UNRRA Headquarters was on the phone. Returning to my office, I was informed by a voice from Vienna that we were about to receive a "shipment" of 22
babies, all orphans, nameless, abandoned on the roadside.
They would arrive by truck, day after tomorrow.

"Delay this shipment a bit," I pleaded, as if dealing
with Macy's. "We've got to find some housing."

"Can't delay. Just picked them up. Better there than
here. We've got only office space. What do you want us to
do, put them on top of our typewriters?" There was a sput-
tering of phone static at the other end.

I yelled into the temperamental army field phone in
my hand. "What nationalities?"

"Who knows? One, two, three-year-olds don't talk. You
don't know what these kids are like. Not only don't they
talk, they don't even know how to smile."

Hurriedly, with the assistance of the *Bezirkhauptmann,* we requisitioned a small house near our quarters,
forcing the friendly Austrian family living in it to evacuate,
and retrieved extra cribs and small beds from a warehouse
in Braunau. With the back-up of an Austrian nurse and
household help, we felt, if not well-organized, at least ready
for the kids.

Scarcely two hours later, the "shipment" arrived.

We may have thought we were ready for the children,
but we were naive. Cheeks the color of ash, sunken eyes,
vacant stares. Boils and pus-filled sores on heads, arms,
legs. No cries, only an occasional whimper. These children
were living in some far away world into which we could
not reach. I thought maybe they were retarded, but Aracy
doubted it. "How can a child become human," she said,
"when it has no name?"

On the logic of this assumption we went from one crib
to another implanting labels with names. Perhaps we got
carried away with whimsy; we assigned some well-known
names: Masha, Pierre, Boris; but we also distributed weird

ones: Androcles (Andy) and Siddharatha (Sid). With each
label a child received a hug and a kiss from Aracy. She
believed in handling children. One touch, she insisted,
means more than a hundred words. The human spirit can
develop only in relation to the world around. Without love
and attention, children have nowhere to go. Without stimu-
lus there is no growth.

Living together in constant contact, the children began
to thrive. Proximity seemed to speed improvement. After a
month, sores and bruises disappeared, cheeks filled out,
eyes became clear and lively.

For several days, one of the little girls stared with interest at a small doll hanging over her crib; the day she
reached for it we almost cheered. Small progress each
week, each month. A year later, when it came time to leave
UNRRA, we could identify only one possibly retarded
child. Even then Aracy was not convinced. With continued
touch and affection, she urged, Anya would still develop.

Inspired by Aracy's success with the DPs and the orphans, Leni, the team secretary, spent as much time as she
could spare away from her typewriter, helping with the
children. Leni found the work so satisfying that on her return to Holland the following year she studied for a Social
Welfare degree and eventually pursued a fulfilling career
working with the underprivileged.

But even with its joint Socialist-Orthodox leadership,
the Jewish camp continued to be saddled with dissension.
The fact that those within the camp were bright and articu-
late, traits highly desirable in ordinary times, only added to
the dissension. Compared to the placid obedience of the
Poles and Yugoslavians in their camps, the Jews questioned
even the mildest decisions of their leaders and UNRRA.
Why should they have to carry coal for their stoves into
their apartments? Get the damn Austrians to carry it. Why
should the DPs have to keep their own apartments clean?
The fucking Nazis should clean the apartments. And why
shouldn't there be bus service between Braunau and the
camp?

Stimulated by this request, we arranged for daily bus

service. Then, even before it started, I received a petition
signed by a dozen Jews demanding that buses be banned in
camp on Friday night and all day Saturday during the Jewish Sabbath.

I consulted the two leaders of the camp. Gelbartowitz,
the Socialist, insisted that bus service was essential every
day of the week. Saturday was a day of recreation and entertainment. If the Orthodox *meshuggas* didn't want a bus
Friday or Saturday, so much the better. The Socialists
would have more seats.

Rubenstein, the Orthodox leader, replied with a snarl
and an explosion of words. I tried to argue with him. In a
democracy, freedom of choice applied to all individuals. If
the Orthodox didn't want to ride the bus on Saturdays, very
well. They could stay in camp. But why should they prevent the Socialists from enjoying their Saturdays?

I hoped this would settle the matter. Alas, the first Saturday morning of the schedule, the bus arrived at ten to
nine. When the Socialists arrived at the bus stop, they
found the Austrian driver in flight, pursued by several
howling Orthodox DPs. Then a small scale riot broke out
with Socialists battling Orthodox.

After another meeting with Gelbartowitz and Rubinstein, we devised an acceptable compromise. The bus
would be available Saturdays, but it would not park inside
the camp. Instead, the bus stop would be next to an open
field. Since the field lay just beyond the camp limits, the
Orthodox had no complaints.

After this episode, I began to wonder if the Jewish
camp would ever operate as a unit. Beliefs were so strongly
held on both sides, agreement seemed next to impossible.
But why should I prize agreement, much less expect it?
America was always rife with conflict and it wasn't doing
too badly. Disagreement at the camp would not prevent us
from limping toward our goal of rehabilitation. In fact, it
could be argued that disagreement was necessary for rehabilitation. I also sensed the major truth that the Jews, although disunited when dealing with each other, would cer-

tainly be united when confronted by an outside enemy. I
didn't have to wait long to find out.

Sometime after midnight I was awakened by a
drunken voice on the street outside yelling, "Mitzi—Where
is Mitzi?" Each time the yell became louder, more insistent.
Since the scream came from the street running through the
middle of the Jewish camp, I knew those within it must
also be awake. The voice seemed to belong to an Austrian
because the garbled words were spoken in a rural German
dialect. Windows hurriedly opened up and down the street.

The Austrian continued calling for Mitzi, each time
with increasing anger. The sound of wild screams in the
middle of the night was like the bursting of many shells at
close range.

As I dressed I heard a Jew yell back to the Austrian,
"Who is Mitzi?"

"Mitzi, *mein liebchen* Mitzi!" The Austrian pounded on
one of the doors. "Open, open!" More pounding until I
thought the man's fist might break through the wood.

I assumed the Austrian and his girlfriend must have
celebrated with a few steins at a beer hall half a kilometer
down the road. Somehow, they must have been separated
on their way home.

By now the man was screaming, *"Mein liebchen, Mitzi,
I save you—these Jews!"* Then more pounding and slobber-
ing. "Dirty Jews—I tell Hitler!"

Doors of the Jewish houses burst open. DPs who until
now may have been amused or mildly annoyed by the
drunken intruder rushed out to the street armed with
sticks, bats and knives.

By this time I was also dressed and out on the street.
In the wavering half-light of the single lamp post, I could
see blood pouring out of the Austrian's nose and mouth. He
was down on one knee, shielding his head with his arms.
One of the Jews, a burly heavyweight whom I recognized
as a Socialist, grabbed him around the middle. Both men
fell to the ground, tearing at each other. Terrified, the Austrian struggled to his feet but was again knocked down. I
saw the wife of Rubinstein, beating the Austrian over the

head with a bat. Pounded and bleeding, he finally broke free and fled into the darkness of a field.

It was a moving incident. I hate violence and bloodshed but I rejoiced to see that the divisive Jewish camp, as I had hoped and suspected, immediately united against a common threat.

My relations with the members of the three camps were friendly, but I was dissatisfied they were not closer. I met with the leaders of all three camps regularly and even held open-air town meetings each week with all three factions to discuss their individual camp problems. Unfortunately never more than three or four DPs showed up.

Until then I had administered the camp from my office. It was a work style I had acquired in Washington as a paper pusher, and, although it was well-suited to the government, the insulation did not adapt well to dealing with DPs. I wondered if I seemed aloof to them, perhaps even austere.

Although I knew a few of those in the Jewish camp well, there were large numbers I did not even recognize. Suddenly the answer came to me. Why not visit the DPs in their homes? I would sit down with each family, listen to their feelings and needs, perhaps get them to open up about their hopes for the future.

The next morning I visited several apartments for the first time. By the end of the week I had visited all the apartments in the Jewish camp. I would not stay long, just enough time to sit down, have a glass of wine or cup of tea, and chat about DP concerns. Within a couple of weeks, the results astonished me. People would greet me genuinely and warmly in the street instead of passing by with a polite "hello." I began to recognize names and faces, to put them together, and before long I knew a majority of the Jewish DPs.

I became attached to some families and enjoyed visiting them more than the others. Margaret and her husband Izzy were among my favorites. They had survived Auschwitz but were eager to forget the past and get on with a new life in America. I had many discussions with them about life in New York. They were good people, warm, intelligent, motivated, and I thought they would do well in the States. We said we would see each other in New York.

In addition to the camp politics, I had to pay attention to the politics of my own team. We were having our own problems of unity. Aracy, Leni, and I usually ate together and often took outings in town on a Saturday evening. The doctor and nurse were an unbreakable duo. Pierre, the cook, and Paul, the assistant supply officer, both French, were usually found together, frequently in the kitchens of the three camps, where they did not belong. (The DPs got their food from the Austrians through the team and were supposed to cook it themselves. Pierre was to cook only for the team.)

Mike, the team supply officer, was a loner from the start. He mixed with none of the other team members, but provided us with necessary food and gasoline supplies. Occasionally he urged us to conserve fuel, use the cars less. He said headquarters was cutting down our gasoline supplies. There just wasn't enough to go around.

About six months after our arrival I received a message from Vienna transferring Aracy and me to Linz. I was to be director of Bindermichl, a much larger camp of over one thousand DPs, compared to the six hundred we had at Braunau. Aracy would head up the large welfare unit in Bindermichl, which was reputed to be a swamp of dissension. In fact, the last camp director had just been fired after feuding with the DPs. Although the transfer meant a promotion for both Aracy and me, neither one of us took pleasure at the thought of moving. We still had much to do before our work was finished at Braunau. The school was running well, but I had recently started my visits to the individual apartments and was only now beginning to know the DPs. As I got to know them, I was gaining their trust. To leave them now would not only mean starting over, but it might leave Braunau with a new director disinclined to continue our work.

Aracy and I drove to Vienna and forced a meeting with Headquarters people who obviously had little interest

in having their decisions questioned. Bureaucracy being
what it is, we got a cold turndown.

Disconsolate, we returned to Braunau. I called a joint
meeting with the leaders of the three camps and unhappily
announced that Aracy and I would be transferred.
Gelbartowitz and the two other leaders immediately sent a
message to Vienna requesting that the transfer be cancelled. He also requested Vienna to send representatives to
a mass demonstration that all the DPs in the three camps
were planning on Saturday evening, three days hence. I
knew UNRRA Headquarters had been pressured by the
United States government to favor Jewish DPs. Therefore, I
suggested that Gelbartowitz sign the message on behalf of
all three camps.

On Saturday, banners and posters suddenly appeared
in all the camps announcing, "Herr Direktor and Miss
Aracy must stay in Braunau. Demonstration at seven this
evening outside office of Herr Direktor." Late in the afternoon three UNRRA representatives arrived from Vienna
and were greeted with hostility by the three camp leaders.
In a sour tone Gelbartowitz told them to join me in my
office. The UNRRA people seemed ill at ease. They sat
tensely on the straight back chairs surrounding my desk.

Gisela Weinstein, the leader of the delegation, immediately defended her decision to transfer Aracy and me to
Linz. She was stressing the need for a top staff at
Bindermichl when Gelbartowitz interrupted. Never subtle,
he pounded his fist on the desk and yelled at her, "I'm a Jew
—you're a Jew! I know your tricks. We have a fine team
director and welfare officer. We demand that they stay. You
in Vienna, what do you know about people? You deal with
figures, with papers. We Jews have suffered in the death
camps of the Nazis—so what do you do? You want to
weaken us. We are human beings, not cattle—you talk like
Nazis. We tell you Herr Direktor and Miss Aracy must stay!
You say they must go. You have no feeling for the suffering
we Jews have endured—you Miss Weinstein, with your
Nazi mind!"

I could see her eyes fill with terror. She must have

been visualizing the protest the DPs would send on to Vienna. Instantly, all three representatives from Vienna gave in. At about the same time, in the gathering twilight outside the building, we saw torches bobbing up and down in the street. Hundreds of DPs were marching, screaming, shouting. I listened with increasing emotion.

Gelbartowitz finished his diatribe with a ringing cry, "Let Bindermichl fuck itself!" I remember thinking I must commend him later for his remarkable progress in English.

Bewildered and somewhat frightened, the Headquarters trio followed the three camp leaders out on the street. By this time, I was carried away by the screams of support from the mobs.

I jumped on the hood of the car from Vienna and gave a rousing speech to the crowd. I have no idea what I said, but everyone screamed with approval. The next morning, of course, I had an emotional hangover, worse than from most I've had from alcohol. Ashamed, I told Aracy what a fool I'd made of myself. With her usual warmth and understanding, she smiled affectionately and murmured, "Any victory over Vienna is to be treasured."

Our transfer orders were cancelled, and the team remained intact for the year of our contract.

After this incident, headquarters accorded me a new respect, yet there was a distinct coldness in their dealings with me. Later, when Aracy and I were resigning, Headquarters paid me back for my rebellion by denying Aracy and me the leave we were entitled to, citing some ridiculous and obscure regulation to support this decision.

The anti-UNRRA demonstration also marked the high point of our team's popularity with the DPs. A few weeks after our victory, the team received a shipment—this time not babies but women's shoes from the American Joint Distribution Committee (AJDC), a welfare organization for the Jews. We rejoiced when the shipment arrived, for shoes were precious after the war, and many DP women were walking with holes in their soles. But when we opened the boxes we were amazed: America had sent us hundreds of

dainty women's evening shoes and slippers, most of them
no larger than size four or five? With sequins and gold
straps, they seemed totally inappropriate to the muddy
paths and roads of rural Austria and, even more, mali-
ciously unsuited to women whose foot size was on the average seven, eight, or nine wide.

But when I consulted Gelbartowitz, he was smiling.

"Wonderful," he murmured.

"What's so wonderful about giving one of our women
this lovely blue and silver model, size five?" I held up an
elegant sequined pair of evening slippers with pearls scattered haphazardly around the toes.

Unfazed, Gelbartowitz answered with what I thought
must have been the optimism of the desperate: "Any
woman can use them."

"Any woman?" I asked.

"Any woman," he repeated.

"How?" I simply could not follow his reasoning.

"Black market, *Herr Direktor,*" He laughed.

So we held a lottery, and each woman in camp ended
up with at least one pair of shoes regardless of the relationship of the size of the shoe to the size of her foot. The
women were obviously confused, surprised and disappointed, and it was equally clear from their veiled com-
ments that *Herr Direktor,* previously noted for his wisdom,
had this time let them down.

Soon, however, on my weekly visits to their apartments, I began to notice cameras, binoculars, suitcases,
and even gallon jugs of basic "load," an almost lethal Austrian drink composed mostly of grain alcohol. These com-
modities had, of course, been quietly bartered for the
shoes.

As the weeks went on, I also began noticing that many
people I had gotten to know had somehow disappeared,
and, in their places, were new faces I had never seen before. For a while, I thought my memory was failing, but
Aracy also soon noticed the same thing.

We had to confront Gelbartowitz for an explanation,
and it was then that he let us in on a generally-known, but

officially secret, enterprise, known as the underground railway to Palestine. Our camp had, literally, become a station on the railway that stretched from Germany to Italy and Cyprus, where the Jews illegally boarded boats to Palestine.

The British, as administrators of Palestine, were trying to stop this immigration by seizing some of the boats filled with DPs. In retaliation, the Jewish terrorist organization, IRGUN, bombed the King David Hotel in Jerusalem with a loss of many British lives. Regardless, I began to support the railway by preparing for the new faces every day and speeding them on their way the next morning.

Since some of the travel inevitably took place on the Jewish Sabbath, the Orthodox in the camp officially disapproved of the railway, but never tried to scuttle it. A few of these Orthodox, eager to get to Palestine and willing to forego religious observances on the Sabbath, may even have taken the railway.

Gelbartowitz had a bad habit of holding back important information, then letting it out only gradually to me or the team. I am not sure why he acted this way. Perhaps he remembered that the proverbial bearer of bad news is the first to have his head cut off.

The most serious example of Gelbartowitz's reluctance to level with us took place just as Aracy, Leni, and I were leaving Braunau at the end of our year's contract. We were all packed, the bags were loaded in the old BMW, and we were saying goodbye to team members and DPs. Margaret had baked a small cake for us to take on the journey home, and she and her husband Izzy were in the crowd saying farewell. Gelbartowitz whispered in my ear. He said he had something important to tell me. A little impatiently I asked if it was important.

He whispered back, *"Herr Direktor,* very very important."

I took him aside. He said he hated to have to report bad things about any team member, but two of my team were engaged in black market activities with the Austrians. Then looking behind him, he whispered, "Herr Mike sells gasoline—Herr Cook sells food." When I questioned him further, he said he had no evidence, but, if I investigated, I would see he was right.

I felt angry and annoyed, especially at myself. If, as I sensed, he was right, I had not been able to keep the team record clean. I would have to admit that I had had my suspicions all along, but refused to allow them to surface. To do so would destroy the lovely picture of team unity I insisted on maintaining, both for myself and also for the DPs. I was also annoyed that Gelbartowitz had waited until the last moments of our stay to reveal this damaging information. Why the hell hadn't he told me weeks ago? I asked for further details or evidence. He only shrugged and slipped back into the crowd.

I called Mike, the team supply officer, aside and confronted him with the accusation. There was an ugly scene. Mike hotly denied the charge and asked for proof. I could only tell him that I was given the information without evidence, and that I would report it to UNRRA.

When I talked to Pierre the French cook, I got a completely different reaction. Instead of being angry, he was astonished, not at being accused, but astonished that I hadn't known.

"Black market," he said, "is like love. *Tout le monde* do it."

He also declaimed that here in Austria he had fed our team well. Was he to be blamed for using some extra rations? I tried to get across to him that black market in France was different. No one was hurt there, but here the DPs could surely have supplemented the sparse rations they were receiving from the Austrians.

Pierre just smiled good-naturedly, perhaps thinking of the ironies involved. Here he was, selling food to the Austrians who were required to give food to the DPs, perhaps the same food Pierre had been selling.

I carried this thinking a step further. Wouldn't it have been more direct for Pierre to sell his food to the DPs? But then, perhaps the DPs were themselves in black market, perhaps selling some of their own food back to the Austrians? Struck by the ludicrous merry-go-round I was imagining, I found myself smiling back at Pierre.

Meanwhile, Leni and Aracy had been waiting impatiently. I called out I would be with them in a moment. In parting, I told Pierre how wonderful it had been to work with him, and how sorry I was that I would have to report the accusation to UNRRA.

In Vienna I told Headquarters about the Gelbartowitz accusations. They were not in the least disturbed. Perhaps Pierre was right. Black market was a way of life. The military and everyone else were in it up to their necks. Cigarettes, coffee, money exchange. And why not? After what they had done for the Europeans, didn't the Americans deserve it? The people at Headquarters reluctantly agreed to an investigation, and I heard later that there had been a desultory inquiry. Both Mike and Pierre were found guilty. The punishment in both cases was a verbal reprimand over the phone with no inclusion in their formal records.

And so, after four and a half years in Europe, I headed back to America.

FOUR

Something International

The war and my service as a displaced person's administrator were over. As I boarded the boat in Southampton I thought, "My God, here I am already 35." I had one known disability, the upper registers of my hearing having been destroyed by some fool sergeant who insisted I put my left ear, without covering it up, close to a cannon he was firing; and one unknown disability, the overabundance of cholesterol clogging up my arteries from four and a half years of fried eggs, bacon, Spam, and fatty gravies.

I began to take stock of what I had learned about myself. How far along had I come in making a career decision? For sometime now I knew I wanted to work in "something international", but beyond that very vague and incomplete aim concept, nothing.

The first thing I did on arrival in New York was to look up Peggy.

That morning she had made the front page of the Herald Tribune by bouncing uncooked eggs from the second floor of the Cornell University Medical Center onto a pad of cellular neoprene. Staged specifically for the journalists, the demonstration showed off the cushioning effect of this new material. When the eggs repeatedly refused to break on contact, the neoprene was considered desirable for use cn the dashboards of cars to decrease injury in case of accident.

Although Peg and I had not seen each other in four and a half years, we knew after several dates that we were in love. The event that was decisive to me was her reaction to my first kiss. She drew back, looked me squarely in the eyes and asked, "What are your intentions?" Any girl so honest and direct was too endearing to let go. We decided to marry.

I was infatuated with Peg and, like many other Americans returning from overseas after the war, I was infatuated with my own country. I gawked at the wide straight streets with their mile-long vistas instead of narrow, twisting alleys and at the luxurious goods in shop windows instead of drab essentials. I revelled in the dazzling brightness of the city at night instead of blackouts. In my exhilaration, I imagined that the excitement of New York was symbolic of my new career: it too would be brilliant, straight, dazzling.

I realized from the beginning that post-war "international" experiences would be vastly different from what I experienced during the war. The hysterical joy of the liberation of Paris, with thousands of French girls kissing any and all Americans, was not likely to be repeated in any international career I could imagine. Even then the honeymoon of the Americans and French was fast wilting. Also, the military uniform during those early days had more presence than plain suits would subsequently have. But, luckily, I was more interested in the substance of international work than in its trappings. As I see it now, I was flowing along on a contagious cloud of idealism. The thought of rebuilding the world on a solid foundation, of decreasing tensions among nations, in fact of helping peoples of all countries to understand each other was heady wine for those times. Not that I wasn't also attracted to glamour and travel. These reasons, when offered by an applicant for any foreign job, are usually enough to disqualify him or her from being accepted. But I would be less than honest if I didn't confess I felt an attraction for both.

Finally, when I juxtaposed these feelings against the remembered dullness of my research work in Washington before the war, I made a firm decision to pursue an international career.

The obvious place to start my search was at the United Nations. Here was the most "international" organization in existence and one, moreover, that directly echoed my desire to contribute to the world. In addition, because of its newness, it must have large numbers of job openings.

In light of the current cynicism about the value of the United Nations, it may be hard to realize that the UN in the late 1940s was the focus of the world's hopes for peace. Its permanent headquarters on the East River were still not constructed, and I haunted its temporary home at Lake Success in Long Island. I first called on a relative of Aracy who held a high position in the social and economic branch of the organization. Though well-received, I was not encouraged to hope for an appointment. Thousands of resumes were being received each month, and already more Americans had been hired than any fair quota system would allow. After innumerable visits to Lake Success over the next two months, although my contacts had increased immeasurably, my chances of a job remained close to zero.

Through a casual contact I was approached by a non-profit organization that was lobbying Congress to admit more DPs into the States. The organization wanted me to travel through the large cities of New England, visit groups like the League of Women Voters, attend their chicken and pea lunches, talk about my UNRRA experience and my knowledge of DPs and try to stimulate these high-minded people to write to their Congressmen. I needed money. The work would give me time to look around for a more solid career. And I believed in what I would be doing. I worked for three or four months and quit when I heard Congress was about to pass a bill allowing significant numbers of DPs to enter the States.

At about that time I also heard that President Truman was starting an aid program for the rehabilitation of Greece and Turkey. The Labor Department, I was also told, was about to start a new program of assigning labor attachés to the staffs of large embassies abroad.

In a visit to Washington I received some encouragement from the temporary offices established to receive applications for the Truman aid program. I would have to be patient, however. The budget had not yet been approved by Congress, and it might take months, many months, before hiring could begin.

When I inquired about the Foreign Service of the State Department I found it was in transition from an élitist organization to one responsive to post-war needs. Instead of exclusively employing the wealthy from Ivy League schools, it now sought officers with varied backgrounds regardless of affluence, and this made me feel that a career in the Service was more desirable than ever.

When I walked into the State Department building, there were no security guards. I was directed to the Board of Examiners of the Foreign Service without needing to flash an identification card at the information desk. I talked to a young Foreign Service Officer (FSO) in the Examiner's office and was elated to hear that the State Department was holding a series of interviews with candidates for the Service. During the war there had been little or no recruitment of personnel. Now, there was a lack of officers in the middle levels. In the past, every applicant was required to take a written exam that only a few were able to pass. Now, however, in order to speed up the recruitment process, State had decided to hire up to 250 officers, waiving the written exam. Recruitment was tied entirely to an oral exam before a panel of Foreign Service Officers and representatives of other government agencies.

I signed up for the interview and spent the next two weeks studying up on long buried knowledge from my college days: United States history, foreign policy, economics, cultural activities. Anything, in other words, that even the most sadistic panel might throw my way.

It was an extremely challenging time for me. Not only was I neck-deep in the pursuit of a new career, but I was out to impress Peggy. I studied and worried and lived more or less on the edge, with Peg proving to be a constant source of unflappable support.

As part of my preparation, I looked over some of the questions on the last written exam given some years before. The more I read, the more I shuddered. How could I answer a question like:

"A market researcher preparing a long range sales forecast would find which one of the following most useful (check one):

    1. Regression analysis
    2. Measure of control tendency
    3. Optimum inventory theory
    4. Quality control analysis"

I went through several economics and marketing books and was still not sure which of these four possibilities I would choose.

I did not sleep the last two nights before the exam. Terror fed on terror each morning as I became increasingly exhausted. How would I be able to overcome my fatigue and pass the exam?

When I entered the examination room I found myself facing six panel members all seated along one side of a long table. I was invited to sit on the other side. Somehow, instead of destroying me, my nervousness and exhaustion added to my already generous supply of adrenalin.

The chairman of the panel greeted me and asked for questions from each member of the panel. Most questions revolved around my military and UNRRA experience. There was a great deal of interest in displaced persons, and the panel seemed impressed with my work in Austria. I was prepared for a question of motivation for Foreign Service work, and, when it came, I carefully steered around the shoals, avoiding terminology like "glamour" and "love of travel."

There was only one substantive question not related to my background: "What would you say if you were asked by a fellow diplomat in a foreign country to explain United States policy toward its Negroes?" I said I would tell the diplomat that the United States recognized it had a problem, that we had to bring black people into the mainstream of American life, that it would undoubtedly take more years, but that we were making progress toward equality. This answer, although noncontroversial now, could actually in those pre-civil rights days be considered daring. And when I saw a frown appear on only one face, my confidence returned.

I went out of the office and waited for the panel to make its decision. After a few minutes the chairman came out and congratulated me for passing. As he talked, I let out a mental whoop of exultation.

Dimly I heard the voice of the chairman. He was asking what kind of work I would like to do in the Service. Without hesitation I burst out with "Labor Attache," since it was about the only job I knew of in the Service. The chairman nodded, consulted a sheet of paper, and asked if I would like to go to Brussels. There was a labor slot available covering Belgium and Luxembourg, and my Social Security background and knowledge of French would be most helpful. Very carefully I controlled the words that were bursting to get out. With a dry mouth, my tongue licking away at the corners, I said firmly, "Yes, that's exactly what I would like."

It was the only time in my long career that I was asked those two questions. From then on, the higher I went in the Service, the less choice I was given.

Peggy and I were married in April, 1947, and in August of that year we sailed for Brussels. By then she was pregnant.

Before leaving we spent a few days in New York. I had the address of my two old friends, Margaret and Izzy, who had left the Jewish DP camp and settled in a small apartment near the Bowery. When I phoned to find out when it would be convenient to call on them, I sensed some hesitation on Margaret's part, thought about it a moment, then cast my reservations aside.

Peggy and I visited Margaret and Izzy the next Sunday afternoon. Margaret graciously offered us a cup of tea. It reminded me of the many times I had visited them in

Braunau. But here something was different. We tried to reestablish the old atmosphere of friendship, but it didn't work. I was uneasy because I sensed their unease. Somehow our relationship had changed. They were no longer two of my DPs, I was no longer their camp director. We floundered through the afternoon together making insignificant and painful talk, edging away from the tragic events of the Holocaust that had brought us together.

Soon I figured out what I should have known long before. Margaret and Izzy didn't want to be reminded of the war or their camp days, and that was exactly what my presence was doing. They were beginning a new life, and all connections with the world of DPs had to be wiped out. I never saw them again.

When Peggy and I arrived in Brussels, I assumed that most of our assignments in the Service would be in Western Europe—after all, that was where my languages and experience could best be put to use. As it turned out, in the quixotic ways of the Service, Brussels turned out to be the *only* post in our whole career of twenty-two years that would be located in Western Europe.

At the start, I was willing to accept the international clichés and stereotypes of the era: Orientals are inscrutable; Muslims are intense and hysterical; Malays are lazy. Fortunately, I was equally able to controvert these clichés year after year as I learned to experience people in all their beautiful eccentricities.

I entered the Service then with expectations of a fascinating and exhilarating life, many of which would be realized. It would take the next twenty-two years to sort out these expectations, compare them with actual experience, pull the threads together, and try to seek coherence in a life that often refused to cohere.

My service career, which started in Washington, ultimately took me to Brussels and Luxembourg, back to Washington, then to Malaya (now Malaysia) and Singapore, again to Washington, then on to Jordan, Yugoslavia, and finally to the most foreign post of all, Texas.

PART TWO

LIFE IN THE FOREIGN SERVICE

FIVE

The Hostess with the Mostest
(Luxembourg)

It was 1947, and I was on my first assignment in the Foreign Service. Peg and I, married only a few months earlier, were adjusting to each other and to our new country.

As Labor Attache, I was to act as a bridge between the trade unions of Belgium and the unions back home. I was to fraternize with the leaders of the Belgium unions, both Socialist and Catholic, attend their conventions, visit their mines, factories and workers' housing, and send Washington my evaluation of labor developments.

When I heard, in 1949, that President Truman was about to appoint Perle Mesta as Minister to Luxembourg, I smiled, then shuddered.

Even though I was attached to the United States Embassy in Brussels, I was also assigned in the same capacity to the tiny neighboring principality of Luxembourg. The more I thought about Mrs. Mesta as my boss, the more amused and annoyed I became. Certainly, I was curious. In 1950 Irving Berlin would immortalize Mesta in song as "The Hostess with the Mostest on the Ball" in his Broadway musical "Call Me Madam." Here was a woman who knew nothing of the Foreign Service. Hers was a flagrantly honest political appointment given as a favor by the President

for services rendered. Mrs. Mesta lionized Truman as a
Senator and had probably contributed heavily to his cam-
paigns. She had also been co-chairman of his inaugural
ball. Now that he was President, Truman probably thought
it seemly to reward her with a "throw away" diplomatic
assignment.

That was precisely the problem. The Grand Duchess of
Luxembourg had only too often seen her principality used
as a "throw away" assignment for one dreary incompetent
American diplomat after another. The appointment of
Washington's most famous hostess as the ranking American diplomat in Luxembourg only served to confirm Washington's apparent lack of respect for the country and its
monarch.

In fact, the Grand Duchess' irritation with this appointment promptly led to a haughty missive to the President, requesting that he reconsider his nomination. Instead, Harry Truman, every bit as stubborn as the duchess,
repeated his request for Mrs. Mesta's accreditation and
added to the document a strong personal recommendation.
The power of these politics proved too much for the Grand
Duchess. Realizing the hopelessness of her position, she reluctantly acquiesced.

While these notes were shuttling back and forth, I pondered uneasily the kind of briefing I would give Mrs. Mesta
on the state of trade unions and the economy in the Grand
Duchy.

First, I tried to deal with the fact that the future Madame Minister was not noted for her intelligence. Crafty
and shrewd she may have been, but could she discuss and
address the intricate political and economic problems of
mutual interest to both the Grand Duchy and America?
Could she interpret United States foreign policy to the
Grand Duchess and her ministers? Could she even explain
Luxembourg's economic problems to the United States
State Department?

Despite my distress, I recognized that every United
States administration appoints 20 or 30 percent of its ambassadors and ministers from outside the Foreign Service:

these are generally friends of the President or those who contribute substantially to his election. So a political appointment, such as Mrs. Mesta's, was in no way unusual. Furthermore, most political appointees breeze through a year or two in a foreign country, collect the coveted title of ambassador, and are seldom an embarrassment to their administration. Uneasily I began to wonder if Mrs. Mesta would prove the exception to the rule, but I consoled myself with the thought that she was not without talent. After all, hadn't she parlayed her fortune skillfully enough to become the most prominent hostess in Washington?

The American Embassy in Brussels was invited by the State Department to submit a schedule to Mrs. Mesta for the day following the presentation of her credentials. Her activities on that day would not only have to set the tone for her whole stay in Luxembourg but should also be impressive enough to land headlines in the New York Times and Washington Post. The publicity ploy, though not stated bluntly, was wrapped up in a lovely sentence: "Mrs. Mesta wishes to make a substantial contribution to her appointment, one that will be appreciated by citizens of both countries from the first day of her arrival."

The political officer of the embassy was given the task of drawing up a schedule for Mrs. Mesta. He suggested a series of appointments with the cream of Luxembourg society with one or two politicos thrown in for seasoning. These were the kind of appointments Mrs. Mesta was used to in Washington and would be most comfortable for her to handle on her first day of diplomatic duty.

Perhaps. But Mrs. Mesta was after bigger game. With her sharp nose for publicity, and realizing that a repetition of her typical Washington day would probably bring her no headlines, she unceremoniously discarded the political officer's schedule.

The embassy then charged me with the task of drawing up a new schedule. No guidelines were suggested, perhaps because no one in the Embassy had a clue to what she was after.

Before coming up with any suggestions, I thought it

prudent to take a good look at the future Madame Minister,
herself. Since I was not about to take a plane to Washington to see her, I gathered clips of various photos in the
Luxembourg and American papers. I regarded her features
closely. Her face was in no way distinguished, certainly not
pretty or handsome or beautiful. If anything, she looked
mean and quite tough. Her only unusual feature seemed to
be her eyes. In them I detected a sharpness and determina-
tion. Even in the worst of the photos, I sensed ego, shrewd-
ness, drive, perhaps even a twist of humor.

I spent a long time studying these photos, and, considering her need for publicity, I proposed a morning visit to a
steel mill preceded by a visit down the shaft of an iron
mine. Trade union leaders would accompany her. In the
afternoon Mrs. Mesta would host a reception for trade
unionists of all levels. I explained in my cable that iron and
steel were the most important industries in Luxembourg,
as well as the largest employers of labor. Therefore, a visit
to both was a unique opportunity to see and understand
the Luxembourg scene. It would also impress the American
public with the seriousness of her assignment, as well as
the AFL-CIO which had great political clout. In other
words, Mrs. Mesta was not to be marketed as the conven-
tional "cookie-pusher" that most Americans in those days
expected of their diplomats abroad.

I received a noncommital reply to my cable the next
day. "Tell me more," it said.

I did tell her more and I sensed from her reply that she
was at least partially hooked:

"What would I wear in the mine?" it said.

Delighted that her curiosity was piqued, I told her she
would be wearing overalls and a miner's helmet. Even
more promptly another cable followed.

"Perfectly fascinating proposal. Be sure helmet fits me.
My beloved John Frederick insists my head size is 7½ but I
always feel better in a 7¾." Then, as if an afterthought, "I
suppose press will attend visit to mine—or will it be too
dark underground to take pictures?" I assured her that
even if it was dark there were always flash bulbs. Besides,

in an emergency, we could always take pictures on the surface in front of the entrance to the mine.

I laughed at her cables but sensed a positive side to all this foolishness. Perle Mesta would not be entirely bad for Luxembourg if she brought it into the headlines and put it on the map for the great American public. Perhaps, I thought, she might even have this in mind.

In due course, the future Madame Minister arrived in Belgium on her way to Luxembourg. The only American she saw in the embassy was Bob Murphy, the American ambassador. Shortly after her visit with him, he called me into his office. On his arrival in Belgium a year earlier, I had arranged invitations for him to visit factories and mines with Socialist and Catholic trade unionists and he was grateful to me for his popularity with both unions. He was always affable, truly charming, and one of the most savvy political minds I knew.

"She asked me for a briefing on Luxembourg," he said. "I was just getting into the political situation when she interrupted. 'Oh, I don't mean that kind of briefing. Harry told me, "Let your staff do all that political stuff. You just show the people and the government what fun they can really have at one of your parties. Like here in Washington." That's what Harry told me. So now tell me about the staff at the Residence. The chef, the Maitre d-, the others.' "

Bob laughed good-naturedly.

"When she asked me for the names of the servants, I had to say I didn't know. When she asked about their efficiency, I had to say I didn't know that either. Eric, I'm telling you this as a warning. You and Peggy are going to be invited to Luxembourg to brief her before she presents her credentials to the Grand Duchess." He looked at me quizzically and somewhat pityingly.

"Perhaps you'd better brush up on Mrs. Mesta's staff at the Residence and forget everything you know about the trade unions in the Grand Duchy."

I was appalled but not surprised. Fortunately the embassy administrative officer supervised the budget of the Luxembourg Residence, and I managed an hour-long session with him. He knew some of the staff and gave me their names and whatever other information he had about them.

As Bob had predicted, Peggy and I were invited to spend three nights at the Residence at Luxembourg the following week.

The first night was a very dull dinner. After Mrs. Mesta told us everything Harry was supposed to have told her over the years, she got up from her chair, as if to make an after dinner speech.

"Mr. Kocher, in diplomacy isn't it *comme il faut* for the men to separate from the women after dinner?"

I nodded, wondering where she wanted me to go.

"At home I never allowed the women to leave the men —it all became too sexless—but here?" She surveyed the newly painted pink of the dining room walls before her eyes descended on Peggy.

"You, Mrs. Kocher, why don't you excuse yourself and go into the powder room? I have business to discuss with Mr. Kocher."

She plunked down into her chair as Peggy rose from the table. I could see Peg was nobly restraining herself. "If you gentlemen will excuse me," she said with a straight face and then walked out.

I looked quickly at Mrs. Mesta and was pleased to see a surprised but admiring expression on her face.

Our discussion, of course, centered on the staff of the Residence, nothing that was in any way confidential or that Peg should not have heard. I could only assume that Mrs. Mesta was trying to change her behavior from hostess in private life and was now behaving as she thought a minister should act.

I told her what little I had learned from the administrative officer in Brussels and tried to broaden the discussion. But each time I mentioned the word "schedule" she pulled the conversation back to the servants and their capabilities. I told her the chef had performed magnificently with his *coulibiac de saumon* and she was pleased to hear it. But immediately she countered with criticism of the baked Alaska which had not been flambéed sufficiently.

Later we rejoined the lady in the living room, and I had a few minutes to sketch in Mrs. Mesta's activities for her day with the trade unionists. She seemed to listen as she bent over a small end table, fists under her chin, a glazed look in my direction. The events themselves interested her vaguely, her guests not at all. I think I detected a slight shudder when I told her she was to be the guest of the Socialist unions.

"Socialists?" she asked. Her voice was very disturbed.

"Yes, the leading trade union organization in Luxembourg."

"But Socialist?" she repeated with even more distaste.

"Not radical at all," I assured her. "Certainly not more so than our own CIO."

"But what will the newspaper readers think—their own diplomat running around with the Communists?"

I realized then that she was only mirroring the current ignorance in many circles in Washington that socialism was synonymous with communism. I reassured her they were quite separate groups in Europe and, in fact, were often at odds with one another. She brightened a bit and said she thought Harry would be glad of this.

"He wouldn't want me to run around with a bunch of dirty Communist thugs," she said.

After a few minutes, the palm of one hand covered a yawn, as artificial as her previous glazed stare.

"You'll excuse me. But you and Mrs. Kocher—please don't go to bed—ask the butler for anything you want. Good night," and she started up the great spiralling staircase to her quarters.

I did not attend the presentation of her credentials the next day. As she left the Residence to enter the limousine to take her to the palace, I noticed she was wearing an enormous diamond ring. I could visualize her during the ceremony, twirling the diamond to show the bejeweled Grand Duchess that Americans also had a few jewels.

Those who accompanied her to the palace were protectively vague about describing the ceremony later. But I imagined that the Grand Duchess and the Hostess with the

Mostest found little in common. In fact, I later learned that
the private conversation that follows each accreditation,
which typically lasts twenty or twenty-five minutes, lasted
exactly two-and-a-half minutes.

The next morning at breakfast, I noticed that the diamond ring was still on her finger. I hoped she would take it
off before the trade unionists called for us, but when they
arrived a half hour later she had not only not discarded the
ring but had complemented it with a huge emerald surrounded by diamonds on another finger. Together, the two
nailed everyone's attention, accenting the squat, coarse fingers. Well, I thought, the iron mine has never seen anything
like that before. I was tempted to warn her that the trade
unionists would consider her another splashy American,
when it occurred to me that that was exactly the image she
wanted to project.

After breakfast two trade union leaders arrived at the
Residence. I shall call them Arnold and Edith. Arnold was
the secretary-general of the Luxembourg Socialist Union
and Edith, his sister, was also an official. I thought to myself all women have something in common; therefore, Mrs.
Mesta and Edith should become friends by the end of the
day.

Alas, from their first greeting in the morning, I sensed
frigidity. Madame Minister greeted Arnold pleasantly
enough, but she barely took Edith's hand, dropped it immediately, then focused exclusively on Arnold.

The drive out of town reminded me how lovely Luxembourg is: only 999 square miles, it lies southeast of
Belgium and borders also on Germany and France. In such
a small country, one need not go far to reach one's destination. We left the Residence and, after twenty minutes of
riding through the restful beauty of hills, forests, streams,
farmland, and medieval towns, we approached the industrial area.

During our visit to the mine, Madame Minister made
an effort to be pleasant. At least she smiled briefly as she
shook hands with the mine foreman. I noticed her eyeing
the row of miners' helmets on a shelf at the entrance. The

foreman picked up the one closest to him and handed it to her. She turned it over and examined what must have been a label inside. A look of displeasure came over her face as she handed it back to the foreman without putting it on.

"I need a bigger size," she complained.

"Madame Minister, all helmets same size."

Hurriedly, I grabbed another helmet from the shelf.

"Try on this one." I handed it to her. "Sometimes they vary slightly."

She tried it on, then looked around as if searching for a mirror. When she found none, she asked me, "How do I look?"

"Just great."

"It feels a little funny," she said. "Very very funny." She put it down and retrieved the helmet she had just given back to the foreman, who was quite bewildered by this time.

"Isn't that funny," she said after putting on the original helmet. "I think this one is really the best. Not too big. Not too little. Yes, just right."

I thought of Goldilocks and the three bears and beckoned to the photographer who accompanied us. He took several pictures, and each time before the bulb flashed there was a slight upward tilt of Madame Minister's head and an appropriate show of teeth.

The visit to the steel mill was much the same, brief smiles, followed by hostile silences. I was crawling with anxiety most of the time, but soon the ludicrousness of the Mesta performance overcame me, and I found myself chuckling. At one point, she seemed transfixed at the sight of molten metal below a plank on which we were walking. Clutching the railing beside her, she looked silently at the fiery mass, then remarked to the foreman, "My steel factory in America also has a lot of molten metal."

During the lunch afterward, she subsided into a kind of sullenness; it was almost as if she resented her hosts for having to spend the day with them in order to get the publicity she wanted.

Edith continued to be ignored. Why the snub, I wondered. Did Mrs. Mesta generally despise other women? Certainly, with her rough clothing and unfashionable pulled-down, felt hat, Edith must have seemed a world apart from the Washington women Mrs. Mesta knew. Perhaps only women of power and wealth needed to be acknowledged; otherwise, save one's energy for the men. But then, as the luncheon ended, I was pleasantly surprised to see Mrs. Mesta patting Edith's hand warmly, smiling brightly and thanking her for the "loveliest luncheon I've had in a long time." Perhaps struck by this sudden rush of uncharacteristic kindness, Edith flushed with pleasure.

We rested briefly before Mrs. Mesta's reception at four. It turned out to be a strange affair. The minister, greatly skilled at entertaining the luminaries of Washington, was hopelessly out of her element with this mixture of trade unionists. Instead of circulating from group to group to gather and spread the latest gossip, as was her social style in Washington, Madame Minister failed visibly to start a conversation, even though most of those present spoke good English.

Instead, this hostess pushed drinks on her guests, in an attempt to get them drunk and relieve the social pressure. But that day, perhaps intimidated by the elegance of the Residence, most of her guests put their glasses untouched on a nearby table.

Finally, Mrs. Mesta spotted the wife of one of the younger trade unionists—a blonde, child-like gamine who seemed lost. Her husband was talking to the other men and their wives were talking to each other. Elise, obviously shy, withdrew to a large corn plant and appeared to be admiring it, when Mrs. Mesta, aware now of Elise's insecurity, drifted over to her and spent several minutes chatting. The conversation seemed at first forced, then the Minister must have said something bizarre. The girl cupped her mouth with her hands as her eyes lit up smiling. A few minutes later, Mrs. Mesta tugged me away from a group of trade unionists, introduced me to Elise and slipped back into the crowd. I spent a few minutes with the girl, finding her amiable but no great conversationalist. I admired Mrs. Mesta's

kindness toward someone who had no wealth, social standing or wit, although I realized they had mutually rescued
each other.

Toward the end of the party, Mrs. Mesta held a press
conference. She had scheduled it at the Residence, so that
her guests would be a captive audience.

When the journalists asked her what she thought of
Luxembourg, she raved about the beauty of the countryside, the people, the royal family, the factories and mines.
At that point, one of the newsmen asked her if she'd had a
chance to visit any factories or mines.

"My dear man," she said, "you cannot imagine how
thrilled I was. Today, my first working day in your lovely,
lovely country, I visited a steel mine. Not only that. I also
visited an iron mill."

There was a stunned silence. In a timid voice the news-
man said almost apologetically. "Madame Minister, can
you repeat that?"

I was about to correct what she had said, but Mrs.
Mesta looked directly at me. I could swear I saw her wink,
as if we were sharing a dark secret.

"Yes," she drew herself up. "I have seldom had two
more beautiful visits—one to your iron mill and the other
to that equally wonderful steel mine."

Her wink, accompanied by the emphasis on iron *mill*
and steel *mine* could only suggest that she quite purposely
committed this malapropism. There were a few titters,
then silence. But she had gotten her headline. Back home
there were direct quotes from her press conference. I did
not see her when she read these headlines. But I could
imagine the knowing smile with which she read them.

I thought a long time about her performance that day.
It seemed she really didn't mind how much a fool she made
of herself. In fact, the more the fool, the more publicity.
She knew she had to make her mark as Madame Minister
somehow, and was clever enough to know she would probably never be acclaimed for her political wisdom. So why
not make her reputation as an oddball? As with everything

she touched, Mrs. Mesta succeeded admirably. At least her name stayed alive in Washington during her absence and for years after her return. She became a national figure as "the hostess with the mostest on the ball," and, at many a Residence party, in apparent annoyance that the decibel level was too low, she would play a record on the record player. Even the subdued noise of conversation would die, as the astonished guests listened to "Call Me Madam," complete with running commentary on each scene and dialogue quoted before it appeared. Ethel Merman sang, but Mrs. Mesta sang with her.

Somewhere in that record, President Truman talks to the Hostess. I have no memory of what the "President" said, but I remember very well the loud clear voice of Perle Mesta, sarcastically interrupting.

"Why, Harry never said that to me. He'd never say a thing like that to me!" Some of the guests laughed, and a few applauded.

The guests were at first fascinated, then embarrassed and finally bored with what soon became the oddest series of parties in Luxembourg's history. They achieved their ends, however.

Although I was often questioned in subsequent years about Mrs. Mesta, I was never asked where or what Luxembourg was.

As a fitting climax to her non sequiturs, Bob Murphy, at one of his subsequent staff meetings, informed me, "You know, Eric, Mrs. Mesta told me you are a brilliant political officer, and she's going to tell the White House."

There was sheer disbelief on the political officer's face; then he smiled. I knew what he thought and I quite agreed with him. Mrs. Mesta knew nothing about political affairs. Her compliment was based on fantasy. But I began to wonder. Might her comment have been deliberately planned, another of her unexpected kindnesses, this time to help along my career?

Two years later, after I was into my next assignment at the National War College, I read that on her departure from Luxembourg, Mrs. Mesta was decorated by the Grand Duchess with the Grand Cross Couronne de Chene, Croix de Guerre.

I wish I had been there.

SIX

Daddy, Go Home
(Belgium)

The Foreign Service of the Department of State exposes the children of its officers to the excitements—and hazards —of living in four or five countries. A lot of pluses and some minuses. Any scars the kids collect from living abroad are not their fault, and probably not the fault of Mom and Dad either. The only villain, if there is one, might be called simply "Foreign Service."

Our first child, Eric Glenn, was on his way before we arrived in Belgium. He was born six months afterwards. After eighteen months, child number two appeared. Terry was a bouncy, friendly, affectionate cherub—blond, blue-eyed, the works. Two years later we had a third son, Chris.

In 1952, our last year in Belgium, we went on vacation to a small resort, Coxyde, on the North Sea. We stayed at a cottage next to white sand and lovely dunes. It was May, a beautiful spring after what had been a gruelling and bone-chilling winter. We all needed sun and warmth, and spent much of the time on the beach.

Peg and I were delighted to watch the older boys romping amiably together while number three looked on. The large expanse of sand and ocean seemed to diminish the sibling rivalry, which had gotten out of hand in the claustrophic setting of a Belgian winter. Instead of howls of conflict, there were now a lot of laughs, splashing of water, and burying legs in the sand.

Terry particularly needed the sun. During the long
winter he had contracted an infection which settled in his
adenoids. Green pus frequently dripped from his nose. Peg
and I were much concerned. We had consulted several Belgian doctors and were told the boy should have his adenoids removed. However, the doctors cautioned, *"at-
tendez."* Wait until the infection clears up. One should
never have an operation when an infection is alive in the
system.

But the infection, instead of clearing up, lingered. Peg
and I learned to live with the constant discharge of pus. No
matter. We had been warned by our favorite doctor, Poulain, that an infection takes time to heal. One must have
patience, not worry. It was Dr. Poulain who suggested a
holiday on the coast.

After the first week at Coxyde, Terry's condition
seemed worse. One morning we were sitting on the beach,
he was listless and sulky. His mood was quite foreign to his
usual bouncy good nature.

"Terry, anything wrong?"

Playfully I threw a handful of sand at him. It was one
of his favorite games. Now he was supposed to throw a
handful of sand at me. Instead, he turned away irritably.

"Come on, Terry." Affectionately I threw another
handful of sand on him. The boy looked at me with a serious, almost tragic glance. His face twisted as if squeezed by
some inner pain. His eyes filled with tears and he started to
cry. Uncontrollably, almost hysterically.

Now thoroughly confused, I picked up the beach ball
and rolled it over to him. Perhaps its blue and orange
stripes would carry to him the message of my love. As the
ball lightly touched his ankle, the foot twisted away as if
the ball were on fire. He kept his eyes closed. His sobs
became louder, more insistent.

It was lunchtime, and all five of us returned to the
cottage. On the short walk from the beach I carried Terry
on my shoulders. At first he resisted being lifted, then began screaming as I neared the cottage.

My confusion increased, and with it my irritation.

What the hell was the boy yelling at? Was I spoiling him? Should I chastise him instead of coddling him? With a sudden anger that I would find hard to forgive in the years ahead, I let the boy down and gave his behind two hard smacks. For perhaps two seconds Terry reacted with astonished silence before turning away with a shrill scream.

At the cottage Peggy hurriedly fixed a tuna salad. Terry was sure to eat some. Just yesterday he had been asking for tuna and this morning she had gone to market purposely to buy a can. When she put the sandwich before him, Terry turned away from the paper plate.

"Too tired to eat, honey?"

When the boy continued sobbing, she picked him up and put him down for his afternoon nap.

After two hours Terry was still asleep. Thinking he needed the rest, Peg and I let him sleep. At tea time—a gathering Terry loved with its buns and biscuits—his eyes were still closed. Again we decided to let him sleep. Supper time. Still the same deep breathing and occasional tossing.

Peg wondered if he had a fever. She felt his forehead and thought it might be warmer than usual. But then, hadn't he been in the sun all morning? Perhaps he was just over-tired. Still, quite a nap. Five and a half hours. But how can one assess the exhaustion, the needs of a child? Everyone has a special rhythm. In any case, the rest would help. It might even cure that damnable greenish flow from his nose. But would he sleep through the night? Hardly. Well, when he awakened, Peg or I would get up and give him toast, milk, a cookie, perhaps read him a bit of Babar, that wonderful French story of an elephant, then gradually lull him back to sleep.

Early next morning Peg and I awoke with one thought. I hurried to Terry's room next door. He was still sleeping! Eighteen hours without waking—without food? This all-night sleep, ordinarily a joy to parents, threw us into a panic. Peg again felt his forehead. The face was hot with little beads of sweat clinging to his temples and cheeks.

Immediately I called the local doctor in Coxyde. When

he arrived a half hour later, he was puzzled. Terry's fever was high. 103. A flu perhaps? A virus? The boy should go to the hospital in Ostend. Even as we bundled him up in the back seat of our Chevy, he began vomiting. The doctor promised to phone the hospital to prepare it for Terry's arrival. I started the car and pressed hard on the accelerator.

The hospital in Ostend was the only one in the surrounding area. It was small, a Catholic-run institution, with nurses in starched uniforms, friendly smiles, and an ambiance of cleanliness and order.

Doctor Van Heuvel was waiting for us in the admission office of the hospital. He was a small serious-looking man, with a dark moustache. On first impression he seemed well meaning but not very perceptive. Initially he thought Terry was suffering from the air at the beach. Some people, the doctor pronounced seriously, find the air on the coast "too strong," *"trop fort."* It was bad for their nerves and they fell ill.

Peg and I were astonished. How could we take such nonsense seriously? But after all, the man was a doctor. He'd been practicing for years. Then the whole idea angered us. With whom were we dealing? Wasn't the doctor's diagnosis really an old wives' tale?

I persuaded the doctor to examine Terry once more. After all, we had taken Terry to the beach several times, and each time he returned healthier than before. Van Heuvel, always ready to please a diplomat no matter how irrational, examined Terry once again, and this time came up with a tentative diagnosis of spinal meningitis. Peg and I were appalled. If true, was it curable? The doctor shrugged uncertainly. Was it contagious? No one in the hospital really knew. In some cases, yes—in some cases, no. But no one knew which case this was, if indeed it was meningitis at all. Terry was immediately separated from the other patients and given a room of his own. The nurse caring for him put on a gauze mask.

Antibiotics were just being introduced in Belgium in that year of 1952. Doctors and hospitals were beginning to experiment with their use. One of the early antibiotics, aureomycin, was given to Terry.

The results were miraculous. In forty-eight hours he was sitting up in bed, apparently cured, as chatty, affectionate, and energetic as before his illness. The fever was gone, and he was eating as much as his favorite elephant, Babar. Even more astonishing, pus no longer dripped from his nose.

Peg and I filled two glasses in Terry's room with water. We clinked them joyously. "To Terry." The boy looked at us with a grin.

The doctor told us no one really knew the way antibiotics worked, but the results spoke for themselves. Terry no longer had a fever, therefore he must be cured. And if he was cured, why give him more pills?

Van Heuvel stopped the medication immediately. *"Eh bien,"* he said, *"le bébé est guéri*—baby cured, *n'est-ce-pas?"*

We accepted his judgment with joy. We also made plans to take Terry back to the beach cottage the next day.

That night, eight hours after the last pill was given Terry, he fell into another deep coma. This time it was even more frightening. Before, we had at least the possibility of a cure for his illness. Now, if it turned out that the antibiotics only gave the appearance of a cure by temporarily silencing the virus, what was the next step? Was there another step?

"More antibiotics," the doctor proclaimed. "We will try a new one. Terramycin. Three times a day."

I could hear the doctors discussing Terry's case in the corridor outside the hospital room. Give Van Heuvel credit. He was bringing together all the expertise of the tiny hospital to save the boy. Still, we were panicked, restless and dissatisfied. We had brought Terry here because there was no other hospital close at hand. What were the alternatives? We could search for another hospital in the area, but it, too, would be tiny and probably afford no greater expertise than here. Should we call Dr. Poulain in Brussels and get his advice? Perhaps he could tell us of another hospital in the vicinity—or—why couldn't we get his help? Perhaps we could induce him to come to Ostend, just for a short consultation.

A few minutes later I was on the phone to Brussels. Fortunately I found Dr. Poulain in his office. After a few moments of indecision, he agreed to come up the next afternoon.

We were uncertain as to how Van Heuvel would receive our request for a consultant, but we told him as diplomatically as we could that our Brussels doctor was coming up the next day. He asked for the name of our doctor, and when we told him, he promptly reached for a huge volume on his shelf and started turning the pages. He settled on the P's and ran his finger up and down a few columns. "First name of this Dr. Poulain?", he asked.

"Georges."

"Ah, oui." His finger seemed to reach the right name. Then dismay spread over his face.

"Ah—this doctor Poulain—is—Socialist, *n'est-ce-pas?"*

"So—?" I tried to be nonchalant but I suspected what he was getting to.

"This is a Catholic hospital, *Monsieur"*, he said. "No Socialist doctor can work in a Catholic hospital."

"Can medicine not be practiced as well no matter what the religion?" I asked.

"Ah, monsieur." Again that sad but rigid expression. *"Ça n'est pas comme il faut."*

"Why should politics intrude in medicine?"

"Ah, monsieur," it does not intrude. It *is* everything. Everything in Belgium is politics. It must be either Catholic or Socialist. Catholics go in one direction. Socialists in the other. It is not for me to judge which is better—but here we are Catholic."

I had a hard time keeping the rage from my voice but I asked "In a matter of life and death, does politics still prevail?"

"Oui, certainement."

"And if a Socialist just might happen to be smarter than a Catholic?"

I got no further. His skin reddened above the white

collar. *"Pas possible, monsieur,"* he interrupted. Then in a
heavily accented English "Not possible, *monsieur.* Nev aire
a Socialist better, nev aire." he intoned.

Peggy and I spent a frantic hour. The barbaric nature
of connecting medicine and religion reminded us of the
primitive tribes that treated ailments with incantations to
the local deity.

After tossing ideas around, we were clear on one
thing. We had to get Terry out of there. I would take him to
Brussels. Peggy, still nursing Chris, would stay temporarily
with the two boys at the beach.

I phoned Dr. Poulain and he readily agreed to prepare
for Terry's admission to the Neurological Institute.

"Any bed or room is O.K.," I said. "Socialist or Catholic—I couldn't care less."

A slight chuckle came from his end of the line. "When
you asked me to come to Ostend, I suspected I would not
be welcome. Anyway, it is better this way. We will take
good care of Terry here."

"Would you object to a Catholic consultant in one of
your Socialist hospitals?" I asked.

"I do not know. The question does not often come up.
Few Catholics would work in a hospital not controlled by
the Catholics."

"Ça n'est pas comme il faut," I murmured.

"Exactly. How well you understand our Belgium."

I tried to find Van Heuvel to tell him we were taking
Terry to Brussels. Unfortunately, the doctor was out on an
emergency call. No one knew when to expect him back. I
went to the office of the head nurse, Mademoiselle Rose.

It was the first time I had met her. On first impression
she seemed hard-boiled, unfeeling.

I announced I was taking Terry to Brussels.

"Oh," she spoke perfect English. "It is decidedly unwise."

I explained that our doctor was waiting for us. Terry
was going to be admitted to one of the best hospitals in
Belgium.

"You are not thinking of the welfare of your son," she said tartly.

"That's exactly what I am thinking of."

She sighed and tried to smile. But all I could see was a movement of the lips that made her look colder than before.

"I am unpleasantly surprised," she said severely. "A father who wishes to risk the life of his son."

"How's that?"

"Your son is dangerously ill—he is in a coma—you do not seem to realize—he might die—you cannot move him."

"Wait a minute," I said. "I'll be right back."

I rushed to the nearest public phone and was lucky to get through promptly to Poulain.

"Is it dangerous to move Terry? He's unconscious."

"Just keep him warm," Poulain said matter of factly. "Go not too fast—our roads are not like American roads— here we have many bumps."

I was tempted to tell him about the pothole in New York that blew out one of my tires, but I didn't want to take the time. "I'll phone just before Terry and I leave for Brussels," I said.

I hurried back to the head nurse, trying to conceal the hatred I felt for her.

"I'll take Terry anyway. The doctor in Brussels thinks it won't be dangerous."

"I do not know your doctor. I do not even care if he is a Socialist, but I must tell you, to move your son is extremely dangerous. Therefore, we will not allow you."

"You won't allow me to take Terry out of the hospital?" I said incredulously. "You do know I am his father, or don't you?"

"You may think you own your son but now that he is in the hospital we are responsible for him."

I paused, not quite sure how to continue. "And if I insist?"

"The police understand our position. If necessary, we will call them." She pushed back her chair and stood up. She was tall, six feet perhaps, gaunt and stringy. She stepped toward me, all the while peering at me as if to convince herself that a person with such outrageous views really existed. "I cannot understand a father who cares so little for his child to deliberately put him in danger. There are so many strange things one hears of America these days." She looked at me accusingly. "Why do you resist what is right?"

"Sorry," I snapped. "I don't think we're going anywhere with this conversation." I walked out of her office and banged the door shut.

Peggy and I made plans for the kidnapping. As I used the word, I was appalled. Parents kidnapping their own child? A non sequitur. An institution that claimed to have the right to decide the fate of our infant? Another non sequitur. We tried to look at the situation objectively, but outrage prevented us from getting very far in our reasoning.

We went to the cottage for supper and waited. At eleven, when the administrative staff, and particularly Mlle. Rose, were off duty, I returned to the hospital with two blankets. By this time, after my visits day and night, I was well known by the receptionist and the few nurses on duty. Without being stopped or questioned, I went into Terry's room. He was still in a deep coma, drawing deep breaths and whistling them out rhythmically. I picked him up, folded the blankets around him, and carried him nonchalantly out of his room.

The duty nurse on Terry's floor was making her rounds. She stopped with a gasp when she saw Terry in my arms.

"Monsieur," she protested.

She was very young and had not yet acquired the authority of a veteran.

"Good evening," I said without stopping. "Just taking Terry for a breath of air. He loves fresh air." Then over my shoulder without turning around, "always gets a violent migraine if he can't breathe a bit of evening air."

Why I said this I hadn't the faintest idea. It was a pure outpouring of stream-of-consciousness words—but they worked. The nurse looked at me in amazement, tried to

puzzle out what I was saying, but by the time she started
after me I was out the front door of the hospital into the
darkness.

Peg was waiting for me in the Chevy. She had just
called Poulain and alerted him to our expected arrival after
midnight. As I drove away, she held Terry in her arms in
the back seat.

God, what a relief. In an hour and a half Terry would
be in the care of one of the best doctors in the country.
Socialist perhaps—but surely as competent as a Catholic.
We'd be through fighting the eternal Belgian battle—Catholics vs. Socialists. Not only did it divide up hospitals, but
politics, schools, families. The separation of church and
state never seemed more desirable to me than on that midnight drive to Brussels.

Poulain and another doctor were waiting for us as we
entered the Neurological Institute. With infinite gratitude I
handed Terry to them. Peg returned to Coxyde to care for
the two other boys. A cot was set up for me in the hospital,
and I enjoyed a good night's sleep for the first time in
weeks. Two days later Peg moved back to Brussels with
Glenn and Chris.

Terry was put on a new mixture of drugs—penicillin,
streptomycin, and a third antibiotic. They were to be given
him three times a day, once after breakfast, once after
lunch, and finally in the evening. Terry responded gradually. In contrast to the apparent miraculous recovery after
his first relapse, two weeks passed before he opened his
eyes, a few more days before he was able to sit up, still
more days before the fever left him and the nervous twitch-
ing of his body attacked him less frequently.

I wish I could say that the Socialist hospital was better
than the Catholic hospital, but malpractice, ignorance and
lack of organization turned out not to be the exclusive
province of either persuasion.

Three weeks after Terry entered the Neurological Institute, a Socialist nurse forgot to give him his afternoon
medication. By evening—before his last dosage of the day
—he again sank into a deep coma. It would be wrong to say

that Peggy and I lost hope at that point. Mine was almost shattered, but Peggy, always more upbeat than I, never allowed herself to give up. We never talked about hope in those days. It seemed too frail a concept to bear the weight of words. But I guessed that even Peggy's hope was frayed and wearing thin. Years later she admitted to me that she had been so troubled during this nightmare that she ate a pound of chocolate-covered caramels each day.

After Terry's second relapse, we tried to adjust. This time we knew we would be in for a longer pull. Much longer. Terry's strength was waning after the long struggle. He seemed to be sinking farther and deeper into the disease. Almost all possible variations of existing antibiotics had been used, separately and in combination. He would need more pills—different pills—and time, much more time if—and here we never voiced this—if he would ever get well.

Immediately after Terry's relapse, I moved into his hospital room. I had a vague feeling that I could offer him something. He would surely have needs that only a parent could understand—but what these needs were I couldn't imagine, except to be sure that he got all his medication on time. I frittered away most nights wavering between sleep and wakefulness, hoping I would be called. Sleeping little and seldom leaving the hospital room, I was getting more and more exhausted. I would get up several times each night and hover over Terry's crib. Surely there must be something I could do for him—and when I found nothing to do, I returned to my cot depressed.

As the weeks went by, the antibiotics fought against the virus without ever entirely winning or being entirely defeated. Sometimes Terry was half conscious. He recognized me, even said a few words to me from time to time. But it was a ragged recovery. The fever persisted, his strength was failing.

One night, perhaps two weeks after I moved into the hospital room, I got up, looking as usual for something to do that would make Terry feel better. There really was nothing—except, well, a bit of the sheet had fallen from his shoulders. Perhaps he felt cold. I picked up the top of the sheet and placed it over his shoulder.

As I patted his face, the motion must have aroused him, for lying on his side in the semi-darkness, with one cheek pressed against the pillow, without opening his eyes, he murmured, "Daddy, you go home."

I experienced a moment of sharp merciless horror, then gradually, relief. I had tried to give him what I thought he needed, but failed. He was stronger and braver than I had imagined, and he wanted to be left alone. I knew I had to move out of the hospital room.

Peg and I talked again about Terry's needs the next day. As much as we loved him, we were giving too much of ourselves, more than he wanted. We were exhausted and were only bringing our exhaustion back to him.

We decided we had to start living again. I went back to work at the embassy for the first time in weeks and attended a convention of the General Federation of Socialist Trade Unions. Peg for her part had an idea for an article for the "Foreign Service Journal," an in-house publication and wrote about new staff arrivals at the embassy, their background and present jobs. I read the article in draft and liked it. I wondered about the advisability of including the name of the new CIA man assigned to the embassy under the cover of "Political Analyst," but I tossed aside my slight misgivings. After all, the Department employed a committee to clear everything written by dependents for publication.

Though we visited Terry every day at the hospital, preferably at different times, Peg was able to finish her article and sent it to the Journal which rapidly accepted it. I sent my dispatch about the convention to the Departments of State and Labor back home and was commended for it.

Getting back to work helped us regain our balance and strength. We even went back to embassy receptions. God, did we go back to receptions. One or two almost every night. Followed by a late dinner at another embassy. Each time we left the children in the care of the devoted couple who were our housekeepers, and each time it was a

wrenching moment to say goodnight to Eric Glenn and
Chris at six in the evening.

Eric Glenn particularly was going through a hard
time. Two of his closest friends' families had been transferred to Washington. In their place would come other
faces. The connection with new children had to be recast to
replace the lost connections. Wouldn't Glenn, deprived of
old friends, and of the constancy of his brother's presence,
need extra emotional support just at a time when Peg and I
were frantically making an exit to start the diplomatic
rounds? This thought riddled us with guilt.

Then there was Terry. Even though we weren't responsible for his illness, we felt guilty anyway. Had we spent
too many hours at cocktail parties and not enough hours
trying to cure the discharge from his adenoids? In retrospect, I think we were covering guilt feelings about Terry
with solicitousness for the other two boys.

One evening we gave a quick kiss and hug to Eric
Glenn and Chris before dashing out to begin our diplomatic rounds. As I was heading for the door, Eric Glenn, a
precocious five-year-old, said rather sadly:

"Gonna have a good time?"

I hesitated, torn between being late for the ambassador's reception and letting Eric Glenn down: then I came
back into his room and sat on the bed.

"Do you think we're deserting you in favor of a glamorous night life? Do you?"

"Yeah."

"My boy, your parents are more to be pitied than envied. Every time Mom and Dad have a glass in their hand,
they feel they're on duty. In fact, they are on duty. The one
unpardonable behavior at a reception is to enjoy yourself.
Either alone or with your spouse. So what do we do—separate and mix, spot the sad-looking guests who need attention. After that the unwritten law tells you to case the joint
—latch on to someone who might divulge some juicy secret
I can report to the Secretary of State. Get it?"

"Naw."

"For example—over there," I pointed to the distance,

"I see a Russian—the counselor of his embassy. Might he tell me what the Russian government thinks of the new Democratic candidate who's just been elected to the White House?" I was speaking out of wishful thinking. Most Americans expected Eisenhower to get in, but I was an Adlai Stevenson fan.

"Huh?"

"Or—how about the Syrian chargé?" I pointed again. "He's talking to the British ambassador over there, but they're searching the rooms with their eyes. Bad sign. They must be bored. Perhaps I should barge in. What's more. The Syrian is red in the face. You know what that means?"

"Booze."

"Exactly. He's Moslem, he's not supposed to touch alcohol. In fact, he drinks most of the Europeans under the table. Perhaps he might tell me something important about terrorism—all those bombs last week in the Middle East. Does any of this mean anything to you?"

"Naw," Eric Glenn yawned.

Without understanding the ways of diplomacy, he seemed to appreciate my effort to make him understand. At least he kissed Peg and me happily, lay down again, and pulled the sheet over his head.

Many Foreign Service children suffer some parental deprivation because of the demands of diplomacy: the frequent need for their parents to attend receptions and dinners at just the time when the kids want to be read to, cuddled, or tucked in. In Eric Glenn's case, parental deprivation seems to have made him a particularly caring parent to his own son. At the time of Nicholas' birth, Eric Glenn took several weeks off from his law practice. He was present at the birth, gave the baby his first bath, and spends much more time with his son than I ever spent with any of our four children. In comparison, I seemed like a heartless villain abnormally wedded to my work.

Perhaps (I hope) Eric Glenn has been compensated along the way for any deprivation suffered. He now seems extraordinarily independent and adventurous. He has climbed to the top of Mt. McKinley and also climbed in

South America, including an attempt on Mt. Aconcagua. He also flies his own plane.

While still a teenager, he became unusually sensitive to the needs of the underprivileged. In Jordan, he visited several refugee camps and carried away with him images of the inequities of the Third World, with its extremes of poverty and wealth. In maturity, he has devoted his legal career to providing advocacy and representation for the poor.

Our boys missed some other basic American cultures: baseball, television, and candy bars, for example. These were pretty much unknown in Jordan and Yugoslavia in the 1950s and 1960s. Chris, our youngest son, particularly remembers how much he missed his beloved baseball. Years later, at Princeton, he was having a discussion with friends. The name Willie Mays was mentioned.

"Who's that?" Chris asked.

He was astonished to hear that Mays was a famous baseball player. He was shocked to realize how much he had missed during his years overseas.

After almost five years in Brussels, I learned that I was being transferred to Washington, D.C. to spend a year at the National War College. Fortunately, I did not have to arrive there until September.

By late July, Terry was sitting up in bed without a fever. He had now been in the hospitals of Ostend and Brussels for two and a half months. Poulain, who had taken personal responsibility to assure that the medication was given three times daily, said that the boy could leave the hospital in another week. He would be well enough to make the sea voyage by the time we were scheduled to leave Belgium. Poulain warned, however, that the recovery would be rocky. Terry had expended more energy fighting the disease than if he had been healthy and exercising twelve hours a day. He was tired; he needed rest.

In our last week in Brussels, the latest issue of the Foreign Service Journal arrived containing Peg's article on new embassy personnel arriving in Belgium. Ten minutes after its receipt in the embassy, the CIA man came charging into my office, accusing Peg of blowing his cover, and thereby ending his usefulness in Belgium.

Without warning, all the emotions I had been repressing for two and a half months exploded and I found myself screaming, "Why pick on Peg? No one briefed her about the Agency. How the hell was she expected to know all that crap about secrecy? Don't blame us. Blame the Journal for publishing it. They must have guidelines about what they publish. Why don't you give them a briefing! And while you're at it, get after the Department's committee on clearances. Why didn't they censor the damn article?"

By the time I calmed down, he was gone. I heard no more complaints from the CIA.

Just before Peg and I left Brussels, we saw Poulain for a final briefing on Terry. He seemed fine now, but would there be after effects? Poulain was straightforward. Because of the prolonged high fever, Terry's brain had been inflated and probably rubbed against his skull. It would be a miracle if the rubbing was not now causing scar tissue to appear on the brain.

"And that means?" Peg asked hesitantly.

"Possible emotional disturbance. Terry's whole emotional constitution has been given a severe shock. He is liable to carry his emotions on his sleeve. Be prepared for surprises. He may react in strange—maybe even illogical—ways in response to things you might consider unimportant. It will be hard not to give in to him in order to spare yourselves a lot of tantrums. But I think you should be aware that if you spoil the child, his later life will be more unhappy than if you treat him from the beginning with love—but firmness."

I don't think we really took in the full meaning of what Poulain was saying. Emotional disturbances? How would we notice them? Were they to show up as tantrums? Could he be a normal playmate? What about his future?

We left Belgium with a host of unanswered questions, and it was only gradually, over the years, that we learned what the good doctor meant. Two years later, in our car on a short trip to Florida, Terry began to tremble without warning, his fingers and legs writhing, his eyes glazed. When we later got to a neurologist, we found that the boy was having small epileptic seizures. Petit mal, it was called.

The petit mal became more frequent and grew into grand mal a year later, when he suffered a first class epileptic seizure: ten minutes of unconsciousness on the floor, biting his tongue, his body lashing out in some unexplained torment, a slight foam at the corners of his mouth. From then on, he was placed on a daily regime of anti-epileptic drugs. Most of the time the grand mal was kept under control with medication, except when Terry, like the Belgian nurse before him, forgot there were pills to be taken.

Years later, in Malaya, Terry was splashing happily in a swimming pool. Without warning, he put his hands to his face and broke into uncontrolled sobs. Peg and I hurried to him. Through his tears he looked at us without really seeing us. Something inside him was causing turbulence, perhaps even pain. Minutes later, when he stopped sobbing, he could not tell us what had happened.

Terry must have associated the torment of those months in Belgium directly with the Foreign Service. Although he eventually recovered his sturdy physique and developed into a great adventurer, when I left the Foreign Service, he swore he would never go abroad again. And so far, secure in the home he has built in Alaska, he never has.

SEVEN

A Joke Book of Questionable Taste (National War College, Washington, D.C.)

"**I**f the cocktails were as cold as the soup, the soup as warm as the wine, the wine as old as the chicken, the chicken as full-breasted as the hostess, and the hostess as available as the ambassador's wife—then it would have been a really great party."

That was only one of the jokes I learned from student presentations given at the National War College (NWC).

With my family, I arrived back in Washington in 1952. All of us were happy to be back, especially after Terry's close call and five years of Socialist/Catholic wars.

Strangely enough, my year at the NWC was a legitimate assignment in the Foreign Service, in fact, a highly-prized one and difficult to get. I received it as a result of record-breaking performance in my previous post as labor attache in Belgium and Luxembourg. During our five year tour of duty there, Peg and I had three children, and I received two promotions from a mid-level rating of FSO-4 to FSO-2, one step from the highest Foreign Service rating. Although both feats broke records, it was the promotions, not the reproduction, that brought me to the NWC.

What really should have been required of each NWC student was at least one highly imaginative dirty joke—for reasons that will soon become clear.

The NWC brought together for one year top-ranking officers of the military (full colonels for the Army and Air

Force, and captains for the Navy) and equally high-ranking officers of the State Department, CIA, and several other government agencies. The purpose of this hodgepodge was to expose the military and civilians to each others' thinking. We would all work together on military-political problems and thereby learn to cooperate better in future wars than we had in World War II. The experience of working together in NWC courses, it was hoped, would diminish future military-civilian clashes and increase the United States' chance for victory in the next war, regardless of the fact that it might be a nuclear war that would devastate the world.

Military officers graduating from the NWC were expected to become generals or admirals, and State Department personnel ambassadors or deputy chiefs of mission. It was assumed by the NWC that all of us would have been promoted to these top ranks by the time of the next war.

I remember my year at the NWC with mixed feelings. I was certainly exposed to military thinking and, I believe, I learned to get along with the "military mind," although I was not always sure what that term meant. I talked and lectured on the Foreign Service and diplomacy; I heard some interesting lectures from authorities in the politico-military field; and, not least of all, I heard some funny jokes.

Each day one of the students would make a presentation to the whole school on some international topic of his choosing. (I say "his" advisedly, since in those days there were no women students.) Almost always the opening of each speech would be a joke. These jokes were eagerly awaited by the school body. When some student was daring enough to barge into his subject without the obligatory introductory joke, there was an audible sigh of betrayal and a scattering of boos from the rest of the student body.

I learned, for example, that diplomacy is the art of letting someone have your way. And I was particularly pleased to find that diplomacy rests coyly in the dictionary between "diplodocus" (a lizard or dinosaur) and "diplopia (double vision). Both are quite adequate descriptions of the art of diplomacy.

In the speech of still another student, I was enchanted to learn of the close relationship between diplomacy and the world's oldest profession: whatever their momentary pleasures, both are deficient in lasting satisfaction.

Not all the jokes during that year were unrelated to the current world problems we were studying at the NWC. One joke about international understanding lingers in my mind. A father was bringing his son up in the most modern of methods. He gave the boy anything he wanted. One day the son announced, "Daddy, I want a worm for breakfast." Without questioning his son, the father went into the garden and brought back a live worm. He put it on a plate and gave it to the boy. The latter started wailing, "No, Daddy, I want the worm cooked." Acquiescent to the demands of his son, the father cooked the worm and presented it to him. "But, Daddy," the son yelled, "I want Daddy to eat half the worm." Again the father dutifully obliged. He ate half the worm and presented the other half to his son. This time he was greeted by hysterical screams, "Daddy, you ate the half I wanted!"

The confrontation between father and son is analogous to many of the world's conflicts. India and Pakistan each wanted half of Kashmir and still do. And Greece and Turkey both wanted half of Cyprus and still do.

I was often so bored with the lectures that I started writing down the jokes. Witticisms are essential to lighten up speeches, and I was often at a loss to come up with appropriate jokes when I was called upon from time to time to make speeches in the Foreign Service. As the semester progressed, however, the jokes got coarser and weirder, and I sensed my collection might not be as useful as I had originally hoped. Nevertheless, I ended up compiling "A Joke Book of Questionable Taste" containing over two hundred jokes ranging from the raw to the slightly stained, and distributed copies to my friends at the end of the year. I still consult my copy occasionally, although I try to know

my audiences so that I don't send them stampeding to the
exits.

Of considerably more interest than the NWC speeches
that year were the speeches delivered in the Senate by Senator Joseph McCarthy who had embarked on his anti-Communist campaign of character assassination. Accusations
of betrayal, Communism, espionage, and whatever other
labels came to mind, were hurled vindictively at individuals in many agencies of government, but focused on the
State Department. I attended some of these hearings and
learned more about dirty politics than dirty jokes.

What followed was ridiculous, tragic, and enraging.
Some of our finest Foreign Service officers wound up being
crucified, ironically, for accomplishing brilliantly the job
they were hired to do: reporting truthfully what they saw
and felt about developments in China. Even before China
became Communist, our China hands were reporting that
Chiang Kai Shek no longer could count on the support of
his people who in desperation were turning to the rebels
led by Communist chief Mao. These reports did not sit well
with Senator McCarthy and many others who had been
supporting Chiang Kai Shek for many years. At first they
blasted the writers of these reports for "ignorance," then,
as Chiang notably weakened and some of his troops de-
fected, the writers of these reports were said to be pro-
Communists, then, finally, traitors. It was not long before
McCarthy passionately announced that "we" had lost
China. The "we" of course referred to the Foreign Service
officers who had written these "inflammatory and treason-
able" reports. One by one these officers were accused of
betrayal and fired.

As the campaign became more rabid, I was disheart-
ened to see that the Department of State was not speaking
up in defense of its China hands. Many of our highest officers were silent, hoping no doubt to escape the whirlwind
shaking up the Department. As a result, we lost many of
our best and wisest FSOs, and our China office was seriously weakened for years to come. This was one of the
most shameful episodes in United States diplomatic his-

tory. Like the proverbial bearers of bad news, our China hands had their heads "cut off."

One of my friends in the Department's International Labor Division was Val Lorwin. He had a membership card from the Socialists and, because the card was red and was seen at a cocktail party, he was accused of being a Communist. Since Socialism and Communism were considered synonymous by the uninformed in those days, he was expelled from the State Department. He went into a teaching job at the University of Oregon and continued to fight to clear his name. A number of us helped with his legal fees and, some years later, when McCarthy had died and the political witch hunt had ended, Val won his case. He was reinstated by the State Department, went back to Washington, collected his back pay for twelve years and the next day resigned. Our farewell party for him was an extraordinarily happy event.

In spring of 1953, as a windup to our year at the NWC, I was given my first exposure to Asia, on an orientation trip to visit military installations. In a jumbo plane with bucket seats, we visited Japan, Hong Kong, Okinawa, Guam, Hawaii, the Philippines and Korea. The Korean War was still raging and we were dumped by helicopter from a battleship into a Pusan overwhelmed with mud and devastation.

In Okinawa we rode in jeeps from the airport to the sumptuous American club perched on top of a cliff overlooking the sea. On the dirt road leading to the club we encountered many farmers trudging along with their overburdened animals. Each time, we honked our horns loudly and insistently until the farmers frantically tugged their animals into the ditches beside the road. I asked the ranking American officer escorting us how the peasants reacted to being honked off the road so imperiously in their own country by foreigners. Or didn't it make any difference how the peasants felt? The American officer looked at me as if I came from another planet. I got the message: These fucking State Department types! But instead of saying it aloud, he only shrugged. I made a mental note of the incident for my end-of-the-term report on the Asian trip.

Briefings by the military in Okinawa and elsewhere impressed me enormously. Not the substance so much as the form. Charts, graphs, polished presentations in a crisp dramatic style. After witnessing these deft and illuminating briefings, I understood why the Pentagon fares so well each year with its Congressional budget briefs.

Despite these endless presentations, we had sufficient spare time to accumulate an enormous amount of trinkets in each country visited, particularly Hong Kong and Tokyo where we acquired *objets d'art* as well as *objets* of utter garnishness.

The reason why I had chosen Asia for my end-of-the-term field trip over other parts of the world was that I was convinced I would never get to Asia during the course of my career. After all, my five years in Brussels plus my war years in Europe would inevitably lead to further assignments in Europe.

As might be perversely expected, on my return to Washington from the Asian trip, I learned that my next assignment would be in Asia as consul to a place whose name I had difficulty pronouncing: Kuala Lumpur. Hurriedly, I looked it up in an Atlas and discovered it was the capital of Malaya (now Malaysia) and a colony of Britain. I also learned that K.L. was the contemporary way of talking about Kuala Lumpur, and that it literally meant "muddy estuary."

Oh my God, I thought with a sinking heart. What am I doing to my family—my wife, my three young kids, now aged two, four, and five? All I knew about Southeast Asia was the oppressive heat. It was close to the equator. I had read Somerset Maugham's Malayan stories and remembered particularly *The Letter*, which starred Jeanne Eagels on the stage and Bette Davis in the movie, stooping to pick up a crucial letter at the foot of an Eurasian woman who had purposely let it drop so that the white woman would have to stoop in front of her. Again, racial problems—as if there weren't enough already in America! And then there

would be cobras—and more health problems. What fright-
ful tropical diseases did we face?

With some anxiety I hurried to my friend Willard
Hanna, a fellow student who had worked and lived in Malaya and Indonesia. To my astonishment, when he heard I
was going to Kuala Lumpur, he congratulated me.

"Fortunate man," he said. Willard was thin and tall
with a razor-sharp mind that relished satire. Surely he was
kidding.

"But it's Southeast Asia," I insisted.

"The most glorious part of the world."

"What's so glorious about heat? My family can't stand
heat. We all get hives."

"Ah—but the houses are built for outdoor living. No
windows. The sides are all open to the outdoor breezes."

"And the flies—mosquitoes—poisonous insects?"

"No flies—no mosquitoes."

He was laying it on too thick to be credible. "Come
on," I said.

"Not only that," he continued merrily. "No malaria.
You can drink the water. No sterilization of vegetables. It's
the garden spot of the world. Lucky man—"

Willard was a practical joker. All his talk of potable
water and gracious living must be sarcasm. Yet there was a
strange note of yearning in his voice.

"What about children? We have three kids."

"They'll thrive—run around all day in shorts—look
like a million dollars after you're there a week. Ah, I wish I
could go back."

I tried to absorb what he said, but my picture of K.L.
still included disease, snakes and sweat. "Where are you off
to?" I asked.

"Tokyo," he said rather sadly.

I wanted to be sure I heard him correctly. "Tokyo?"

"If only I could trade with you." The yearning was
now out in the open.

At that point I would gladly have traded assignments
with him. But later I found out he was mostly right. True,
in K.L. we did occasionally sleep under mosquito nets. But

Washington D.C. had more mosquitoes than Malaya. British inspectors kept standing water to a minimum, and malaria was limited to jungle posts. The British had done a remarkable job in bringing health to Malaya, and, during the next three years, all the Kochers blessed them for it.

The end of my term at the NWC approached. All that was left was to work up a five or ten minute report on the Asian trip to present to the rest of the students, some of whom had travelled to Europe, others to the Middle East.

When my turn came to report to the school, I stepped to the platform and silently scanned the faces of the students in the auditorium. I was in no hurry to begin. In fact, I wanted to unnerve them a bit by my silence. My first sentence was an apology—I had no joke with which to start. At this point I got several expected boos. I admitted I was a renegade. But bear with me, I continued. There just wasn't anything funny about the trip: bucket seats for fifteen hours at a stretch, mud and devastation when we got to Korea, and as for Okinawa—still no jokes there. But there was a story I should share with them. Their faces brightened at this point, thinking I would not disappoint them, after all. Then, without emotion, I told them about the peasants on the dirt road in Okinawa, mercilessly honked into the ditch, cattle and all, by an American jeep with no need to hurry.

When I finished, I looked at the faces in the auditorium. They were suddenly serious, more serious than I had probably ever seen them.

"All year long," I said, "we've been talking about the military mind and diplomacy as if they might be the same. The incident in Okinawa clearly illustrated the complete difference between the two. The military mind means: get those goddamn peasants out of the way. Diplomacy means: get those nice peasants out of the way.

"In our long careers ahead, there will be plenty of occasions to blow the horn imperiously. But when there's no emergency, fellows, shouldn't we try a softer horn? It always helps to keep the public on our side."

EIGHT

Over the Fence with Nixon (Malaya)

"You must find things for Vice President Nixon to do that have never been done before by any American visiting Malaya."

There it was, a cable in the most challenging of terms from the Department of State in Washington to Eric Kocher, American Consul in Kuala Lumpur. Nixon was about to make his first trip to Southeast Asia, a year after his election as Vice President in 1952.

I had only arrived in Kuala Lumpur a few weeks before. We were still adjusting to our new post, comparing it with our previous assignment in Belgium. From a raw, wet climate to persistent tropical heat, from democracy to colonialism, from a mid-level job as labor attache to the slot of number one American representative in the whole country. There was obviously a lot of adjusting to do.

Clearly the purpose of Nixon's visit would not be sightseeing. The Vice President had a reputation for working long and gruelling hours. We would certainly not see a repetition of the visit of Senator Estes Kefauver, the renowned expert on crime in America, who, according to my staff, in a day and a half in Singapore some months before my arrival, spent his entire time writing post cards to his moneyed constituents, wearing—in the dripping heat—his famous coonskin cap from Tennessee, and patronizing a local brothel. Nor could the Nixon visit afford to imitate

most Congressional delegations that travelled abroad on
fact-finding missions, finding facts that could more easily
have been found at home in the Department of State.

We were well aware of the dark side of Nixon's reputation: his rabid anti-Communism. He had started his career
as a Congressman from California, a race he had won by
vilifying his opponent for alleged Communist leanings. In
addition, he was a fervent supporter of the obsessed Senator Joseph McCarthy. By trading on the anti-Communist
hysteria of the time to further his career, Nixon had gained
a reputation for being unscrupulous and vindictive.

Rumors from the other posts Nixon was planning to
visit were ominous. In addition to broadening his international horizons, he intended to evaluate the political leanings of Foreign Service officers at each post. He wanted no
Communist sympathizers, closet or otherwise, to represent
America abroad. Fair enough. During my few months in
Kuala Lumpur I had never sensed Communist leanings in
any of the consulate staff. But though we were "clean," we
still shared a foreboding that the Nixon visit would bring
us no pleasure.

Nixon's demand for a unique activity was an obvious
ploy for a headline back home: "Vice President Nixon in
Malaya has _____. First time ever for any American." Now
it was up to the consulate to fill in the blanks.

Although we resented this assignment at first, we soon
realized it was not unreasonable for an American VIP to
want a few headlines in the *New York Times* and *Washington Post* to build up his reputation for daring and initiative.

And so we set to work. Our consulate was small—one
political officer, one economic officer, and one officer who
combined administrative and consular functions. Knowing
Nixon's anti-Communist concerns, we should have found it
easy to work up an engrossing schedule. Obviously the
anti-Communist measures taken by the Malayans and the
British should be highlighted. A year or so before, the British High Commissioner had been assassinated by Communist guerrillas as he drove through the jungle to a hill station. At that time the Communists seemed to be gaining

control of a large part of the country outside the main cen-
ters of population. If security now permitted, it would
make sense for Nixon to visit one of the jungle outposts
from which the British launched their attacks against the
guerrillas. Of course, there would be obligatory briefings
by the British and ourselves, as well as the lunches and
dinners that visiting dignitaries have to suffer through.

But that sticky phrase "never been done before" continued to haunt us. The trouble was we were trying to find
the unfindable. Adlai Stevenson, the defeated Democratic
candidate for President in 1952, had been in Malaya for
two months. His purpose had been to steep himself in the
life and problems of Malaya, and he had literally done it
all. Tin mines, rubber plantations, aborigines in the jungle,
leprosarium, military outposts, jungle warfare, British,
Chinese, Malays, Indians. Tigers, elephants, cobras. Everything. Everyone. Everywhere.

Each time Oscar, our political officer, an imaginative
Chinese language specialist, came up with a suggestion, the
administration officer who kept all the records of previous
visits would glance through his papers and sigh: "Adlai already did it."

After our third meeting on the Nixon visit, not one
new idea had emerged. I consulted the British High Commissioner, Field Marshal Sir Gerald Templer, who smiled
cynically and suggested, tongue in cheek, that a ride on an
elephant at dawn might be just the thing to cause a yawn
back home.

"As for Nixon's visit," he said, "I must warn you
blokes. You'll have some competition."

"What competition?"

"Lee will be arriving at the airport about the same
time as your Vice President."

"Who's Lee?" I asked quizzically.

"Of course you wouldn't know." Sir Gerald raised his
eyebrows in that wonderfully British supercilious way, "A
great movie and singing star—the idol of Singapore."

"When does he arrive?" I asked.

"Right after Mr. Nixon's plane. We wanted to postpone

Lee's arrival but he's due at the theatre at noon. Can't disappoint the mobs."

We held one more meeting of consulate officers on the Nixon visit. We had gone beyond seriousness in our ridiculous quest for uniqueness. The admin. officer suggested that Nixon might be fitted with cleats and pushed up a coconut tree, hopefully causing a coconut to fall on his head. And our economic officer thought Nixon would look great, if, dressed in a loin cloth, he blew a dart from a blow pipe at a tiger. That surely had never been done before by any visitor, American or otherwise. With our laughter, we dissipated some of the tension and foreboding that seemed to be closing in on us.

Somewhat apologetically we sent a cable to Nixon, still in Washington, recommending a schedule for his visit. We admitted that the recommended activities, though not unique, were included to give the Vice President necessary insight into the country. Tin and rubber were basic to the Malayan economy, so that excluding a visit to a tin mine and rubber plantation would be a disservice to the Vice President. Ditto for the British handling of the Communist "emergency." We stressed, however, that we had not given up the quest for a unique activity despite the difficulty of finding one after Adlai Stevenson's long and detailed visit.

It was necessary to keep the promise of originality alive in Washington, realistic or not; it would surely not endear the consulate to the new Vice President if he had to scratch us from his schedule for lack of positive response to his request.

There was silence from Washington for a few days. When the answer came, it was brief. The schedule suggested was acceptable. But the need still existed for a unique activity so that the Vice Presidential visit would stand out above all other American visits. We groaned in despair.

Even with the crucial part of the schedule still in shadow, we started planning the logistics. Details of each part of the program were attended to: the number of cars;

the exact time and place of departure and arrival of each vehicle, the names of each person in each car.

All too soon the time came for our last cable to Nixon. He would leave Washington day after tomorrow, fly to Hawaii, Singapore, and other posts that have escaped my memory, before arriving in Kuala Lumpur. It was with a feeling of the greatest unease, mixed with a crazy what-the-hell attitude, that I dictated the final sentence: "Consulate still searching for unique activity for Vice President."

The morning of Nixon's arrival, Peggy and I were at the airport at nine. His plane was due to arrive about ten. The two cars the British High Commissioner had loaned us for the visit were already parked on the tarmac. A U.S. Security detail that had arrived three days earlier was scouting the building.

The sun shone over the top of the palm trees, and a humid breeze was cutting across the runway. The brilliant orange-blue sky, typical of Malayan mornings, gave no hint of the black rain clouds that would inevitably form on the horizon at lunchtime and flood the landscape before evening. Even though the morning, hot and muggy as usual, induced torpor, I felt something between exhilaration and foreboding. Nixon was probably the most important visitor I would host in a long Foreign Service career. Yet the most crucial part of his schedule was still not in place.

Kuala Lumpur airport was barely equipped to receive large international planes. Its single runway was narrow and usually shot with potholes. Its technical equipment provided only minimal safety. On ordinary days the monotony of the terminal's grey wooden walls was hardly relieved by the drab green sills of small windows. The paint was peeling off walls and window frames, and the wood underneath was visibly rotting.

Still, the government tried to measure up to Nixon's visit. It decorated enough of the outside of the old building to give it a measure of youthful grace. Three enormous flags—British, Malay and American—hung over the arched entrance. Bunting festooned the windows and door.

Nixon's plane first appeared as a black speck escaping

the white mists enveloping the hilltops. Soon, in a long downward curve, it landed on the runway, then taxied toward the terminal. As I walked to the runway, the plane rolled to a halt.

With friendly waves, Richard and Pat Nixon came through the huge door and stood on the top of the ramp. Grinning, arms high over his head, he seemed to be celebrating an election victory. Pat, behind her husband, was less ebullient. Immediately, the two photographers went into action. Before each click of the camera, Nixon's smile seemed to become broader, warmer, ever more flashing. Mrs. Nixon, more reserved, smiled briefly, then descended the ramp after her husband. Behind her came three aides with briefcases.

After greeting Nixon and his wife, I introduced them to Peggy and the Deputy High Commissioner who represented the British government. The two men spoke a moment, then, as if by pre-arranged signal, the Army band started playing the British and American anthems. Visitors as well as hosts stood at attention. Nixon inspected the two lines of soldiers in full ceremonial dress, standing rigidly in front of the airport building.

As soon as the inspection was over, Nixon came to me. By the time he reached me, the smile he had adopted for the ceremony had faded.

"Have you thought of anything unique?"

I was just about to say "not yet" when I became aware of a jumble of forms behind him. With a swift glance I found myself staring at countless faces behind the five foot wooden fence surrounding the airport: Malays, Chinese, Indians. With their laughs and cheers, they seemed in a holiday spirit. Some of them were even hanging over the fence.

Then I remembered that Lee, the great Singapore star, was also arriving at the airport. The people were waiting for Lee. Still, it was a crowd. And the crowd was in high spirits. Primed for cheering and greeting and shaking hands. And here also was Nixon. Why not bring everyone together?

"Mr. Nixon," I said cautiously. "There is something Adlai Stevenson never did here. Or any other American for that matter."

He turned toward me with new interest. "Oh?" That single word was charged with more meaning than you usually find in several sentences.

"When Stevenson was here, he was comparatively unknown. At least there weren't crowds eagerly hanging over the fence waiting to greet him."

"Oh, there are crowds?" I never imagined Nixon to be this coy, but that's how he was shaping up.

"More people than I've ever seen for an American. Many more. They're eager to see you—greet the great American from overseas—shake your hand."

"Do you suppose?"

"They would be touched if you went over and said a few words—"

"If you want me to—."

"I'll notify the photographers—wait a second." I went to the consulate political officer who was standing a few feet away and told him to get the photographers over near the fence.

I returned to Nixon. "Two photographers will follow you."

"In that case—" His face came alive and his smile was eager. He walked at a brisk pace towards the fence, a distance of perhaps a hundred yards, two photographers trailing behind him.

"I should warn you," I called out. "The British may not like it. They may think it's too aggressive, too—American."

Without even turning, he muttered something like "fuck them," then headed at an even faster pace for the fence. With some consternation two British and one American security police followed him.

The Vice President headed directly for an old man with deep furrows on his face. Seizing the gnarled hand, Nixon tried to shake it. The old man snatched his hand away as if he had been bitten by a cobra. Nixon contemplated his quarry for a moment. He seemed to be evaluating the man, analyzing his motivation, trying to devise a breakthrough. He offered his hand again. This time his gesture was low key, his look almost gentle.

The crowd fell silent, probably confused. Nixon didn't look like Lee. He didn't even look like a movie star. Still, there was something about him. That Army band. That music. The limousine of the British. But why did he come rushing over to the fence? Then that white hand stretching toward the Malay—the Malay backing up—what was it all about?

With a warm smile and his hand extended, Nixon kept his eyes focused on the old man. Slowly, very slowly, the Malay put out his hand. The two hands met, and their owners exchanged tentative smiles. When the old man giggled, the crowd exploded in screams of delight. Who the strange white man was might never be known, but the crowd was enchanted. Nixon was now pumping dozens of hands reaching out toward him. Children, urged on by parents, tried to touch him. Babies were held up, their grimy fingers directed toward his hand.

When the Vice President came back, Pat sighed with relief. "He's always running for election," she said with gentle amusement. "But should he trust your crowds? What do you think?"

"They're enchanted," I said.

"How did I do, Pat?" He put his arm around her. "Did I win the election?"

"You have my vote," she said.

I saw the Deputy High Commissioner frown as he came over to our group.

"Excellency," he said. "You're having lunch with the American Consul, I believe—"

"I nodded."

"Later in the afternoon you will come to the High Commissioner's?"

Again I nodded.

Nixon was being put up by the British at Government House because my Residence, large and comfortable though it was, lacked the elegance of the High Commissioner's mansion with its platoon of servants and huge gardens.

"The Vice President will be at Government House at four twenty," I said. I was glad I had memorized the schedule so I could rattle it off without consulting the piece of paper in my pocket.

"A very pleasant visit then, Excellency."

The Deputy High Commissioner and his aides walked toward their Rolls Royce, as I guided the Nixons to the consulate Chevy. The Nixons rode with Peg and me. The American flag was flying on one fender, the Malayan flag on the other. Nixon's aides and U.S. Security personnel followed in the other two cars.

After leaving the airport, we came to the outskirts of a village. Small huts on stilts, sheltered by groves of coconut trees, lined the road. In front of each hut, silent peasants crouched on wooden steps. They seemed to be relaxing, chewing betel nut, dreamily watching the occasional passing car.

"No great enthusiasm out there. Do they always sit on their hands when they see the American flag?"

Nixon seemed gloomy. The silence of these peasants must have been a disappointment after the cheers and screams he had just experienced.

"I often drive on this road," I said. "It's the only road between town and the airport. The people don't know there's someone special in the car today."

"Stop, driver," Nixon suddenly said to Hamad our driver.

"What's on your mind?" I asked.

"Just mix—see and be seen—shake all their beautiful black and brown and yellow hands."

Hamad, confused, had cut his speed without stopping. Now he put on the brakes.

With his smile firmly in place, Nixon leaped out of the car and strode toward five peasants crouched on the steps in front of one of the huts. I jumped out after him.

I wondered if he would start pumping hands all over again. Apparently, however, he had learned from his last

encounter at the airport. As he approached the five peasants, he slowed his step, gave a boyish smile, and very
slowly extended a hand. Several seconds passed that must
have seemed an eternity to someone as eager as Nixon for
a quick victory. Eventually a hand met his, accompanied
by a slight confused bowing of the head. Still dreamily
chewing betel nut, the other four peasants slowly took the
Nixon hand and languidly shook it. They waved gently as
he left.

When he got back to the car, Nixon's smile was rooted
in triumph. It was as if he had encountered some of his
constituents and knew he had won their vote.

"If only I could run for election in Malaya," he said a
bit wistfully.

"What are you after?" Even though Pat smiled, I
sensed a note of concern in her voice. "Want to be Vice
President of the world?"

"No—just President." Nixon burst into laughter, then
suddenly stopped. "No one ever did that before. Or did
they? Did any American mix with the peasants on the airport road?"

"Nobody ever had the interest—or the guts," I said trying not to betray my knowledge of why the crowds had
gathered or feel thankful they had not called out for their
singing idol Lee.

"Brashness might be a better word," he said. "When-
ever I see a challenge, I feel like a coward until I face it.
Those dumb farts were a challenge. God, were they stupid.
I thought they really had me for a while."

With mixed feelings I watched the last dreamy waving
of hands as we left the village. The peasants did not know
that Nixon despised them, that all the handshakes and
smiles were part of a game. I resented him exploiting them.
But perhaps his feelings toward them were not important.
What mattered was that they felt they had been greeted as
an equal by a white man.

As we entered the outskirts of Kuala Lumpur, we had
to slow down. Throngs of Malays, Chinese, Indians, Ceylonese, all in their ethnic clothes, pressed together. Brown

and rust-colored sarongs, black shorts, green and purple saris. Water buffalo, pigs, and carts shared the narrow street with them.

"What local color!" Pat said, her head hanging out the window.

"Like that." I pointed to a youngster. No more than five, he was naked except for a buttonless shirt. His emaciated face was bent over a tiny rivulet of blackish water in a gutter. Flattening himself on his belly, he poked his hand into the water and wiped his face. Apparently refreshed, he stood up and urinated into the rivulet.

"All in my honor." Nixon laughed. "Now look at that."

A Buddhist temple was on our left. Like a world on fire, its gilded dome glinted in the sun. Two old men, after taking off their sandals, started climbing a flight of stone steps leading to the door. They were eating bananas, and, as they finished, tossed the peels on the step. All along the stairs mangosteen and banana skins oozed.

"Why did those men take off their sandals?" Mrs. Nixon asked. "Out of respect?"

"More likely to keep their sandals from getting dirty," Peggy said wryly.

Nixon turned to me. "From the plane, Malaya looks like a jungle paradise. How much jungle is there?"

"Eighty percent, only twenty percent cultivated."

"Hunter's paradise? Tigers—elephants—samba deer?"

I nodded.

"Don't tell me the Department didn't mention it all in your briefing books."

"Those goddam books—a real bore. Hell, I learn more about a country in a few minutes being there, than I do in a week of reading. How do you assess the Communist situation here?"

"Difficult. But the British are doing a magnificent job."

"Templer sounds like the kind of anti-Communist fighter I'm proud of. He comes across sharp and straight. And he isn't afraid to be ruthless. How the hell do you suppress those bastards without a bit of the old frontier spirit? Get the job done and then see how to justify the means. It's a lesson we should learn in America."

"We have a briefing set up for you in half an hour. Before lunch."

"Good."

In another ten minutes we reached the Residence. Five minutes later, after washing up, Nixon and his aides were ready for the briefing. Mrs. Nixon, travel-weary, wanted to "put her feet up," and we left her on the rattan sofa in the living room, legs up on an ottoman, overhead fan moving the torpid air. In order not to disturb her coiffure, she kept on her hat, one I remember because it was the kind worn by Hollywood ingenues of the period.

As we took Nixon and his aides to the consulate for the briefing, Peg checked on the lunch for forty which was scheduled for one o'clock.

At the briefing, the Political Officer and I went into the current political and economic picture in Malaya with an emphasis on the Communist threat.

I well remember Nixon's first question after we finished our presentations: "Any chance of the Communists taking over here?"

"A year ago, yes," I said. "But now the balance is on our side."

He seemed disappointed with my optimistic reply, a reaction I only understood later when I heard that his first question after a briefing in Japan was the same question he asked here. One of my friends, the Deputy Chief of Mission in Tokyo, who gave the briefing, told Nixon there was little chance of Communism succeeding in Japan. The real threat, he said, was fascism. Shortly after, the officer was transferred to New Zealand, a post of far lesser importance in the Foreign Service.

"What's the problem," Nixon next asked. "The British have all the equipment and fire power. Can't they find those goddam Commies?"

"Usually no. The jungle is so thick you can drive along almost any road in Malaya and not detect a Communist camp, even if it's only ten feet away. The terrain gives them an enormous advantage. Why, everyone swears the number two Communist leader is bivouacked somewhere near the golf course—"

"The golf course? In Kuala Lumpur?" Nixon interrupted.

"He could hide there—probably is there—then orchestrate attacks against the British—and still never be found."

Nixon turned strangely silent as I saw him mulling over what I had said.

We soon adjourned for lunch. The guests started pouring in at once. A large canopy had been erected in the garden, and we had set up tables there and in the living room. Peggy had worked long hours on the invitation list, the menu, the cooking, the schedule for Mrs. Nixon.

At that time, spouses of Foreign Service officers were not compensated for work performed for the United States government. Most of them pitched in willingly with only an occasional complaint that the State Department was getting two for the price of one. The Foreign Service paid me but got the free services of Peggy as well. Even Henry Luce, the founder of Time Magazine, found himself enrolled in embassy functions when his wife, Clare Boothe Luce, was ambassador to Italy, not only to help his wife but also to enhance the American image.

The lunch went well. Afterwards, Nixon gave a short speech about the beauties of the country, the importance of Malaya in the world, the marvelous reception accorded him by the extremely kind and hospitable Malayans, in short, all the usual but necessary cliches. After that we broke up. Peg and Pat Nixon went to visit an orphanage, and I went with Nixon, his aides, a couple of security police, and a representative of the High Commissioner to a rubber plantation and tin mine.

As we started out, I gave instructions in Malay to Hamad.

"Where did you learn Mayalsian," Nixon asked. He seemed impressed.

"Started off with an Army language manual," I replied,

"Peg and I studied and quizzed each other for three weeks on the boat coming over. By the time we reached Kuala Lumpur, we had learned quite a few greetings and a goodly amount of vocabulary. Since then, we've been taking lessons with a Malay in the Consulate."

"Must be a complicated language," Nixon said.

"Not really. The Malays have two dialects—bazaar Malay for all practical and social occasions, and a second, more formal, dialect for conversations with the Sultan. Since Peg and I have no royal aspirations, we study bazaar Malaya. Fortunately, it's relatively easy. You can get by with a thousand words or less. Even better, it has no tenses, no articles and no prepositions."

"Great language," Nixon commented, "It makes me wonder if all the subtleties in English only make life more complicated."

The plantation owner, a tall thin Indian in a flowing white robe, was critical of United States efforts to develop artificial rubber. What would happen to all the wonderful natural rubber in Malaya? Quite cleverly Nixon deflected the criticism: the need for rubber everywhere, he said, is expanding at such a rapid rate that there will always be a demand for both natural and artificial.

But most of Nixon's interest was focused on the tin mine. A lone Chinese woman was at work. She wore loose black pyjamas, a wide bamboo hat and a faded orange scarf tied around her cheeks and forehead to shield her from the sun. She was standing with a huge dragon of a hose squeezed against her chest. Her whole body was trembling as the water burst out of the hose with the force of a cannonball, separating the tin from the clay. The pressure of the water was so brutal it seemed to tear apart her body as it broke down the hills of clay in front of her.

It was an appalling sight, but it fascinated Nixon. "She's probably Communist, wouldn't you think?"

"She should be but I doubt it. No time, no energy, no thought of anything except that hose."

Nixon gave me a strange look and I began wondering.

How will he evaluate me on my Communist leanings? Fifty percent? Eighty percent?

Later that afternoon Peg and I escorted the Nixons to the High Commissioner's mansion, a grandiose palace-like structure resting on top of one of the great hills of Kuala Lumpur with a glorious view of jungle and town below. Sir Gerald Templer, the High Commissioner, took great pride in pointing out the scene of some of Somerset Maugham's stories: over there on the left was the Dog, the fabled British club, not far to the right was the small hotel by the railroad station which was frequently invaded by monkeys to the delight—or horror—of visiting tourists. And there on the extreme right, a golf course, near which the number two Communist was seen just last week. Again that look on Nixon's face—half yearning, half torment. He seemed racked by conflicting thoughts with which he was unable to come to terms.

The dinner that night was in the best British colonial tradition. Elegance, ritual, protocol, yet tempered with good humor, even occasional jesting. After dinner Lady Templer led the women to the lounge outside the powder room. Sir Gerald took the men to the garden. He stopped at a bed of canna lilies where the men, as if by rote, unzipped their pants and relieved themselves. I explained to the astonished Nixon and aides that urinating on canna lilies was in the best British tradition, at least in the colonies. Nixon gave me a sharp look as I gravely unzipped my pants and followed the others in the ritual of watering the plants. Somewhat reluctantly Nixon did likewise. The aides looked around with worried expressions as they followed the Vice President.

"No worry," I said. "Lady Templer and the women know all about our jungle habits. They'll stay on the other side of the house."

The Nixons departed the next day. On our way to the airport I gave him a copy of the English language Kuala Lumpur Daily Mail and pointed out a large headline: "Nixon Chats with Common Man," followed by "The

American Vice President, Mr. Richard Nixon, yesterday found time to stretch his arm over a five foot fence and offer his hand to an ordinary citizen of Malaya."

"Well, now, isn't that something?" He said in high spirits. Then he asked us to pass by the golf course. One of the aides began to take photos of the various holes.

Nixon gave me a small smile.

"Any chance of faking it? You know, getting my picture taken with a Malay—long beard, emaciated, as if he'd been hiding away for months in the jungle—then sending it to the papers back home?"

I tried to hide my distaste.

"As if you'd just discovered the number two Communist in Malaya?"

"Well—" Then suddenly as he saw the disbelief in my eyes, he sharply changed tack. "It wouldn't work, would it?"

Before I could answer, he changed the subject and started talking about the hospitality of the British. He considered Lady Templer one of the great ladies of the world and had invited both Templers to visit Washington.

Before getting on his plane, Nixon looked longingly at the fence surrounding the airport. No crowd. In fact, not even one person.

"The crowds—," he said unbelievingly, "What happened?"

I wanted to say "if only you knew how to sing like Frank Sinatra." Instead I said, "It's a special holiday for the Muslims. Most everyone is at the Mosque."

"Can't fight religion," he shrugged.

Pat Nixon seemed relieved her husband was not running around shaking hands. "He does too much of that," she said. "He should relax more and forget his image."

She thanked Peg and me for our hospitality and said she had a really good time. I believed her and appreciated her sheer amiability. Lady Templer, however, saw Pat in a different light. "Pat Nixon," Lady Templer said the following week when I met her at a reception, "A nice woman but . . ." she stopped. ". . . Some women can keep up with their husbands but not Pat Nixon. Too bad."

I was surprised that Lady Templer was so blunt about her feelings, particularly to an American. She did not recognize that Pat had no desire to "keep up" with her husband, certainly not in the complementary but independent way Lady Templer kept up with Sir Gerald by being the grande dame of Malaya with her own projects, hospital work, homes for children and the like. She had her own office and her own schedule during the day. The idea of a wife giving emotional support to her husband by "being there" was obviously unacceptable to Lady Templer.

Three weeks after the Nixons left Kuala Lumpur, the number two Communist in Malaya was found off the ninth hole of the golf course. Someone had shot a ball way off mark—it soared into the jungle. Annoyed and undaunted in the best British tradition, the golfer had grabbed a machete and started whacking his way through the brush and creepers. He never found the ball, but he did come across a small tent with a sleeping Communist in it. Two days later the picture of both men appeared in the Kuala Lumpur Daily Mail; the native man grim, bristling with beard, the other glowing in a fat satisfied way as if the man next to him was a golf trophy, as in a way he was.

I never had the heart to tell Nixon.

NINE

The Voting Booth
on Elephant Hill
(Malaya)

A year later, I was up to my ears in local, grass-roots issues. Nixon's visit and its reminders of civilization as we knew it back home were already a distant memory.

Campbell, the game warden, was pointing to the headline in the Kuala Lumpur Daily Mail of October 19, 1954, "Wild elephants rampage for second night in Bukit Gajah." His craggy brows wrinkled and he let out a laugh that sounded a little wicked.

He continued reading, "Crops destroyed—huts wrecked," another laugh rippled upward from his paunch, which had grown noticeably larger in the six months I had known him.

"Now what do I do?" It was a question he might better have pondered alone, but he was looking directly at me. Somehow he seemed to want to draw me into the problem.

"You're the game warden," I said, "Don't you know what to do?"

"I'm torn, bloody torn. The natives want the British to protect their homes and crops. I want to protect them, but Sir Gerald . . ." His voice trailed off.

Campbell was talking like no other game warden I knew. Far from protecting an endangered species, he seemed tempted to exterminate a couple of misbehaving elephants.

"Surely the High Commissioner wouldn't object to helping the natives, would he?" I said.

"You talk like a real Yank."

I had known Campbell ever since my second week as American consul in Kuala Lumpur. We talked easily to each other now, so I was not insulted by his sarcasm.

"Sir Gerald, my boy, is an ecologist." He said the word scornfully. "He wouldn't object to keeping the elephants in line—but it would be just that—a line of elephants padding through the jungle softly."

I had to laugh. Campbell approached everything with cynicism.

"You can laugh, my boy, but you don't work for Sir Gerald—moreover, you haven't answered my question. What do I do?" Then before I could answer, "Want to come with me to investigate Bukit Gajah tomorrow?"

"That's two questions," I said. "First you make up your mind if you're an ecologist or a hunter, then you go about being it. As for your invitation, I'm really busy, I'm—"

Campbell interrupted with a hearty smack on my back as if he was trying to keep unwelcome words from coming out.

"I know you blokes. Take a day away from the office— you're wasting the taxpayers' money. Well, if elephants can't lure you to Bukit Gajah, how about elections?" He was winking impishly, as if he had thrust a piece of bait before me.

"What elections?" I looked up from the Daily Mail which he had placed in my hand.

"First elections ever in Malaya. First step toward independence."

I had heard the British had vague plans for a series of elections in villages as a prelude to nationwide elections and independence.

"You mean tomorrow?"

He nodded solemnly.

"How come I didn't get an invitation to observe them?" I was annoyed. "What's the Consular Corps for except to keep track of what you Brits are doing?"

"Use the mind, old boy. London may not want you to report to Washington all our bloops."

"Perhaps you won't make any."

"The whole thing is a bloody awful mistake; these stupid Malays aren't ready for independence. When the British leave, the Malays will start a fucking war—Malays against Chinese—that sort of thing, you'll see."

"Oh, I don't know," I said vaguely. If I argued in support of independence we would end up in a first class row. "Anyway, I wish I could go with you but—"

"Oh, but you can."

"How do you know, Campbell?" I suppose he had a first name, but I'd never heard it.

"I want you to come," he said peremptorily. He was so obsessed with his work that he could not understand why everyone else was not similarly obsessed.

I had hoped to spend the day at the consulate writing a dispatch on all the millions the British must be raking in from a colonial dependent, but I was vastly tempted to go with Campbell. I could learn a lot from him if we spent the day in the jungle.

"Well—" I began.

"Good," he said promptly. "We'll be picking up our Malay trackers at Bukit Gajah. From there we walk. Ten kilometers should do it."

"Do what?"

"Find the fucking pachyderms. Now we're on."

As if he was consummating a deal, he shook my hand briskly. I thought I saw a tiny sparkle in his eyes and wondered what it meant, but it lasted only a moment.

At sunrise the next morning he showed up at the Residence in a jeep. I noticed a rifle on the floor.

"I thought you were going to investigate," I said.

"With a rifle you can investigate better. Elephants—and Communists."

"Communists?"

"Guerrillas in the jungle. All around us. We may come up on one or two of the buggers." He picked up a rifle from behind the seat similar to the one lying on the floor. "Here's yours, my boy. Know how to use it, I suppose?"

"In the Army they gave me an M-1. I practiced on the shooting range a lot but never fired at man or beast."

"Well, maybe today's the day," he said ominously. "You Americans see all the gangster films—think how Cagney and Eddie Robinson use their guns before you shoot."

As he handed me the rifle, I thought of all the gun control petitions Peggy and I had signed. Campbell met my guilty look with an open warm smile. Peggy's smile when I said goodbye to her was neither warm nor open.

"Why do you need that?" She pointed to the rifle in my hand.

Mumbling a few non sequiturs about investigating elephants and Communists, I hurriedly hugged her goodbye and jumped in beside him.

Campbell and I drove out of town. The last small huts soon yielded to jungle.

After another five minutes, the asphalt road narrowed and turned into dirt. Without the dampening effect of recent rain, a powdery yellowish dust prevailed and swirled over the jeep. Six or seven kilometers later, the dirt road disintegrated into a jungle path covered with low reeds. At first the jeep maneuvred successfully around bumps and decaying stumps of trees. After another kilometer, the jungle closed in around us. Vines slashed at the sides of the jeep. The path disappeared, and we plunged through tall grass that sheltered us from the sun.

All at once, ahead of us in a small clearing appeared two Malays in sarongs. They were on bicycles; next to them two other bikes leaned against a giant baobab tree.

"Out with you, my boy," Campbell yelled in excitement, as he jumped out of the jeep.

"Here's yours." He thrust a bike at me.

Campbell said a few words to the two Malays, slung his rifle over his shoulder, and jumped on the other bike. Leaving the jeep in the clearing, we followed them.

The path was no more than two feet wide. After a kilometer, it narrowed even further, until we were pushing away branches and vines clawing at us.

Abruptly we arrived at a large clearing surrounded by tall coconut and casuarina trees that allowed only filtered light to reach the ground. Ahead of us was a small village or *kampong*. We parked our bikes against a coconut palm.

As we walked into the village, we passed an orange drink shop with a round table and two empty chairs on the front veranda. In the background stood rows of sand bags in front of a barbed wire fence.

A few yards beyond the drink shop was a hut on stilts with five wooden steps leading to its entrance. The roof was attap, and the sides were made of tree branches. Naked children were playing in the cool shelter under the hut. An old Malay woman, sitting in the open doorway, was chewing betel nut, her stringy white hair hanging over her face, her broad bare feet resting on the top step.

"Slamat," I greeted her.

She smiled dreamily and spat out a mouthful of red juice. I had visited many kampongs before and each time had seen people stoned on betel, as addictive a substance as the coca leaf. (As I looked at the kids playing under the hut, I wondered if one day they too would be chewing betel nut.)

On a slight rise ahead of us stood the skeleton of a wooden structure. It had no roof and its sides were only half completed. Its smallness and booth-like character lent no clues to its identity. A pile of lumber lay next to it. On the other side of the lumber was a small wooden platform about a foot high. A few Malays in dirty brown sarongs were listening to an old Malay man who was speaking on the platform.

"You want to see the elections?" Campbell nudged me and pointed to the Malay on the platform. "A candidate, wouldn't you say?"

We stopped to listen. The old man on the platform was speaking slowly, and I had no difficulty understanding his Malay.

"This is why we want new latrine and that is why I call my party Latrine Party."

One of the listeners suddenly yelled.

"No latrine! School is better. We need school!"

"I tell you again why *kampong* need latrine," the old man continued in his soft voice. "Now only one latrine. On other side of *kampong*. Far, far. Second latrine will be here"—he pointed to the ground beneath him. "For all families on this side of *kampong*."

"For your family," the young man jeered.

"Yes, yes—for my family," the old man said proudly. "Why should I not help my family? If I help all other families, my wife—my children—get angry. They say I no longer belong to them."

"He is right!" another listener shouted to the young Malay who wanted a school. "You want school—so you start School Party. Why? Because you have five children."

I heard footsteps behind me and turned to see a small wiry Englishman immaculately dressed in a white polo shirt and new khaki shorts.

"Campbell, so delighted you could come." The man tapped Campbell on the shoulder with a swagger stick. His debonair manner would have been more appropriate at a fashionable garden party in London.

"Ah, you have brought your American friend," he continued.

Campbell introduced me to him. He was District Officer, Ronald Bingham.

"I'm really pleased you could come, Consul. I wasn't allowed by headquarters to invite any foreign blokes to our elections, but how can I complain if you arrive on your own?"

"When are the elections?" I asked.

"This afternoon—when the voting booth is finished." He pointed with his swagger stick to the skeleton of the wooden platform. "The last lumber just arrived. Soon a work squad will finish the booth." He paused and shook his head. "Dear God. Quite an election. What would you say in

Washington if you had to choose between a Latrine Party and a School Party?"

I smiled. "At least it's an issue. Clear cut and no fuzziness. More than you can say sometimes for our Democrats and Republicans."

As I was talking to Bingham, I noticed again the sand bags and barbed wire in the background. I asked if they were related to the elections.

"Totally. The barbed wire surrounds the whole kampong. It's intended to keep the Communists out. But really, Headquarters have gone quite crazy on security. They assigned twenty soldiers to this kampong. More than we'll ever need."

"Let me be naive," I put in. "Why would the Communists want to come into the kampong?"

"Elections. The first ever in Malaya. The Communists know that if elections succeed here, there will be more elections in the rest of the country and eventually independence. A population headed for freedom is not the best hunting grounds for Communism."

"Then you expect the Communists will try to break up the elections?"

"They may try all right. But not a chance." He smiled confidently.

"Let me be naive again," I said. "Why hold the first elections here? In the middle of the jungle you're much more vulnerable to Communist attack. Aren't there kampongs closer to Kuala Lumpur where it would be easier to protect the elections?"

"That's just the point, Consul. The big boys took days to find the most vulnerable kampong. Here we are. Bukit Gajah. If elections succeed in the middle of the jungle, we can surely go the rest of the way without problems right into national elections."

Campbell's eyes were drifting away from Bingham. He must have been bored, perhaps even annoyed.

"We're here for elephants," he said. "Did they come again last night?"

"Let me show you."

Bingham led us a couple of hundred yards to the other side of the kampong. We passed holes where crops and trees had been uprooted. Manioc, cassava, papaya, mangosteen, bananas all littered the ground.

"Looks like you had a visitation," I said lightly.

"Five or six bastards." Then Bingham added, "More elephants—more hunger." The pointed way he said it embarrassed me. I must have appeared insensitive to the full effects of the disaster.

"Ronald, are the trackers ready?" Campbell asked.

Bingham pointed with his swagger stick to six Malays sitting under a coconut tree.

For a moment I wavered between staying in Bukit Gajah to witness the elections and going on with Campbell, but the latter persuaded me I could do both. We could surely track down the elephants and return by five that afternoon in time to see the end of the elections.

The trackers led the way. The elephants presumably had returned along the same path that brought them to the kampong. It was easy at first to follow their trail of devastation; bushes were trampled, small trees uprooted, grass and reeds battered. After a kilometer, however, we came to a path that wound between high trees on which only an occasional elephant foot could be seen. Until then I might have been able to follow the trail myself. Now I would surely have lost it. The ground had become rocky, resisting all imprint.

Unfazed, the trackers took a sharp right, then in a few minutes an equally sharp left. We followed, silent, admiring. Once we sat down to rest in the half-light and, in moments a host of red soldier ants appeared overwhelming our legs and feet with their ravenous bites. Quickly we scrambled to our feet, brushed them away in disgust, and continued crashing through the jungle. "Shouldn't we be quiet," I asked Campbell. "Must be a lot of snakes in the brush."

"The only thing not to do," Campbell said drily. "is to be quiet. Make all the noise you can—step on all the dead sticks you can find—kick up the earth—yell if necessary. The more noise you make, the faster the snakes slither away. There's only one exception. The king cobra. The only aggressive snake in Malaya. But don't worry. They usually stay close to streams on the outskirts of kampongs."

An hour later we followed the trackers up a slight incline. Suddenly the head tracker put up a warning hand. We stopped abruptly. Dropping to the ground, he crawled slowly on his belly up the hill. As he reached the top, he stopped and gestured for us to join him. On hands and knees we approached. As we reached the crest of the hill, we saw one elephant standing thirty or forty feet away, eating bark and leaves, presumably guarding the five or six other elephants resting lazily on the ground. The scene was beautifully peaceful and quiet.

I remember the total silence so well because of the thundering gunfire that broke out only a moment later. The trackers must have had a pre-arranged signal because I heard what sounded like only one shot blasting simultaneously out of seven rifles. Then Campbell was on his belly firing away. The Malays, some on their bellies, some standing, were shooting separately with crazy excitement. Swept away by the shouts and hysteria, I suddenly found myself shooting wildly at no elephant in particular but at a fused image of six or seven elephants together.

The guardian elephant was brought to its knees, limbs sagging gradually, then lashing out with its trunk and legs as it fell. The other elephants, still half asleep, stumbled to their feet and lumbered away from us downhill, crashing through the brush.

The outcome of the slaughter was one dead mother, her baby, and a male. The other elephants, presumably untouched, had disappeared, bellowing off in a swirl of crashing branches.

We made no attempt to chase them. The Malays believed that attacked elephants change their feeding and resting grounds. And so it turned out. Bukit Gajah had no more elephant visits. Unfortunately a kampong some twenty kilometers away was attacked a week later, losing most of its crops and several of its huts.

For two hours the trackers labored over the dead elephants. All four legs of the dead animals as well as the penis of the male were hacked off with huge ax-like knives. Legs were then strung up on poles, two legs to a pole, each end carried by a tracker. The penis was carried in a leather pouch, eventually to be cooked, the broth guaranteeing virility to all men who drank it.

Throughout these proceedings I was curious and excited, then dismayed. I asked Campbell what they intended to do with twelve elephant legs.

"Waste baskets," he said promptly. Then indicating several legs, "These are your four."

"My four?"

"You shot an elephant, didn't you?"

I protested that I had shot wildly and that it would be madness to suppose I had hit anything at all, but Campbell and the head tracker, undoubtedly trying to flatter an honored guest, insisted I had brought down at least one of the three. To make the gift more appealing, Campbell said he'd send my four legs to the tanners, then in a couple of weeks deliver four waste baskets to me. I was slightly nauseated at the thought of bleeding elephant legs, but must admit to some curiosity and even pleasure at the prospect of receiving the unique waste baskets, one of which Peg and I still have in our den at home. I have occasional twinges of remorse, particularly at the thought of the slaughter of a mother and its baby, but I console myself with the knowledge that a lot of people in Bukit Gajah now have enough to eat and a roof over their heads as a result of the killings.

By the time we returned to Bukit Gajah, it was late afternoon and the elections were under way. Two British soldiers with rifles were posted near the completed voting booth, in front of which a Malay attendant sat at a small table. Heading the line of five voters was a gray, stringy child not yet in his teens. Second, stood an old woman in a ragged brown sarong and an even more ragged blouse.

Then three young men in shorts who might have been carpenters or farmers.

Bingham was scolding the child. Even from a distance I could hear Ronald saying in none too gentle a tone, "For the third time—no—you're too young to vote, m'boy."

The child spoke back with his hands, waving them in the face of the district officer. When Bingham's voice became even harsher, the boy yelled back: "My father tell me —vote for Latrine Party. I do what father say. Now let me vote!"

Bingham firmly took the shoulders of the boy, turned him around, and gave him a gentle push away from the booth.

"You tell your father you need a lot more years to vote. Ten is no good. Twenty-one is what I want. Will you tell your father that?"

For a moment I thought the boy was incensed enough to hit Bingham, but then he sullenly turned and ran away.

When Bingham saw Campbell and me approaching with the Malay trackers, he came to us.

"A successful day, eh?" He pointed his swagger stick at the still-bleeding elephant legs. "You've just come out of the jungle. Seen any Communist guerrillas?"

"None," Campbell said.

"I've been getting reports all day. Two guerrillas east. Three more over by the hill. I've alerted my men. If those goddam Communist bastards attack, well—" He moved his hand swiftly along his throat as if he was slitting it with a sharp dagger.

"Anyway, glad you're in time for the elections. Come and watch."

The old woman next in line gave her name to the Malay attending the booth and was asked to sign a slip. Pushing a bony finger through her hair, she scratched her head.

"Any problem?" Bingham went to the poll attendant.

"She cannot sign her name."

"Can you make an X?" Bingham asked the woman.

"X? What is that?"

"Let me help." He slipped a pencil between the thumb

and forefinger of her right hand. Then he guided her pencil into a primitive cross.

The woman began to laugh. "That is an X? That is how you write my name?"

"That's it."

"Then I must make X three more times. I vote for husband. My son. His wife."

She picked up the pencil and started in on an X.

"Whoa." Bingham took the pencil from her hand. "Only vote for one person. Yourself."

"My husband, my son, his wife," insisted the woman.

"Didn't you read the voting instructions?"

"Cannot read."

"Then you must have attended the meeting yesterday. I scheduled it for late in the afternoon when most women are back from the river."

"Baby sick. I stay with him."

I must have looked surprised, for Bingham said, "Most women fetch water twice a day. The nearest river is two kilometers away. That makes each round trip four kilometers. And twice a day eight kilometers—half of them carrying a heavy jar filled with water on their heads. Not bloody easy."

"Give her credit for at least coming to vote," I said.

"Damn right." He patted the old woman on the back. "Sorry about this but you can only vote for yourself. Not for the whole family.

"Now go back and tell husband and son and wife to come to see me. I will help them vote. Doesn't it make a difference to them whether the Latrine or School Party wins?"

"Yes, yes. Latrine Party." With a glow the old woman hobbled away.

"How many people registered to vote?" I asked Bingham.

"One hundred forty-three."

I looked at the line of voters. It had now swollen to 33 people. On examining the line again, I realized something: out of 33, there was only one woman.

"Why only one woman"? I asked Bingham. "The rest are fetching water?"

"Exactly."

"How about a Water Party?" I offered. "Didn't anyone suggest digging a well or two in the kampong?"

"There's a Yank for you," Bingham said good-naturedly. "Don't you know in these parts water under the ground is considered dirty, unfit to drink, unfit even to wash clothes? No, my friend–"

Several boys playing bola had just finished their game and were lounging near the booth looking vaguely interested in the voting process. My mouth was feeling dry, and I took a Life Saver out of my pocket and started sucking on it. I beckoned to the boys. Immediately they came at me, some with hands outstretched, others clutching at my clothes. I offered the Life Savers around.

In a few moments the package was emptied. I pulled out a second package and a third, then all the Life Savers were gone.

"Sorry, kids," I said pulling away. "All gone."

The boys mumbled something I took to be thanks, and drifted away.

Campbell, who had remained quiet until now, frowned. "You confused them by showering gifts on them."

"Those Life Savers?"

"I'm surprised it wasn't chewing gum." For the first time since I had known him he seemed angry. "You're turning them into beggars. Remember their outstretched hands?"

"I also remember their joy and thanks. You—" At that moment, out of nowhere a Chinese man in black pyjamas ran up from the left, one of his arms raised. He passed so close to me that I instinctively stepped back. He was almost certainly a Communist terrorist, for no Chinese lived in the kampong, and most of the terrorists were Chinese.

I could hear Bingham yelling, "Get him! Get the bastard!"

Campbell had left his rifle leaning against a papaya

tree fifty yards away. He looked quickly over his shoulder
at the tree, then must have made a split-second decision not
to go after the rifle, for he plunged head first toward the
Chinese guerrilla. Before he could get to him, the terrorist,
with a wild desperate gesture, hurled something at the
booth. He was mowed down in a blast of gunfire at the
same moment as the building exploded and burst into
flames. Bingham grabbed a jar of water that the woman on
the voting line had put to one side and threw it at the fire. It
was useless, of course. In a few minutes the booth was a
fiery skeleton, and then as the beams crumbled, the entire
structure fell with a crash.

Desolately, silently we stood looking as the fire turned
into glowing ashes. When the voters drifted back, the old
man we had seen that morning campaigning for the Latrine Party stumbled over to Bingham.

"Where is Latrine Party?" he said, tears in his eyes.
"We want latrine. How do we get latrine?"

Before Bingham could answer, the young man who
had campaigned for the School Party pushed the old man
aside and pounded on Bingham's chest.

"School—we want school! When do we get new
school!"

Bingham stepped back and brushed his shirt.

"Elections are cancelled. I'm as devastated as you.
There'll be new elections later, I guarantee. Then perhaps
you will get your school. And you," he patted the old man
on his back, "your latrine."

As both Malays moved away dejected, Bingham became reflective, then annoyed. "Well, we Brits do learn the
hard way. Maybe starting with the most vulnerable kampong was about the stupidest way to begin the process of
national elections and independence."

"No sure way to nirvana," Campbell put in cheerfully.
I could tell he wasn't at all unhappy the elections were cancelled.

I knew Campbell wouldn't like what I was going to
say, but I wanted to cheer up Bingham.

"A small defeat today—a big victory tomorrow," I said.

"What big victory?" Bingham asked almost resentfully. His eyes narrowed with pain.

"Elections haven't really been set back," I went on. "Only a few weeks' or months' delay. So what? Malaya will still have its independence. Most important, you people have prepared them beautifully for it. The efficient Civil Service you're leaving behind. The excellent police forces. The friendly well-trained leaders. Hell, you'll see Malaya emerge as the most constructive influence in Southeast Asia."

"Hmm—" Bingham muttered noncommittally, but he looked at me with what I thought might be gratitude.

"Balls!" Campbell snorted.

I didn't argue with him, nor was I surprised at his reaction. After all, what would independence do for Campbell? One thing was certain. It would do him out of a job. Like most of the British, he would return to England. Fat chance of getting a game warden job there. Not only that. He would lose his spacious bungalow next to the golf course along with his number one boy, his number two boy, his gardener, and his cook. From a colonial aristocrat he would suddenly find himself demoted to an unemployed proletarian.

Despite my optimism about an independent Malaya, I was almost proved wrong.

A few days after the cancellation of elections in Bukit Gajah, Tengku Abdul Rahman, the leader of the United Malays Nationalist Organization and the father of Malayan independence, had a quite inconsequential spat with the British and was promptly dumped in jail. Distressed, I spent a miserable night. Not because my optimism about Malaya's future was proving unwarranted, but because in my sleeplessness my thoughts focused on the savage pre-independence conflicts taking place in Indonesia and Indochina. Was Malaya also to be turned into a bloody war ground between a colonial power and local leaders? Wisely, however, the British, remembering the price paid for the turmoil and riots that followed their jailing of Gandhi in India, released the Tengku the next day.

Despite this temporary setback, Malaya did achieve its independence and manage to remain friendlier with the West than any other country in the area. It still remains so today.

TEN

Hindu Mysticism
(Malaya and Cambodia)

From the first days of my assignment in Kuala Lumpur, Peg and I were eager to experience Malaya in all its facets. Not the ordinary day by day living—we would soon have enough of that—but the unusual aspects we might miss without the guidance of a pro. In Devan, the foremost Indian political leader in Malaya, we were fortunate enough to discover this pro. Or did he discover us? In any case, our need for guidance fit well into his desire to share his adopted country with two uninitiated foreigners. Less than a minute after we met him at the reception given in our honor by the staff of the consulate, Devan invited us to come with him the following week to observe the ceremonies of *Thaipusan,* the annual day of punishment and atonement for the Indians. We accepted with pleasure.

Thaipusan is one of thirty-eight holidays in Malaya, reputedly the country with the largest number of official holidays in the world. In Malaya we celebrated not only all British and American holidays, but Malay, Chinese, and Indian holidays as well. It seemed the consulate was closed most of the time.

We arrived early at the place where we planned to meet Devan, a stream about twelve kilometers from Kuala Lumpur. Towering over the plain and the stream was the sacred cave of Lord Krishna on top of a cliff where he was said to have once spent the night. Several hundred steps carved out of the face of the rock led to the cave. The steps were dangerously steep, but a figure clothed in white was laboriously climbing them. As I took in the sheerness of the cliff with its solitary occupant I was reminded of a fly climbing a vertical wall.

The stream was already filled with thousands of penitents, women in white saris and men with white cloths wound around their waists. They were splashing their faces, then sitting in the turgid brown water. The process of purification had started. Without any desire for purification, I envied them. My shirt and trousers were wet with sweat. Even a muddy stream would provide welcome coolness.

On the bank a Hindu priest in a long white garment piled skewers onto a table under a tree. Next to the skewers he placed long straight pins and smaller safety pins. The penitents moved closer. Their tongues, seemingly eager for the entrance of the sharp metal, passed between their teeth. The priest whirled a bright yellow ball on the end of a string. He chanted a few bars of music. The range of incantation was narrow, encompassing only three notes. When he reached the third note, he lingered over it softly, caressingly, before repeating the cycle. A low murmur came from the group. But the sound was feeble. Like an orchestra conductor, the priest raised his arms in a sweeping motion. He seemed to be pleading for greater volume. The penitents followed him in relentless repetition of the three notes until a wave of sound engulfed the hillside. The yellow ball glinting in the sun continued to spin feverishly. An old woman tottered. A hideous yearning on her face made me think of a tormented spirit. Her tongue came out serpent-like in quick, flicking motions. Her mouth agape, she pushed aside two men and on infirm legs stumbled to the priest. With loving skill he pierced her tongue with a skewer. Next, pins were deftly fastened through the flesh on her arms, neck, back. Metal weights were hung on the pins. Bedecked with the exquisite elegance of the penitent, the woman swayed before the priest, her knees slightly bent, the unseeing eyes rotating.

"How can a child become human
when it has no name?"

UNRRA Yugoslav Displaced Persons Camp

(Braunau am Inn, Austria – 1945)

"A very domestic affair"

Peg and Eric Kocher on their wedding day
with Theresa Helburn of the Theatre Guild

(Carlyle, Massachusetts – 1947)

"The Hostess with the Mostest"

Perle Mesta (third from left) with assorted
trade unionists on her way to a coal mine

(Luxembourg – 1950)

"Politician vs. Rock Star"

Eric Kocher, the Nixons, and Peg

(Malay – 1953)

"The Battle Against Communism"

The Sultan of Selangor with the Nixon Party

(Malaya – 1953)

"The Family"
Peg, Terry, Chris, Eric Glenn and Eric Kocher
(Malaya – 1954)

"A somewhat pitiful absurdist figure"
President Diem and Eric Kocher

(Saigon – 1957)

"Bridge on the River Kwai and Holiday on Ice"
Eric Kocher with King Hussein
(Jordan – 1960)

"Missile crisis and sorrow"
Eric Kocher with Marshal Tito and Mrs. Tito
(Belgrade, Yugoslavia – 1962)

Peg and I were revolted but fascinated. We saw no wound, no blood. The woman apparently felt no pain. But Peg began to gag. She clutched me and I felt something churning in my stomach. We looked at each other, smiled bravely, then assumed the interested but uninvolved expression appropriate to a visitor.

Shrieking, the woman turned and sped blindly toward the steps leading to the cave of Lord Krishna. Her fragile legs, ordinarily barely strong enough to support her, propelled her forward with the power of a dynamo. Like a tormented marionette, she clawed her way through the crowds lining the steps to the cave. My eyes followed her until she was a speck at the top. I thought I saw her body falling, limp like a pricked balloon. As she sank down, a priest bent over her. He must have been removing the skewer from her tongue.

I felt a hotness in my tongue as I slid it over my teeth. The inside of my mouth was dry. As the saliva returned, it tasted like blood and I spat in disgust.

Near the stream were other priests, each with a group of disciples. Dozens of penitents, also bedecked with skewers and pins, were now in front of the cave. The insistent screams made me want to stuff my ears. I saw that Peggy was fighting hard to keep her expression placid. The shrieks of the penitents, released through ecstasy, mingled with the cries of the cold drink vendors. The long gasp of relief—the aaah at the first touch of the skewer, soared like a winged creature over the crowds only to be cut down by the voice of a vendor— "so—daaa or-r-aaaaaange, waa-ter mellllll-on, so-dasssssssss." The voices soared over the crowd, imparting a carnival spirit to the melancholy surroundings.

"Isn't that Devan over there?" Peggy pointed to an Indian squatting near the water, his back against a tree.

I squinted. "Good. Yes."

"While you're with him, I'll take on the wife of the Health Minister—if you can take on anyone in this madness."

Peggy was keeping her detachment better than I. Even

in these macabre surroundings, she knew she was on duty. Whether at a cocktail party or a bacchanal, Foreign Service officers—and their wives—were supposed to slip from one group to another, gathering juicy tidbits of information that might sometime be of use to the State Department or at least afford a further understanding of the people and country that would be reflected in their cables and dispatches to Washington.

As I approached the stream, Devan was talking to a handful of young men. Their faces were bright with attention. He was a guru to many young Indians. All at once, as I approached, Devan got up, waved at his disciples, and walked into the stream. He splashed his long thin body with the muddy water. Then, raising his white garment, he sat down so that the water flowed over his head. As he emerged, his black hair fell over his forehead, leaving a thin line of curls above the long aquiline nose. Squeezing the water from his garment, he walked back to the tree. The young men had scattered.

We greeted each other.

I noted how kindly the Indian looked. Usually kindness comes with old age. Yet here was a relatively young face alive with humanity.

Devan motioned to the grass. "If you do not mind with your good trousers—." He picked up a pouch he had left on the bank and fitted an American cigarette into a mother-of-pearl holder. Apparently he had not lost the taste for elegance he had cultivated as a child in a rich family.

"So this is how it feels to be one of your disciples." I sat down.

"Those young men?" The Indian smiled. "Just a little talk about politics. With instructions not to follow the examples of my colleagues."

"What examples?"

"Look at the administrator of hospitals over there. Yesterday he let out a new contract for a new hospital. That means he is five thousand Malayan dollars richer. And over on his left—the administrator of prisons. Bloated and happy. A criminal was released from jail last week. Odd—

but the administrator is eight thousand dollars richer to-day."

Even here in this primitive country, I thought, the smell of corruption is just like at home.

A bell rang sharply behind us. Two priests were lining up hundreds of Indians on the path leading to the cave. Devan stood up.

"Joining the procession?" I asked.

"I am a coward, my friend. I do not atone for my many sins through pain. I only walk in a procession." He laughed in derision.

"When does the procession start?"

"When the man from the temple—how is he called?—rings a third bell." Devan's vagueness could only mean that his knowledge of Hindu ritual was not profound.

As he walked to the rear of the line, he was met by the administrator of prisons and the administrator of hospitals. They too, perhaps, were expiating for their crimes, probably in their cases only too real. All three followed the priest leading the procession. They were soon lost to sight as they trudged laboriously up the stone steps of the cliff.

Peggy joined me and we sat on the bank of the stream. An Indian lurched weakly against me. Staggering as he passed, the penitent spat. Again, I was astonished to see that the spittle was without a tinge of blood.

Then a wild beating sound behind us made me turn sharply. An Indian woman with whitish hair was pounding her fists against a tree. Her eyes flickered though the eyelids were rigid. A long iron skewer hung through the lifeless tongue. The beating stopped. As she fled in her frenzied path to the cave, a sound came from the stricken throat, an inhuman rasping and creaking like a wooden door swaying in a violent wind.

Half an hour later Peggy gestured toward a group of Indians returning from the cave. "There's Devan."

Next to him were the two government administrators. As he walked, the Indian lifted his fists to his chest and brought them down with an angry motion. Perhaps he was confronting them with their corruption, I hoped. Devan ad-

vanced rapidly with huge strides leaving the two administrators behind.

He came over to Peggy and me.

"Your two friends have received penance?" I asked.

Devan replied drolly. "They think they have. Notice
their smiles. Now they have a whole year for more corruption before they join the procession next year for more
penance."

Peg and I were about to leave when he stopped us.
"You have seen the worst and the bloodiest of Hinduism—I
want you to see the other side. Often sweet—even poetic."

Peggy, a hater of violence, was tempted. I could tell it
from the lifted eyebrows and the sudden interest in her
eyes.

But perhaps she was also thinking of his last invitation. Night before last he had taken us to a performance of
the Kathakali dancers in Kuala Lumpur, a performance
filled with blood and cannibalism. Peggy had gagged at the
end of the evening.

"What do you have in mind?" she said guardedly.

"A shadow play. *Wayang kulit.* Tomorrow evening. In
a small village a few kilometers from Kuala Lumpur."

Peg and I knew the importance of these puppet shows
in the culture of rural Malaya, but we had not yet seen one.

"Great idea," I said before Peggy could answer. "Don't
you think so, Peg?"

"Yes," she said, but I thought she was still suspicious.

Devan told us the performance was to start with the
first darkness of the evening and last until dawn.

"Really, that late?"

This time the uncertainty came from me. I hated staying up after midnight, much less until dawn. The thought
of no sleep reminded me of the only time I had stayed up
all night—my sophomore prom at college. In those days I
didn't mind staggering through the day with a dreary head-
ache, but now?

"Oh, you won't have to stay all night," Devan said
quickly. "Just get a whiff of it, then leave. No one will object. In fact, the audience moves in and out of the perfor-

mance, falls asleep, wakes up, sees more of the *wayang kulit,* then goes back to sleep. It is ultimately boring—and very tiring—but you won't know Malaya until you've slept through at least one performance."

Theatre at sunrise (Malaya continued)

Just before sunset the next evening we arrived at the small kampong. Devan had been with us for an early supper at the Residence and was a little drowsy after the Cointreau at the end of the meal. He introduced us to the *ketua,* the leader, who escorted us with many salaams and much waving of the hands to a large enclosure that served as a theatre. It was simplicity itself. Coconut and banana trees on two sides, bare ground, two backless wooden benches for guests. Because of the large number of Indians in the kampong, we were to see the *Ramayana.* Even the Malays, though usually Muslim, enjoy this Hindu epic poem from the fifth century.

Wayang kulit stories are both entertainment and a protection against the spirits. Each villager, while in the audience, is supposed to become immune to the spells of the evil demons. With these two incentives, a mass turnout was guaranteed.

The *wayang* is held for every event of importance in the village: birth, marriage, birthday, feast day, religious holiday, death. That night the celebration was in honor of the birthday of the ketua's daughter, a straggly child of seven or eight who, bewildered by the attention she was getting from the village, spent most of the night on the lap of her father.

When we sat on one of the benches, the gamelan orchestra that was to accompany the play was already practicing. Rows of small bronze kettle-shaped discs with raised nipples were hit with sticks. The resulting sound ranged from a tinkle to a deep boom. A row of small bronze slabs suspended by cords over a row of resonant tubes was beaten by wooden sticks, and a set of convex metallic keys was hit with small mallets. A single flute was the only wind instrument. The sound of the gamelan has been likened to "moonlight and flowing water." During the practice session, however, the orchestra emitted the dissonance of an electrical storm.

The villagers began to drift in. Most women and men wore dark brown sarongs. Naked babies were in many arms. After the benches were filled, the new arrivals sat on the ground in front of a white sheet hung on a wire between two coconut trees.

Behind the sheet was a lantern already lit. Next to the lantern, various puppets, two to three feet long and made of water buffalo skin, were stuck in the trunk of a banana tree by means of the pointed end of a long buffalo horn handle. I recognized the main characters of the *Ramayana:* Rama the hero, Sita his wife, the demon Ravana, and Hanuman the monkey chief. The other puppets probably represented the gods. I thought they might be Brahma, Vishnu, Ganesha (the elephant-headed son of Shiva). All were elaborately cut out and decorated with gold paint. The puppets would be manipulated by hand between the lantern and the screen so that the audience on the other side of the screen would see only shadows. The performer could stay out of sight below the screen because of the length of the buffalo horn handles.

Even before the performance began, the kids were running through the audience as if they were in a playground. There was little discipline; perhaps none was required, because the people, at least the older villagers, smiled indulgently even when the children stumbled over their feet.

When the play started, the commotion increased. In addition to the continued scrambling and shouts of small children, the older villagers got up to walk around, chat, eat and drink.

With shouts and applause the *wayang* began. We sat through the kidnapping of Sita by Ravana the demon. Sita's husband Rama had been away chasing a gazelle. When he returned and saw that Sita was gone, he enrolled

the help of Hanuman, the monkey chief, to find her. Together they learned she was being held captive across the
ocean in Ceylon. With shouts of good will from the audience, Hanuman and his warrior monkeys built a bridge
across the ocean. In a single bound they left India and arrived in Ceylon to rescue Sita from the demon.

The play dragged on and often seemed dull, but I felt
moved at times. Devan was right; a bit of poetry shone
through the performance.

Devan himself was asleep on the floor. I nudged Peg
awake. By then it was three in the morning, but we had
decided at midnight to stay the course and experience Malaya, as Devan had suggested. We watched some more, then
went to sleep, then watched again. I particularly enjoyed
Sita's trial by fire and shouted approval with the rest of the
audience when she emerged safely, thus proving she was
not damaged goods despite her kidnapping. Hanuman had
his victory. Sita was restored to Rama. Happy ending.
Amen.

It was dawn. The sun was rising behind the coconut
trees, its light shining through a hazy mist. Some of the
spectators were still in place. The lantern was removed and
the puppets set aside. The *wayang* was over. Devan was
sitting up stretching his long arms. Peggy's eyes were
glazed. She had been napping for hours on my shoulder
and was just now awakening.

"God, isn't that remarkable." I said with a huge yawn.

"Boring," Devan said.

"Not in the least," I objected. Peggy was looking at me
critically. I knew she was suspecting me of an in-house
Foreign Service crime, the "diplomatic lie."

Tired as I was, I was impressed. Not so much with the
substance of the *wayang,* but with what it represented.

We had seen a show that lasted all night, and it involved a whole village. Those who had not directly participated in it, either as puppeteer or gamelan player, had participated by watching it for ten or more hours. The
performers would soon be going into the fields to work all

morning, come home for rice and fruit, and then rehearse again, possibly to play in another festival that evening.

I tried to imagine what they would make of America, its culture and art. Most Americans were not performers, but observers, paying $30 or more to observe a play or listen to music. They would sit for several hours beside people they had never seen, and would probably never see again. They would return home, with no additional connection to the art or entertainment, until they were ready to repeat the process. There was a clear separation between daily life and art in America.

The Malayans did just the opposite: they integrated everything—their lives, their entertainment, their work and their play. They would probably find our reaction to life most odd. Perhaps they would laugh at us, then, later, feel sorry for us.

However, our revulsion at *Thaipusan* and our delight at the *wayang kulit* did not prepare us for what happened at Angkor Wat in Cambodia.

Death at Sunset (Cambodia)

Peg and I were on holiday from Kuala Lumpur. We had just spent several days in Bangkok before going on to Cambodia. We had deliberately chosen to visit Angkor Wat, one of the largest religious monuments in the world, at the last moment. The border between Cambodia and Thailand, frequently closed because of endless fighting between the two countries, was open. To delay our visit another week might mean the borders would be closed.

Angkor Wat was built by the Khmer kings of Cambodia during the golden years of their empire from the ninth to the twelfth century. With the collapse of the Khmers soon thereafter, their many temples deteriorated and were swallowed by the voracious jungle. They lay forgotten for centuries, until a French explorer in the 1860s rediscovered them. Some of the temples, like Angkor, were restored; others, still undiscovered, exist, and presumably continue to deteriorate in the vast jungle.

On our arrival at the small, primitive airport at Siem Reap, we checked in at the sole guest house. It had been built in 1904 and was called the Grand Hotel, but it had no electricity at night, no air conditioning at any time, and, in the late afternoon, bats flew in and out of the lobby.

We hired a rickety pre-World War II Citroen to take us to the temple. The driver told us a young woman tourist would join us there. She had borrowed a bicycle from one of the workers at the guest house and was already on her way to Angkor.

We rode several miles over rough dirt roads until we rounded a curve and beheld Angkor Wat stretching before us. A broad straight roadway extended for a quarter of a mile from the western end of the monument across a huge moat to the main part of the temple. The bridge across the moat was decorated with serpents' heads carved in stone. The water under the bridge had long since evaporated, and in its place were clumps of soggy mud, curled up like tiny waves about to break. The driver told us that Angkor was originally built as a Hindu temple but in recent years had become a monastery for Buddhist monks.

We left the car at the entrance of the outer gallery. It was the only car there. Thank God, I thought. The most magnificent sight in the world and still unspoiled by tourism. No fee to pay, no gates to shut, no opening and closing hours. No guards, no gift shops. Just one small push cart displaying a few postcards, its owner nodding in the shade.

The driver led us to the bas reliefs with scenes from the Hindu epic poems *Ramayana* and *Mahabarata*. Details of these stories were sculpted in stone for the next half mile. Many of these scenes were episodes of torture. Kneeling people slain by blows to the back of their heads. People burning. People being fed to crocodiles. The same horrific methods of execution used by the Communists hundreds of years later. The whole perimeter of the temple, its courtyards and towers, totaled about four miles. Its unique combination of magnificent outer structure and exquisite

sculpted interior detail was beyond comparison to anything we had ever seen.

We walked into the inner court of the temple. Open to
the sky, it was bordered on each side by huge pillars of
stone and sandstone that rose up and faded into the distance. In the middle was a high central tower. Four Buddha
shrines surrounded the base of the tower. A flight of stairs
led upward to the last landing before the top narrowed into
a pyramid.

At this point the woman from the guest house joined
us, having just arrived by bike. Sweating profusely, Emily
greeted us in a strident voice. She was about thirty, flushed
from her recent exercise and seemed overly nervous by the
way she picked at her fingers. She wore shorts and a shirt
on which was printed "Love Your Baby." She also wore a
camera slung around her neck and carried a large shopping bag in her hand. She said she was from California.

Our driver turned us over to a Buddhist monk, whom
he addressed as "Bonze". As caretaker of the temple, he
would be our guide. He was dressed in a long flowing saf-
fron-colored robe. The driver would wait for us at the car.
He said we should hurry along: an hour later it would be
too dark to see any more of the temple. Besides, brigands
and ruffians were known to invade the temple after dark.

We followed Bonze as he climbed.

"My book on Angkor said it would be magic here."
Emily looked around as if she was disappointed.

"On top there is magic everywhere," Bonze said mat-
ter-of-factly.

We climbed up another flight of stairs. Even though
small patches of sun filtered through from outside, the
shadows seemed to be lengthening on the steps.

We paused as Bonze pointed out several small Buddhas, green with moss encased in small shrines recessed
into the wall. One statue had only one ear. Emily seemed
particularly interested in it. She examined it closely, at first
from a few feet away, then approached it and rubbed her
fingers on the place where the ear had been.

Bonze spoke in a resigned voice edged with anger, "Broken—stolen—what tourists do."

"But that's terrible," Emily said. "Tourists can be so cruel. Imagine—stealing an ear. It's precious, isn't it?"

"As precious as any part that belongs to a whole."

We continued climbing another minute. Peg turned around and saw Emily behind her. She was panting.

"Tough climbing, isn't it?" Peg said.

"You mean because of my condition?"

I hadn't noticed Emily's "condition" before. Now I saw the slight roundish bulge of her stomach.

"A baby doesn't keep you from climbing," Emily said. "My baby won't keep me from doing *anything* I want," she insisted, with an emphasis that hardly seemed warranted. "And if I thought it would—" She laughed. "But I just know it won't—"

"I love the slogan on your shirt," Peg said. "Love Your Baby—original."

"A gift from my husband. He had it printed. Ridiculous, isn't it? I don't have to be reminded I'm going to have a baby, nor do I need to be reminded to love it. I almost threw the damn thing away, but this is my last clean shirt." Nervously she took a pill from her bag and swallowed it.

Bonze went up the last four or five steps before the top narrowed into a pyramid. We followed him as he went to the parapet and looked over the edge.

"There is magic," he said with a wave of his arm.

Emily looked down. "How high are we?"

"One hundred, twenty-six feet. High enough to die if you jump off."

"Who would want to jump off?" Emily laughed uneasily.

"Many people jump from here. This is a sacred temple."

"But they would be killed," Emily protested.

"That is what they want."

"Who would want that—except a crazy person?"

"Perhaps not crazy when they jump into another life. Maybe better than this life?"

Emily took another pill. She noticed Peggy watching her. "Just to enlarge my consciousness," she said seriously. "See reality—feel more deeply."

"I see," Peggy said, although I suspected that she didn't.

"Most of all," Emily continued, "to flow with the universe." She turned to Bonze. *"You* know what I mean."

"Sometimes flowing is easier without pills," he said.

Perhaps Emily felt harshly judged. At least she stepped away from him.

Peggy and I exchanged glances, as if to confirm our mutual desire to get away from Emily and her particular craziness. We were primarily interested in examining Angkor. But somehow Emily held us captive. She seemed vulnerable and overwrought, weird but interesting.

Bonze was still at the parapet, looking down. "Now look," he said. "Trees, jungle. Have you ever seen another view like this?"

"Oh, it is a miracle," Emily said exultantly. "Doesn't it make you want to breathe deeply?" She held her breath several moments and then let it out with a whoosh.

To me, the view was certainly not a miracle. Nor did it make me want to breathe deeply. In fact, it seemed quite ordinary, lovely perhaps, but not spectacular. Trees. Jungle. Intertwined. Everything seemed right, but somehow unsurprising.

"Angkor was once the center of a wonderful civilization," Bonze said. "Over there," he pointed to the left, "a palace. Next to it a terrace of elephants. Alas, civilization declined, then the jungle came back. Look at the roots of those huge trees: They're strangling the temples and the huge stone faces underneath. The incursion of the jungle— it is like a devastating tidal wave. It demolishes everything in its way."

Emily was watching him closely. "You talk as if you'd seen it." Then in sudden excitement, "Did you live a thousand years ago?"

"I do not remember."

"Don't you believe in reincarnation?"

"It is taught. I know nothing of it."

"I thought all Buddhists believed in reincarnation."
Emily seemed disappointed.

"Do all Americans believe in capitalism? Does everyone believe in what they are taught to believe in?"

Emily remained undaunted. "I bet you lived another
life. Probably right here. What could you have been?" She
kept on talking, as if to herself. "Probably a slave. Piling
stone on stone. Wearing out your body to build Angkor.
Now you are being rewarded. A caretaker. Divine justice."

"To caretake is not a reward."

Emily touched a stone projection jutting off the wall
next to one of the Buddha shrines. "Why in heaven's name
would anyone want to sculpt a peculiar projection like
this?"

"It is a lingga," said Bonze.

"Lingga?"

"A stone phallus. Symbol of fertility."

"Ah hah," Emily laughed uneasily.

"Sterile women come here to pray," Bonze explained.

Emily took several pictures with her camera, first of
the lingga, then of two Buddhas in their shrines, then a few
more of the lingga.

We saw Emily take another pill and began to worry
whether she was drugging herself out of reality. She
backed away, focused her camera, and took several more
pictures. All at once, as though overtaken with curiosity
and desire, she reached out her hand to pick up one of the
smaller statues. In her eagerness she fumbled it. The statue
crashed on the stone. The Buddhist monk abruptly stepped
away from the parapet. He stooped to pick up the apparently undamaged statue and put it back in its niche.

Emily was all remorse. "I'm sorry, how dreadful of
me, I wanted to touch, only touch, not to steal. I'm not a
thief, am I?" She turned to Peg and me.

I felt no particular sympathy for her. In fact, I half
believed she would have stolen the statue had Bonze not
been watching. Before I could commit myself to an answer, Peg stepped in. "Of course we believe you," she said.

Emily tugged on the caretaker's robe. "Don't you believe me? I'm not a thief." She screamed shrilly with a vehemence out of proportion to the nature of the incident. "I'M NOT A THIEF, I'M NOT!!!"

Bonze was casual. "Thief or not, please help." He went on his hands and knees.

"What can I do?" Emily asked, her voice breaking.

"Try to find it. One of the Buddha's ears."

"Is that what's broken?"

"The left lobe," Bonze replied.

Emily picked up an object on the floor. "Here it is. I'm really sorry. You can't mend a broken ear, can you?"

"Tomorrow I will try." He paused. "Do you think I should throw it away?"

"That's up to you," she said. Then eagerly, "but if you do throw it away, well . . ."

"You would like to have it," he said irritated. "Well, it is sacred." He put the lobe next to the Buddha. "Every day I walk through the corridors of this old temple. Every day I find broken statues. Pieces of stone chiselled from the old pillars—ears—fingers. Vandals . . ."

As he started to move away, Emily said hastily, "Can I take your picture? Please . . ."

Bonze paused before replying. "If you take my picture, you may not like the result."

"I'm sure I will," Emily said. "Now please—right against the pillar. A Buddha over your head. The lingga beside you." He started moving into position. "A little farther left. Perfect." She looked through the lens, then puzzled, raised her head and looked at Bonze. She wiped the lens and looked again.

Bonze was smiling for the first time. "What do you see?"

"You're still there," she said. "And yet—" She looked again through the lens. "I see someone else."

"I told you you might not like the result," he said.

"Perhaps it was the poor light," Emily said. She looked through the lens again. "No, there's another man—young—heavy beard—dressed in rags—a dirty turban. Someone who might have lived a hundred years ago." She stopped. "Was it you?"

Bonze spoke without emotion. "When I was a young Hindu I came to Angkor to worship my Hindu gods. But I did not know it had become a Buddhist temple. I came to worship Shiva and Krishna, but when I walked along corridors, up the stairs, going higher and higher, I came to the top and there were four shrines, and in each a statue of Buddha. In a rage, I picked up the four statues and hurled them down one by one. Then I ran through the corridors breaking every Buddha I could find. By the end of the day I had smashed thirty-six Buddhas."

"So that Hindu of years ago—you—you're the one I see in my lens now?"

Bonze shrugged.

"Now you worship Buddha—mend him—care for him." She went on as if caught up in a dream. "Is that your penance?"

Bonze did not answer.

I was fascinated by their conversation. I borrowed Peg's camera and looked through the lens.

"What do you see?" Peg asked.

"Bonze. What else?" Again I thought, Emily and her pills.

Emily was smiling. "My friends won't believe me when I show them your picture. It's so weird—I'll just have to add you to my museum."

"What museum?" Peg and I both asked at almost the same time.

"Curios from all over the world. A rose from the garden of Versailles. A stone from the cathedral of Chartres. A square of porcelain from the great porcelain temple of Bangkok. Some ash from Vesuvius. A large red stone from a Balinese temple. Even a towel from the Queen Mary."

"Collections," said Bonze. "Aren't they for people who are empty?"

"How do you mean?" Emily said.

"Empty people need things, but your body is full. You have a life inside you. Is it your first child?"

"First and last."

"It should bring you much happiness."

"My husband wants a child very much," she said.

"And you?"

"I'm a decorator," Emily said. "I love things. Beautiful things. I travel a lot looking for exquisite *objets d'art.* For a long time I didn't want a child. I'm always so busy. Even now I'm not sure." She gave a slight laugh. "Men are funny. But my husband—when he heard a child was coming, he insisted I take a trip around the world. He had some notion I would be tied down—no work—no travelling for years to come. So he bought my plane ticket—do you see now? To give me a last whirl."

"It was very kind of him," Bonze said.

"Bill is very kind," Emily said. "I really love him. That's why I finally agreed to have the baby. But I'm not the sort of mother he wants for his child."

Peggy and I were drawn more and more into the conversation. We had heard the beginning of it while we were examining the small Buddhas in their sanctuaries. Now we went back to the corner near the stairs where Emily and the caretaker were standing.

"My husband wants me to devote full time to the child," Emily said. "I know I won't. Let's face it. I'm selfish, and there's one thing I detest in people, self-sacrifice. I wouldn't sacrifice myself for anything or anybody."

A Cambodian woman came up the steps carrying a large bundle. The light was dying now and I couldn't see her distinctly. She appeared old and ragged and groped around as if she was looking for something.

Bonze said a few words to her in Cambodian—or at least in a language with which I was not familiar. Perhaps he asked her if he could be of help. She shrugged and sat on the stone floor.

I heard the sound of many gongs far away.

"I must inspect the next shrine," Bonze said. Then to Emily, "Don't be afraid to enjoy the baby."

"And don't you be afraid of material things," she said.

He placed his palms together, touched his forehead, bowed slightly, and went down the stairs.

The Cambodian woman got up with her bundle and stumbled over a stone. There was a faint moan as if from some stricken animal.

Peggy went to her. "Are you all right?"

The woman looked at her sourly, then turned away.

"She doesn't understand English. Who knows Cambodian?" I said foolishly, knowing in advance that none of us did.

The woman sat for a moment, presumably resting. As she shifted her bundle from one arm to the other, we heard the same moaning sound.

Peggy said to me, "Do you think she has a baby?"

"Perhaps."

Emily went to the woman. "You have a baby, don't you?"

The woman clutched her bundle to her body and looked with hostility at Emily.

"Don't force it," I said. "Why question her? It's none of our business."

Emily went on, "But if there is a baby—"

"So what?" Peggy put in. "Suppose she does have a baby—is that illegal?"

The woman stumbled to the parapet with her bundle. Again I heard the same stifled moan.

"But why is she here?" asked Emily. "She's not a tourist." Emily reminded me of a ferret tracking down its quarry.

"This is a sacred temple," I said. "She may want the baby to receive a special blessing from Buddha."

All at once the woman rushed to the edge of the parapet, raising the bundle high over her head.

"Careful," I called. "It's coming apart." Remembering she didn't understand, I hurried toward her.

"It will fall!" Emily screamed.

Before I could reach the woman, something fell out of the bundle and over the side of the temple. The unmistakable cry of a baby receded in the distance. Peggy and I stood there, chilled. Then Emily screamed.

"Don't kill it. Don't kill it!" Then in a wild uncontrollable cry, "I WILL KILL MY CHILD!"

In sudden shock at the enormity of what she had just released, she stopped and covered her face with her hands.

Bonze returned swiftly just as the old woman came back from the edge.

"I heard a scream," he said.

Emily was now weeping softly.

"We thought we heard the cry of a baby," Peggy said.

"Yes," Bonze said quietly. "She had a baby."

The woman was now smiling. Bonze talked to her a few moments. "She has six, seven children—she forgets the number. She is desperately poor. She has no food for these children."

"I understand all about poverty," Emily said. As I looked at this spoiled and tortured woman, I was skeptical.

A warm smile still glowed on the face of the woman.

"How can she be happy?" Emily asked. "The baby—"

"The baby is happier in its new life," Bonze said. "The Buddha has given it a special blessing."

Emily clutched at him. "What does it mean, Bonze—what I just said? Why did I say I would kill my child?"

"I do not know," Bonze said quietly.

"I don't want it to be like that," she cried desperately. "I will not kill—"

"Didn't you say you didn't want the child?"

"The child won't interfere. It won't! I can plan things—day care, nurse, schools. But even if the child does interfere, that doesn't mean I will kill—Bonze, could it have been a slip of the tongue—a thought?"

"Perhaps," the Bonze said.

Emily was pale. "Then you think—I will kill the child?" She was speaking softly, as if she was talking to herself. Then slowly, as if in torment, "If I do—If I kill—something will happen to me. What will happen?"

Bonze came close to her. "It is too early to say."

"Everything today has a result—and a cause. How will

I suffer? A hundred years from now, poor, like that woman? All my treasures gone?"

Suddenly Emily stepped back in fright as she saw another Cambodian woman come in. She was poor and ragged like the first woman, but her teeth were painted black to hide the yellow stains caused by the betel nut she was chewing. Slowly she prostrated herself before the lingga and rocked back and forth mumbling the words of a chant.

Emily said numbly, "She is bending, bowing like a slave, to that?"

"The god of fertility," Bonze said.

Emily whispered, "What is she saying?"

"She is saying, 'Oh god, great god of seed and spring, it is winter. The ground is dry and barren. You are asleep. But sleeping you listen.'" He paused as he listened to the woman chanting. "Now she tells the god she has been married fifteen years. She has no children. The family will die if there is no child. She is old, perhaps too old to have a child. But just one child, she begs—just one."

The woman kissed the phallus, then ran her tongue along its length, at first slowly, then with increasing passion.

I shivered slightly.

"So that is what will happen to me." Emily was whispering. "I will want a child too—desperately—so desperately I will even pray to . . ." She laughed wildly. *"Bonze,* there I am, punished, barren, a hundred years from now, on my knees, scraping, worshipping a stone god. Are you pleased? Are you!"

Bonze turned away. He announced, "I must visit another shrine."

As he left, the moon was beginning to rise over the mysterious stone faces of temples half covered by the roots of huge trees. Hundreds of chattering parrots flew home to roost in the tall gum trees.

The horn of the car suddenly sounded from below.

"Let's go, Peg," I said. "The driver is waiting."

Emily went to the phallus and gently, almost rever-

ently touched it. "In a hundred years I will be here." She
laughed wryly. "I hope you will still be here."

She tore herself away with an effort, then stopped suddenly before descending. She retraced her steps and
paused near the shrine of the mutilated Buddha.

The horn of the car again sounded insistently from
below.

As Emily gazed at the Buddha, she seemed to become
possessed of an uncontrollable impulse. Her hand reached
out quickly, picked up the statue, and put it in her bag.
Swiftly she ran down the stone steps.

"Coming!" I called as Peg and I followed her.

I could not sleep that night, and it wasn't because of
the dirty pallet on my narrow cot, or the lizards on the
ceiling that threatened to fall on the bed, or the mosquitoes
that torturingly found their way to Peggy and me through
the holes of our sagging netting. I thought of Emily and her
baby, of the Cambodian woman with too many children, of
the other, barren woman with her desperate need for a
child.

I knew then that I had to return to Angkor in the
morning, to see it in full light of day, to mount the stairs
and look over the edge. The ragged bundle that was thrown
into the wind—that baby, could it really have been a baby
—would it be below?

Hurriedly at dawn I dressed, drank a cup of tea, and
rushed back to Angkor. Since a taxi was not available at
such an early hour, I borrowed a bicycle from one of the
workers at the guest house. Even though I pedalled vigor-
ously, full light was dawning when I arrived, and the sunrise as dazzling as the sunset the evening before. Now, at
least, I could be free of the shadows, rein in my imagination, and be able to separate the real from the unreal.

I left the bike as soon as I crossed the moat in my
haste to get to the central tower. The serpent heads on the
bridge seemed closer, bigger than the day before. Now they
seemed threatening, as if they were about to open their
mouths and spit their poison directly into my body. I
started running over the stones sunk into the roadway. I

mounted the steps of the central tower at a speed that surprised me. By the time I reached the top I was drenched in sweat. The top of the tower was just as we had left it the evening before, except that rays of light were now illuminating the dark corners. I looked over the edge of the parapet. A brown cloth lay below on the bare ground. In great excitement I ran down the stairs and around the tower until I reached the rear of the monument. I looked around, bewildered. The rag was gone and in its place was a dark brown stone. I shuddered as I turned it over. Nothing. Of course, vultures and other scavengers might have visited during the night. A dead one-day old baby would not last long in the Cambodian darkness.

Many unanswered mysterious questions still provoke my thoughts. Did Emily have her baby? Did she ultimately love it or destroy it? Which of the forces warring within her would have won?

Then the Cambodian mother—did she go on having babies, a seventh, an eighth, a ninth, another each year? No need for abortion here, not when a one-day old baby is as easy to dispose of as a fetus. No need for birth control either. And the barren woman? The way she caressed the lingga suggested it might not be a means, but an end in itself.

I would read, years later, that Angkor Wat had been captured by the Cambodian Communists. They had been camping in it for years, using it as a fortress to defend themselves. Worst of all, they had smashed many of the precious statues, laying hammers and blunt instruments to the sandstone, and piling up mounds of broken stone as barricades. The magnificence of the temple was reduced to a ruin. If Emily read of its vandalizing by the Communists, she would probably berate herself for not taking more statues to add to her collection.

Perhaps she—and the two Cambodian women—are still haunting Angkor Wat in search of their future.

ELEVEN

The War without a Beginning (Washington, D.C.)

There is never any logic to war. There is even less logic to a war that has no beginning. Yet in the United States-Vietnam conflict, with its monumental devastation of lives and property, there was no declaration of hostilities; no record of a first shot fired, a first plane downed, a first ship sunk.

If there was no overt act to mark the beginning of conflict, was there perhaps some covert action? In searching my memory of those days, I finally came upon an act in the autumn of 1958 which, secret and unrecorded, I believe, in retrospect, sparked the beginning of the overt hostilities a few years later.

The rememberance of that act still shocks me—not because the action itself was shocking but because I participated in it.

In 1955, I was transferred back to Washington from Malaya. Although with the zeal of the young I had asked for Africa for my next assignment, the State Department assigned me to Headquarters in Washington in 1956.

I still had no taste for headquarters jobs, especially in Foggy Bottom, where the piles of paper are notoriously too high, the bureaucracy too rigidly ingrained, the conferences and meetings altogether too frequent. I thought about trying to get my assignment changed. Hadn't I known with certainty even as early as my UNRRA days that work in the field was infinitely more satisfying? It gave me more freedom; it was more creative; it brought me into closer contact with people of other countries. And it was more fun.

Still, a position at Headquarters fit the shape of my ambition, which during those years became very strong. I would become known and appreciated by the senior officers. I would enhance my reputation—why, when it came time for my next assignment perhaps I'd even become—well, why not?—an ambassador. My attitude in those early days in Washington was one of curiosity and cautious optimism. It might be a damned nuisance to spend my time shifting papers from my IN box to my OUT box, but surely it would be enlightening, perhaps even rewarding, to see how policy was made, who was actually involved in making these awesome—and sometimes foolish—decisions, and how they ultimately got carried out.

My fancy title in the State Department was Deputy Director of the Office of Southeast Asian Affairs in the Bureau of Far Eastern Affairs. The Southeast Asian (SEA) part of the title was reasonable enough. The office had jurisdiction, policy-wise, over seven countries in Southeast Asia: Thailand, Burma, Laos, Cambodia, Vietnam, Singapore, and Malaya (before it became independent and changed its name to Malaysia to reflect the increasing number of Indians, Ceylonese, and particularly Chinese in the population).

But the Far East part of the title was deceptive. The United States had adopted it from the British, for whom it had been accurate enough. For the United States, however, that part of Asia fronting on the Pacific was really Far West rather than Far East. In any case, before long the Bureau's name was changed more realistically to East Asia.

The director of the office was Ken Young, a remarkably sensitive and effective officer, and a fine human being as well. I enjoyed working with Ken tremendously and was sorry when he left a year or two later even though I was appointed director in his place.

The seven countries in SEA for which I was responsible varied economically from relatively well off to downright poor, and politically from stable to chaotic. Each country was handled by a desk officer. SEA desk officers without exception were ambitious, hard-working, dedicated and highly intelligent. I supervised and coordinated their work.

The dissensions, rebellions, and ethnic, cultural and religious conflicts within and between countries caused me many sleepless nights. Particularly on weekends when the NIACT (Night Action) cables requiring immediate action would flow in. And particularly where the problems involved Vietnam, Laos, and Cambodia. These three countries, ravaged by the recent Indochina War with France, were volatile, almost schizophrenic, distrustful of colonial power, yet desperately needing its technical knowhow.

At 4:30 one morning a thundering ring of my home phone awakened me as sharply as if I had been dumped into a cold bath. It was the duty officer of the State Department.

"Sir," he may have thought he was keeping a tight rein on his voice, but I detected a tremor, "We have a NIACT from Saigon."

Since the cable not only required overnight action but was classified as SECRET, the subject could not be divulged over the phone.

"I'll be right in," I said, trying only half-heartedly to conceal a lot of grumpiness.

"Yes, sir," he said again.

As I hung up, I had the strangest feeling I had aged appreciably overnight. All these "sirs." They could only come from a very junior officer thinking he was addressing a very senior one. On my way out of the house, it was no consolation to bang into a small table in the hall which fell over with a crash and awakened my wife.

Driving in the dark, I had visions of all the catastrophes that could possibly be rocking Saigon. A riot—a military coup—an attempted assassination—maybe even a successful one. I pressed down on the accelerator until the car roared ahead through the empty streets.

Whatever the contents of the NIACT, it was likely to concern Communism. Most cables from Southeast Asia did. Many Americans in these days thought of Communism as sinister, ominous, destructive, but almost never comic. In Southeast Asia, however, Communism did have its frivolous side. I tried to focus on it in order to counteract the intense foreboding that was now gripping me as I rode through the dark. Frivolity in Saigon? Hardly. But how about Laos? In that benighted country the number one Communist leader Souvannapong was the brother of the anti-Communist Prime Minister, Souvannapouma. Even more bizarre, relations between the two brothers remained friendly, even warm, despite their political differences. During the week the Communist brother would be in the hills with his Communist troops attacking government forces and making forays into government territory. Come Friday, however, he would leave his guerrillas in the hills and jungles to pay a friendly visit to his brother's Vientiane palace. After a pleasant weekend of champagne and temple dancers, the Communist leader would return on Sunday evening to the hills to prepare for new attacks against his brother's troops. The material in Foreign Service files would make a splendid comic opera.

Even today, Laos continues to excel at peculiar contradictions. Recently the Communist regime, which won its battle in the 1950's, welcomed Princess Anne of Britain to Vientiane, scarcely a decade after dumping its own royal family into a prison camp where they are reported to have died a miserable death. It would have been easy to be enraged by such inexplicable behavior, but, on that day long ago, spurred by my own ambition, I speeded toward Washington and smiled faintly in affectionate resignation.

In Saigon, as in Laos, there were contradictions, but they were bizarrely concentrated in one person: President Diem of South Vietnam. Though his life ended tragically with an assassin's bullet, he lived it as a somewhat pitiful absurdist figure.

There was nothing of the Oriental stereotype about Diem. He was brought up in France, was ardently Catholic in a Buddhist country, wore Western clothes and spoke impeccable English. All of these attributes made him highly acceptable to the State Department. Unfortunately, they also made him almost totally unacceptable to his own people, among whom he was accounted a stooge of the Western imperialists.

When I first met him in his Saigon palace during a briefing trip to Southeast Asia, Diem wore an immaculate white linen suit and was delicately sipping a cappuccino. He was courtly, friendly and an obsessive talker. He regaled me with endless stories of Vietnam history, current Saigon gossip, and ponderous political commentary, all of it wildly optimistic of Vietnam's future under his leadership, and all of it lasting for hours. Each time I would try to break away, Diem would increase the speed and volume of his delivery. At the same time, the increasing distance in his eyes told me he wasn't really talking to me but to some imaginary audience. His style was a kind of autohypnosis that left me puzzled and uneasy. When I finally left his office over his protests, I began to ponder the effectiveness of a leader who had three hours to kill with a mid-level officer of the Department of State. I heard subsequently that Diem treated every one of his many visitors with the same stories, the same windiness of discourse, the same empty civility.

Thereafter, I began to give serious thought to the question of why the State Department was putting its faith—and its money—on a man who had nothing better to do. Shouldn't he be visiting villages—speaking to village leaders, being seen by his people, trying to unify them, trying to understand and resolve the unrest inexorably spreading throughout his country? Then the next question occurred: Shouldn't the State Department, which had taken upon itself the role of savior to the anti-Communist regimes in

South East Asia, be searching for a new leader of South
Vietnam?

I let up on the accelerator as a few cars, their lights
still blazing in the pre-dawn, began to emerge from the side
streets. Ten minutes later I parked on C Street near the
entrance to the State Department building. I showed the
guard my pass and dashed up the stairs to meet the duty
officer. The NIACT was worse than I thought. It was a complaint against the American Military Attache in Saigon by
the International Control Commission (ICC). A complaint
against the United States brought by an international commission might not be thought much of in these days, where
American contempt for U.N. pronouncements is not un-
common, but in those days the ICC held the fragile balance
between war and peace in Southeast Asia.

The Commission, created by the Geneva Accords
which ended the French-Indochina War, forbade foreign
military interference in Vietnam. The mission of the ICC
was to monitor the uneasy peace between Communist
North Vietnam and anti-Communist South Vietnam, the
two states into which Indochina was carved after the war.
South Vietnam was the area that the United States, for
whatever reasons of pride, geopolitics, and eventually pure
obsession, vowed to keep out of Communist hands.

To make United States relations with the ICC even
more complicated, it was composed of three members: a
Canadian, a Pole, and an Indian. The latter, Nehru, was the
chairman. These three countries were presumably non-
aligned, favoring neither Communists nor anti-Commu-
nists, but it was no secret that the membership was skillfully created to reflect political reality. Canada would take
the United States point of view, Poland the Russian, and
India, hopefully, would mediate between the two extremes
to reach a compromise acceptable to all three.

The ICC complaint against the American military attache cited a visit he had made to the commanding general
of the South Vietnamese Army. It was perfectly appropriate for such a visit to be made, since the major function of
the attache was to keep in touch with military develop-

ments in South Vietnam. But, unfortunately, an informant, someone on the general's staff, must have reported to the ICC that the American attache, after expressing concern about the infiltration of Communists from North Vietnam into the South, promised to provide the Saigon government with military equipment—artillery, three-quarter ton trucks, rifles, ammo, small and large guns—all of which was forbidden by the Geneva Accords. Whether the approach had been made at the initiative of the Vietnamese or Americans was not stated. The main concern of the ICC was that any military buildup in North or South might well lead to a resumption of hostilities between the two Vietnams.

When I finished reading the cable, I knew we were in for serious trouble if the complaint was correct.

It was vital to contact the Pentagon to get a confirmation or denial of the cable. There was no reason to doubt what the Pentagon would tell me. In those days it was just as unlikely for one government agency to lie to another as it is likely, especially on sensitive matters, to happen today.

I called the Pentagon duty officer to see if Defense had gotten a copy of the cable from Saigon, and if the Pentagon officer in charge of Saigon Affairs had also been routed out of bed and was even now at his desk. The answer was yes—the cable had been received—but no—the officer in charge of Vietnam Affairs had not been routed out of bed. The cable just didn't seem significant enough to call anyone at four in the morning.

Not significant enough? In what fantasy world was the Pentagon operating? Didn't they know the difference between war and peace? Didn't they care?

It seemed useless to return home for sunrise and breakfast. Instead I made myself some coffee in the office machine and sat at my desk, alternately looking at the glow of the sun rising in the east and at a pile of unread papers still in my IN box.

At nine, still seething, I called the Pentagon and got an appointment half an hour later with my opposite number; I shall call him Colonel Wesover. As I entered his office, I noticed the colonel had an empty desk top, an empty IN basket, and an empty OUT basket. Either he had finished his work for the day, or the Pentagon—like the State Department in those years—was vastly overstaffed. His immaculate uniform, tidy little moustache, and no-nonsense handshake seemed to put him slightly on the side of efficiency.

"Of course the cable's accurate," he said in a rasping voice that always reminded me of a broken flute. "Our military attache in Saigon talked under instructions from the Pentagon with the top military brass in South Vietnam."

Normally, the colonel and I were quite friendly, but that morning I felt edgy and my tone was cold.

"Don't you think you might have consulted with State before authorizing your man to break the Geneva Accords?"

"What's so sacred about the Accords?"

"Just the difference between war and peace." I said icily. "I hope you have a good explanation I can give the ICC."

"Why explain anything to the ICC?" He seemed honestly astonished at my concern.

"If you scrap the Accords," I continued, "You scrap the whole peace."

"And what's wrong with that?"

Again he was looking at me. Not a shred of embarrassment. Just honest curiosity and perhaps a little annoyance.

"America has its destiny," he went on quite calmly. "You people at State are a little wacky if you let some crackpot organization scare the lead out of your pants." Then, with his next statement, he betrayed the real truth: "Peace can be worse than war—especially if it's a Communist peace. Don't you agree?"

With a jolt I thought of the recent McCarthy hearings in Congress that had investigated Communist influence in government. They had scared the hell out of the State Department and forced us to fire several Foreign Service officers who had objectively reported the reasons why the

Chinese people preferred Communism to the corruption of Chiang Kai-shek.

"God, no," I snapped back. "Only an idiot prefers war to peace."

On the surface I pretended to remain brave. But inwardly I was backing up in my thinking. Why hadn't I recognized from the beginning the obvious fact that the Pentagon would be only too eager to see the war resume? To the military, the Geneva Accords were only a temporary measure, just enough to allow a strategic buildup for the final victory. With American help, South Vietnam could then drive through to Hanoi, overthrow Ho Chi Minh, and unify all of Vietnam into one big safe anti-Communist country.

"Don't run down the ICC," I went on, although more and more I felt I was defending a dead horse. "It monitors North Vietnam pretty damn well. As far as we know, there's no military buildup in the North."

"That's not what we hear," the Colonel said. "The North has already started drafting fourteen-year-olds."

"Where did you get that?"

"Oh—from our sources," he said mysteriously, looking out his huge window toward the Potomac as if he were afraid that a solitary glimpse of his eyes would tell me too much.

"Strange," I said drily. "I've just read a CIA report. It specifically states there's no evidence of any military buildup in the North."

"Anyway," the Colonel sniffed quickly as if he wanted to change his tack. "The ICC is as worthless as a third tit. What the hell do they know?" His voice was rasping more than usual. He was probably annoyed at my implication that his denigration of peace in Vietnam was the thought of an idiot.

"Another war in Vietnam," I said, "will destroy an already ravaged country. At least State thinks so."

I realized I was dodging a confrontation, taking shelter behind the State Department line instead of proposing my own beliefs.

"Are you sure that's what State thinks?" He was smiling in a snide, superior way. For the first time, I began to dislike him. "I'm sure it does," I said as I stood up to go. "By the way—who in the Pentagon gave authorization for your military attache to make his approach to the Saigon military?"

"The Secretary of Defense," he said without hesitation. "Who else?"

I hurried back to State and barged into the office of my superior, Walter Robertson, Assistant Secretary of the Bureau of Far Eastern Affairs. Robertson was a courtly Southern gentleman, as long as he was not crossed. When crossed, however, his words would sputter out like a string of firecrackers about to explode. As I told him about my talk with Colonel Wesover, I sensed ambivalence in his feeling toward the ICC complaint. As a rabid anti-Communist, Robertson would probably support any military plan against North Vietnam. Still, as a proper gentleman reared to observe the proprieties, he would expect Defense to consult State before adopting a radical change in United States policy.

"I'll let you know how the secretary reacts," he said, a trifle vaguely as he hurried out the door, probably to barge into the office of the secretary of State in the same way I had just barged in on him.

An hour later the phone in my office rang. It was Robertson and he had just returned from the office of Secretary of State John Foster Dulles.

"Foster never gives his hand away," Robertson offered.

I had a momentary vision of an impossible conversation between a completely placid secretary and an agitated assistant secretary, wearing his emotions plainly on his sleeve.

"But what did he say?" I asked.

"Just that he would invite Secretary of Defense Neil McElroy to have a fish lunch with him tomorrow."

"Fish lunch?"

A gentle laugh came over the phone lines.

"Foster and I have this little code. A fish lunch means the problem to be discussed is not controversial. On the other hand, a beef lunch means blood might be spilled during the meal. Metaphorically, of course—"

I puzzled over fish and beef and their relationship to Vietnam. Did the fish lunch mean that Dulles expected to get full agreement from the secretary of Defense? If so, on what points? That the military attaché in Saigon had exceeded his authority? Hardly. When did the Pentagon ever concede it was wrong? Or did the fish mean that the Department of State would support Defense in tearing up the Geneva Accords?

The rest of the afternoon, I cleaned out my IN box only to find before going home that it was filled with new cables, despatches, airgrams, aides memoires, intelligence assessments, policy guidance, inter-office memos, third person notes. In disgust I visualized exactly how Parkinson's Law must apply to paper: one sheet of bond inevitably led to another, until the whole voracious system spiralled into endless reams of paper piled as high as the Washington Monument.

The next morning I went to two meetings. One on the dreadful state of the Burmese economy, the other on racial problems in Singapore. Both were strangely refreshing—like a couple of hours of vacation away from real trouble.

In the early afternoon I was summoned to the secretary of State's office with Assistant Secretary Robertson. It was the first time I had been in the Secretary's office. Dulles was slouching at his desk, sandwiched between an American flag on one side and a Department of State seal on the other. Overwhelmed by symbols that far exceeded his own stature, he looked small, even insignificant.

"I've just had lunch with Neil McElroy," Dulles said. I noticed he said nothing about a fish lunch. Had it somehow turned into a beef lunch?

"We talked about the ICC complaint against our military attache in Saigon," Dulles went on. "How do you suppose the ICC ever got wind of a meeting that was supposed to be secret?"

I was distressed. The secretary seemed primarily concerned that a secret meeting had been discovered, without questioning the validity of the meeting itself.

Walter Robertson, sometimes intimidated in the presence of the secretary, was silent.

I hesitated before barging in. "Mr. Secretary," I said, "When I saw Colonel Wesover yesterday I assumed that State was not aware of the démarche of our attache in Saigon. Was I right?"

Robertson registered surprise, even alarm, but remained silent. Dulles never met my eyes. His head remained lowered as if he was intently observing some insect on the desktop.

"Mr. Kocher, does that make any difference to you? That is, if State knew about the démarche in advance?"

"I think it would make a great deal of difference, Sir, to the Department and the United States Government. For one thing, a difference between trust and mistrust between two equal Departments of the government. Also the difference between war and peace."

The bowed head rose to meet my gaze. His words instantly increased my distress. "In a world running toward war, there's not much room for peace. Now is there?"

"How do you mean?" I asked.

Robertson had been fidgeting nervously, picking away at his fingers. Now he cleared his throat, a loud honk as if it came from a goose.

"Eric, the secretary told me—and I am telling you—to work out something with the Pentagon, anything, perhaps an end run around the ICC. Those damned Communists must not win. We all want that, don't we?"

"The ICC is supposed to be neither Communist nor anti-Communist." I tried to keep my voice calm to belie the turmoil raging inside me.

"Supposed to be" the secretary repeated, heavily accenting each word. "Those cursed Communists will bring destruction on the world—these evil godless people—"

Years later, recollecting these words, I thought of Reagan and the evil empire he called Russia.

But there, in that office, facing the secretary and the

assistant secretary, I felt like a pawn cornered by a king and queen. The panic must have shown on my face.

"I know you're a bit confused," Dulles went on. "I don't blame you. State Department policy on Vietnam has been confused. We have all been wavering between our emotional hatred of Communism and our bureaucratic duty to support an organization no one believes in. But my lunch with the secretary of Defense showed me where State should have stood all along." He stopped and looked at me as if he expected some comment.

"With Defense?" I asked incredulously.

"Exactly." A small fist beat weakly on the desktop. His voice rose as if he felt he had to defend his actions.

"Sir, what of President Eisenhower? Would he agree?"

It was foolhardy of me to challenge the secretary's power to change United States policy, but I spoke instinctively, out of anger.

With a wave of his hand Dulles brushed aside my question.

"Ike leaves foreign policy to me. Thank you, gentlemen." And, with an abrupt gesture, he dismissed us.

On my way home that evening I stopped the car and walked. A cool wind, almost sharp, beat against my face. A few leaves were changing color already although it was only the end of September. I kept on thinking about Vietnam. What the hell were we getting into? I had been in World War II and all I could think of was the difference between good wars and bad wars. World War II was a good war. All the flames and casualties and deaths were regrettably needed. If we hadn't fought it we would probably not have survived. But Vietnam—?

I slept poorly that night for I knew what I had to do the next morning. I got to the office early and put in a call to Colonel Wesover. I told him we had better get together. I had been instructed to work with him on a highly important matter. He was not surprised. Nor did I have to explain further. He had probably been waiting for my call, had perhaps even cancelled his morning appointments. I will put in a good word for him here. Even though I sensed his high spirits, perhaps even an inward gloating over his triumph, he came over the phone perfectly matter-of-fact. And he did do me the courtesy of offering to visit me. A gentleman. *Noblesse oblige.*

Twenty minutes later when Wesover came into my office, I fully expected him to show me a shopping list of all the arms the Pentagon would ship to South Vietnam. Instead he explained he had worked up a plan to bypass the ICC. He talked about it as scientifically as if he were describing a triple bypass of the heart. He had devised, in his words, a "marvelous imaginative scheme" to build up Vietnamese strength without even slightly annoying the ICC. If you're not going to annoy them, I thought to myself, does that mean you'll kill them first? Aloud I only admitted that in my experience the Pentagon was always one of the more imaginative departments of the United States government.

Proudly he outlined his scheme: The Pentagon would send United States military to South Vietnam in civilian clothes. Civilians were not prohibited by the Geneva Accords.

"What are these military civilians going to do?" I asked.

He seemed so proud of himself, I thought his chest was going to inflate. "Ah, nice idea, very nice. They're going to collect all the arms on the roadside in South Vietnam— the arms that the French abandoned after Dien Bien Phu— and incidentally, the same arms the Americans sent to them. Our civilians will inventory these arms, and then under cover turn them over to the South Vietnamese Army. At the same time, our civilians will begin training the South Vietnamese, turning them into the finest army in South East Asia."

"And Diem—does he know?"

"Of course—he calls it a superbly outstanding idea."

By then it was becoming clear that Diem had lost whatever small amount of support he had earlier been able to rely on in South Vietnam. While its ruler was treating his visitors to rhetoric and wind, the country was falling apart.

"When will these military civilians go to Vietnam?" I proceeded.

"Almost immediately."

"But don't you have to recruit them—train them?"

"Oh yes . . ."

"Well," I said a little impatiently.

"In our usual farsighted fashion, we've been training them for quite some time—"

"Unknown to the State Department?"

"Oh, let's say unknown to certain echelons of the State Department. And say, I've even thought up the right name for them."

"What's that?"

"Temporary Equipment Recovery Mission. Great acronym too. T-E-R-M. TERM. Clever, uh?"

"Very imaginative," I said. "So they're quite ready to go?"

"Travel orders have already been cut."

"When are they leaving?"

"In two weeks."

"Don't you think Nehru and the ICC will find out they're military?"

"He knows already. We've talked to him."

"And he accepts it?"

"What can he do?"

"Make another protest—even stronger."

There was a pause. Then Wesover smiled. "Will it make you feel better to know Nehru is on our side?"

"How so?"

"We've talked to him confidentially. He knows."

"No, it doesn't make me feel better," I said. "Why did he make the protest?"

As I asked the question, it suddenly became gratuitous. "O.K.," I said bleakly. "I know the answer: for the record."

Then I thought, clever man. He protects himself and the ICC. He antagonizes no one. Neither the United States nor the Communists.

Some months later, I requested a transfer out of the Office of Southeast Asian Affairs.

Not long afterward, State started counting friends and enemies. Anyone publicly speaking against United States involvement in Vietnam was on the enemies list. I was told by another office director who attended the assistant secretary's daily staff meeting that the day after Martin Luther King spoke out against our involvement, Robertson denounced him, and his name was turned over to the FBI for investigation and surveillance.

I realized my request for a transfer arose out of strictly emotional reasons. It was also equally clear that wherever my next assignment might take me, I would only be substituting one set of insoluble problems for another. But then, as our French friends would say, *"Plus ça change, plus c'est la même chose."* Literal translation: "The more things change, the more they stay the same."

TWELVE

The War of Words (Jordan)

In 1959, Loy Henderson was Deputy Under Secretary for Administration. It was a position that lent itself to abuse, a position that had only two supervisors, the Secretary of State and the Under Secretary of State, and neither occupied himself with assignments below the rank of Ambassador. As a result, Henderson ruled the personnel functions of the Department with an iron, and often capricious, hand.

I had finished my tour of duty as Director of Southeast Asian Affairs and had been assigned as Deputy Chief of Mission in Pakistan, the number two position in the embassy. Peg and I had not been overly excited about the assignment, but were studying the country and its problems. We had started learning Urdu and were making reasonable progress when a morning call from Henderson's office asked me to come up immediately.

Our meeting could not have lasted more than three or four minutes. Henderson greeted me politely.

"I am sorry not to have seen much of you in the last years," he said noncommittally, "but I have to inform you that I cannot send you to Pakistan.

"I have to send my boy Bill Hall there," he said hurriedly, as if trying to wave me out of the office.

"My wife and I are well into Urdu already," I protested.

"Oh, that will take care of itself." he waved his hand in a meaningless way. "You and I know that the Foreign Service demands of its officers every bit of knowledge they can accumulate. I'm sure you will find Urdu of great importance some day—no matter in which country you serve."

He was talking nonsense and I was about to protest. Then I realized that I would only antagonize him without reversing his decision.

"So what will you do for your boy Eric Kocher," I asked?

He pulled himself up sharply.

"Something good—something good I am sure," He smiled warmly.

"So what is my next assignment," I insisted.

"Oh, you will hear very shortly."

"But I thought you said—no other Deputy Chief of Mission jobs are coming available."

"Oh, something will turn up. Something always turns up. Now thank you for coming."

It turned out that Hall, one of Henderson's favorites, wanted a field assignment and the only suitable opening at that time was Pakistan.

I waited a month without news. My phone calls to Henderson's office were not returned and I realized I had better look around for another assignment on my own. I had several good friends in the Middle East area and heard that Amman in Jordan might soon be vacant. I was more interested in the Middle East than in South Asia and immediately put in a bid for the job.

Soon Peg and I were on our way to Jordan with three kids in tow and another on the way.

I was ready to go to Jordan, far from the many-layered bureaucratic levels of Headquarters. I now had only one boss, a kindly and conscientious ambassador. As the number two man in the embassy, I finally had all the freedom I had never enjoyed in Washington to define my job and go about my business as I thought best. More satisfying still, I was part of a developing country where, as in Malaya, I would not only be an observer but to some extent an involved participant in its evolution.

My job title was Counselor and Deputy Chief of Mission. I supervised the staff of the embassy, and, as most DCMs are wont to do, involved myself wherever I felt needed. I worked closely with the ambassador on whatever he was working on and somewhat more independently on whatever matters he didn't want to work on.

Actually, my first days in the Middle East centered around a matter of some domestic importance. One afternoon Peg gave birth early to our fourth child and first daughter. It was all we could do to get to the hospital on time. In the absence of any doctor on the premises, a midwife expertly delivered Debra. By early evening, when mother and daughter were settled in for the night, I passed the delivery room on my way home. A sheikh was coming out and another sheikh going in. With some qualms I realized their desert outfits conjured up reminders of the antiseptic clothing visitors wore in the delivery room of the Brussels hospital where all three boys were born.

(Debra did not succumb to germs, but to the spell of internationalism. At an early age she specialized in Russian studies and also pursued a semester of study at Leningrad. She now has a job in London with Cable News Network.)

After I was in Jordan a year, the ambassador was scheduled to go on home leave. During his absence I became Chargé. It was late August of 1960, near the end of an unusually quiet summer. In the volatile Middle East, one can ordinarily count on a couple of riots each month with or without cause, a few noisy demonstrations against Israel, and several threats from Egypt, which at that time claimed to be the leader of all Arabs, although the majority of Arabs claimed otherwise. That summer there had oddly been no demonstrations, no threats, no riots of any kind.

A few days before the ambassador's departure for the States, he sat moodily at his desk looking out the window. He was shaking his head and murmuring, "Too quiet."

"What's too quiet?" I asked.

"Don't trust it," he warned. "Anytime we have a week or two of this—no intrigues from Egypt, quiet on the Syrian front, no rumors or threats from Israel—well, just don't trust it."

"At least it's a breather."

"It won't last," he muttered. "It's so quiet I dread leaving."

I understood what the ambassador meant. He was an activist. He loved intrigue, fast action, melodrama. The thought of leaving me in charge to enjoy what he was convinced would be a series of political and military crises must have fully depressed him.

"Do you think I should leave—or stay?" he asked me. "After all, I don't have to go back to the States."

It was apparent that with a little persuasion he would stay on. But the prospect of all the disasters he was predicting exhilarated me, and I realized it would be much more exciting if I could handle them from the top. My response, accordingly, was not wholly objective, and in the end he went.

For two days after his departure the quiet continued. With each day I became more tense. I must be catching Mid-east fever, I thought—that strange gnawing expectation of disaster without rational basis. The heat pressed on me more heavily than ever.

On the third day I was talking with the embassy political officer (I shall call him Sandy) about the West Bank and its agitators when we heard a deep rumbling in the distance. This noise swiftly escalated to a wild roar and then, just as quickly, subsided. The embassy shook and the windows rattled as if a heavy wind had beaten against them. It sounded like an explosion near the center of town.

I listened again but the only sound was the heavy hum of distant traffic. Suddenly a gunshot rang out. Hurriedly I rose with a feeling of exhilaration and relief. The long wait was finally over.

"We're on our way!" I yelled to Sandy.

"Where to?" He rushed after me.

"To run down my feeling of disaster."

As Samaan, the embassy chauffeur, drove us through the marketplace, several shots sounded on the left. As the gunfire got closer, pedestrians fled in panic, jamming the narrow arteries leading out of the marketplace. It became obvious that it was useless to try to drive through the tangled masses of human beings, pushcarts, and donkeys.

"Let's go on foot, Sandy. Samaan, take the car back to the Embassy."

Sandy and I pushed our way through the clogged streets. There were armed cars and mounted machine guns at every circle. Once we had to dodge behind a stone pillar because of approaching gunfire. The sound promptly died out. Again we continued our slow progress toward the highest of the seven hills on which Amman was built. On the top we would be able to observe the center of town and the effects of the explosion, assuming it had been an explosion after all.

Sandy and I arrived at the top of the hill, both of us puffing mightily. Below on the right was Government Row, with the main government offices. At the end of the long line of pink stone rectangular buildings was the Prime Ministry. Smoke and flames poured out from gaping holes in the right wing. Half the building had been destroyed. A section of reinforced concrete, once part of the third floor, now hung down like a steep ski slope.

"That's where the Prime Minister's office is," Sandy murmured.

"That's where the Prime Minister was," I added.

But why was the Prime Minister a terrorist target? Likable, mild, but efficient, Hazza Pasha Majali was no threat to any group. Besides, he was easily replaceable by King Hussein without crippling the country.

I shivered slightly. The sky was ablaze with a reddish sun, and a thin wisp of cloud drifted carelessly over the mountains of Moab far away. Two vultures circled noise-lessly over the town. The sound of intermittent gunfire flowed up from below.

Sandy nudged me. Soldiers in army uniforms were lining up along Government Row. They rammed the butts of their rifles into pedestrians, pushing them off the street.

Then two trucks suddenly appeared in front of the Prime Ministry. Soldiers sprang from them and poured into the burning building. All at once there was heavy fir-ing. It was impossible to tell from where it came, because little puffs hung over the whole street. Sweating, I squinted through the blinding sun. A heavy barrage of rifle fire came from the right. When I tried to trace the sound, I saw two more trucks hugging the side wall of the Prime Ministry.

"Let's get back while there's still time," I whispered, although there was no one but Sandy who could possibly hear me.

On our way back to the embassy, streets were almost empty. Most peasants and vendors had already fled from the marketplace. The last metal shutters were clanging in front of the shops. The town was closing down.

We turned on the radio in my office. The government station was repeating a short announcement *ad nauseum.* The Prime Ministry had blown up. No one could ascertain the fate of Majali, or, for that matter, whether he had even been in the building at the time of the explosion. Groups of unknown origin had tried to take over the country, but were apparently unsuccessful. Some of them were shot, others arrested. A curfew was now in effect. No one would be allowed in the street from five in the afternoon to five in the morning.

At that point I received an urgent call from Peggy. Eric Glenn's school had telephoned her. Its transport could not be used because of the curfew. Could I fetch him right away?

I had no pass to get through the checkpoints in the city. But I told Samaan to put the flags on the car. With them, plus our diplomatic license plates, we might not be stopped. Without traffic, we sailed along the deserted streets at a good pace. The flags and license plates did their job. With no problem, we soon picked Eric Glenn up at school. On the way back to our house, he sat up proudly in the back seat, acted every inch an ambassador, and once, when we were saluted by a policeman, returned the salute with a wave of his hand.

Back in the office, I dictated a cable to the Secretary of State, summarizing the events of the last few hours. Later, when we learned the facts of the attempted coup, I would send Washington an assessment of the effect, if any, of these events on United States–Jordanian relations.

I hurriedly convened a staff meeting and assigned each officer a specific duty. Sandy was to keep in touch with the Foreign Ministry; the military attache with the military personnel in Jordan; the economic officer with his counterparts in the Economic Ministry; and I with King Hussein and ambassadors of the diplomatic corps. Clerks, coding personnel, and secretaries were placed on a duty roster. The admin officer was to contact Security and get passes for our embassy personnel to be allowed to go to and from their homes in spite of the curfew. I was still puzzling over the motivation for the attempt on Majali's life when the British ambassador phoned. We talked freely, since phones in Jordan were not bugged in those days. He asked if I had heard the rumor that Hussein was in the Prime Ministry when the bomb went off.

Immediately, the scenario began to make sense. Motivations for the king's assassination were legion. Jordan had two disparate populations: the Palestinians on the fertile West Bank, then part of Jordan—intelligent, literate, politically rebellious—and roaming bands of Bedouins on the dry barren East Bank—politically conservative and extremely orthodox in their chosen Islamic tradition. Perhaps one group or the other was incensed that Hussein was not more aggressive toward Israel. Perhaps they suspected he was even negotiating with the Israelis. Perhaps the Syrians, no friend of the Jordanians, wanted a more tractable ruler on their border. Perhaps President Nasser of Egypt was enraged because Hussein had prevented Jordan from being tied to Nasser's United Arab Republic.

If Hussein were dead, what would it mean to Jordan? Certainly, for a while, chaos. The Hashemite dynasty itself might be endangered. After all, Hussein's grandfather Abdullah had been imposed on the country by the British just 37 years ago when they were administering Jordan on behalf of the League of Nations. The next in line of succession was Hussein's brother. At a large reception, just two weeks before, when the African leader Lumumba was killed, the same brother took me aside and told me he wanted my government to know that Lumumba had been eaten by the natives. As he told me this bit of grisly news, he licked his lips as if personally enjoying the feast. It was inconceivable that such a man would function as head of Jordan.

The next day the government radio confirmed that Majali had been in his office and was now dead. Still no word of Hussein. We used all our sources—government contacts, diplomatic friends, colleagues—but without effect. The lack of news about the king could be interpreted in two ways. If he were dead, the palace might be trying to keep the fact secret for a few days to prevent chaos in the country. If Hussein were alive, he might still be a target of assassins and therefore could well remain in hiding until those responsible for the bomb were identified.

Driving back from the Foreign Ministry in the late afternoon I noticed for the first time how silent the town was. Empty streets and alleys—no cars—no donkeys—no vendors or stalls—no buzzing and chipping of stone cutters— not even the stinking garbage of decaying fruit. Overnight, a bustling brawling town had become a corpse.

Hussein's principal source of strength was the Bedouins on the Left Bank. Conceivably, he might have been in touch with the most powerful tribe to confirm its support. I asked Sandy to send Samaan, the embassy driver, to the ruling sheikh with a request that he receive us urgently. The Arab temperament of instant hospitality served us well. We were told to come immediately. The chief of the tribe would wait for us. There would be Arab horses to ride before we sat down to eat.

An hour later Sandy and I were in our jeep. On our way out of town we passed through several small Bedouin settlements: makeshift shelters with scraps of tin for roofs and ragged black blankets for sides. A few goats or sheep were tethered or wandered between shelters. An occasional camel sat or sprawled on the dry dirt. A sudden roar above stilled our conversation. Four jets of the Royal Jordanian Air Force zoomed overhead. They seemed an invasion of the twentieth century into a two-thousand year old civilization.

Soon we were in the desert. Unlike the sandy Egyptian Sahara, the Jordan desert is rocky, hard, barren of life. I could see no tracks. Yet Samaan drove ahead swiftly and fearlessly. How did he not get lost? All I could see was an endless unmarked plain of rock and gravel.

An hour later, we spotted the first oasis: a few toy-like tents half a mile in the distance and small black dots that turned into tethered horses as we drew closer. The sheikh came out to greet us as soon as the jeep pulled up beside the first tent. He was wearing a white caftan with long sleeves, tied at the waist by a golden cord. Despite the intense heat he wore a long burnoose cloak over the caftan. Around his head was the traditional *kaffiyeh* held in place by a braided *agal*. He escorted us inside the largest, most luxurious tent.

We sat on huge soft cushions of red and orange under a canopy of pink silk hanging from the canvas top. Arab hospitality demands the strict observance of amenities. It is not enough to greet guests with "how are you" and get right down to business. Each guest must be greeted with questions concerning family, both immediate and extended, before entering a wide uncharted area of three or four additional minutes on any subject except business. I was writhing on my cushion with impatience after two minutes. After four minutes, I started to ask a question about the king but recognizing my *gaucherie*, I managed to choke off the question and turn it into a cliché about the weather.

I spread my legs and tried to look at ease as I lolled back on the soft cushions, but inwardly I felt only turmoil. When could we stop this wretched overture and get on with the main act? After five minutes I raised my cup of hot tea in greeting.

"Honored Sheikh," I said in my imperfect Arabic, glad that my Arabic teacher was not present to be disgraced by my pronunciation.

"You have such a beautiful country. Jordan is to me the most enchanting of all the countries in which I have served in the Foreign Service." The sheikh nodded his head appreciatively.

"I am honored to work in your country," I went on. "The problems are vast and difficult to solve. But if there is anyone who can solve them, it must surely be your own King Hussein. I am greatly impressed with his wisdom." I looked at the sheikh, and again he was nodding his head. Still no indication if he knew the whereabouts of Hussein. I trusted his devotion to the king and felt I was on firm ground once I kept to praise of country and monarch. "Sheikh," I tried to look worried. "It is most tragic what happened to the Prime Minister three days ago. You knew Hazza Pasha well, I think?"

"Yes, of course," the sheikh said simply. "He was one of us."

"Do you know of any motive for his assassination? He seemed a very kind, even modest man, and one without an enemy."

"That is true. But there are things more important than motive to consider."

"Of course."

"Whoever has done this execrable crime must suffer when we know who is the murderer—and we will know."

For the first time I sensed the heat of his emotion. His words came faster, even softer, but his eyes were glaring and his face flushed.

"An even more terrible thing," I said. "Your king—it has worried our country and me personally—no one knows where he is—how he is—Do you know how his Highness is?"

"I have not seen him, but we have exchanged messages. He assures me he is well."

"Excellent," I said, breathing lightly again.

"Justice and—revenge—you Americans cannot understand how we Arabs feel about revenge—when we know who has been the murderer, that person must be punished. It is not enough to kill—he must be killed painfully—with torture—with blood. I know you in the West try to devise the ways of death that are the swiftest and least painful. Here we have—if you will pardon me—the wisdom to devise the most painful and slowest tortures. But this is not a pleasant subject for an honored guest." Abruptly he got up. "Perhaps you would like to see our tents—our people?"

"Thank you. Yes."

He told me to follow him. Outside the tent we found ourselves in the blazing heat of the afternoon sun. The sheikh led us past the other tents. Through the open flaps of one I saw several women in silk veils crouching in the dark shadows, probably to avoid being seen. The horses we approached were small, sleek, and black. All were without saddles. The sheikh suggested we ride. Since I fancied I was more valuable to my government alive than dead, I respectfully refused the offer to accompany him. After a few minutes, Sandy who had been hanging sideways onto the flanks of the horse while madly clutching the reins, slid off with a sigh of major relief.

The sheikh smiled briefly and escorted us to a tent where a *mansif,* a feast prepared for honored guests, was waiting. It usually features a freshly roasted lamb and is eaten without forks, spoons, knives, or even sticks. The fingers grab any desired part of the roasted animal, the teeth chew the meat, and the tongue cleanses the fingers. Sandy grabbed a great hunk of the lamb's side and started chewing. I looked analytically at the animal, trying to decide whether I favored the side or the rear end when the sheikh touched my outstretched arm and gently pushed it aside. He reached toward the lamb and pulled out what I most

feared he would—the eye. This part of the anatomy, considered the most succulent, is traditionally given to the guest
of honor. In semi-revulsion, as the sheikh offered me the
dripping eye, I passed it slowly to my mouth. With half-
closed eyes I chewed and swallowed as fast as teeth and
throat would work. At the end, as I licked my fingers, I felt
slightly nauseated and distinctly light-headed, but trium-
phant.

The conversation was desultory. I tried to get the
sheikh to talk about his message from the king—did Hussein say where he was?—but the sheikh dodged each question and ended where we began, with family, health and
the weather.

The rules of Arab deportment which require long peri-
ods of conversational inanities before eating or doing business may not favor the guests. But the postprandial protocol which dictates an immediate departure, somewhat
compensates them.

Our last mouthful had hardly been swallowed when
Sandy and I said our farewells. Under my breath I murmured *"hamdulillah,"* as the Arabs say when thanking
heavens and the deity.

We weren't in Amman more than half an hour when
our office radio, which was customarily kept on twenty-
four hours a day, stated that King Hussein was about to
speak to his people.

When the king came on, his statement was short. He
revealed he had planned to be in the Prime Ministry at
eleven on the day Hazza Pasha was assassinated, but by
one of those strange but heaven-sent interventions of Allah,
Hussein had been forced to postpone his visit. The bomb,
certainly intended for him, was placed in the top drawer of
Majali's desk. How the bomb got into the drawer was still
being investigated.

"Hamdulillah," the king concluded. "Allah has saved
my life so that I can serve my people. My first duty will be
to find the murderer of our Prime Minister and punish him
according to Arab law."

How charmed Hussein's life already had been. Then

only twenty-five, he had already survived several attempts on his life.

I phoned the palace and left a message expressing the joy of the American government, the embassy, and myself that the king had been spared.

Over the next few days, the mechanics of the plot against the king began to unravel. A Syrian cleaning woman, recently hired by the Prime Ministry, was thought to have unlocked a door of the building during the night before the bomb went off. A trained technician presumably entered with two bombs, rigged one up in the Prime Minister's desk to go off at 11:10, just after the king was scheduled to arrive at the Prime Ministry. A second bomb, in the other wing of the building, was also timed to go off at 11:10. The first bomb went off as planned. The second bomb fizzled.

The Syrian woman and technician had miraculously disappeared. There were indications, but no proof, that they had slipped over the border into Syria. The Jordanian government demanded that the Syrian government locate them and return them to Jordan to stand trial. The Syrians in reply said there were thousands of cleaning women and technicians in Syria. It was ridiculous to expect the government to know them all. Was King Hussein becoming paranoid?

The Jordanian army then mobilized and moved its forces near the border of Syria. The Syrian reply was to mobilize its own forces. Within a few days, both armies, fully mobilized, were snarling at each other across the border.

The State Department was concerned. It instructed me to see the king and persuade him not to take any provocative action that could lead to a war with Syria.

Within a few hours I was in the king's sitting room, sipping a blackish coffee from a delicate porcelain cup.

For a moment I wondered whether I needed to fill up the next five minutes with the usual greetings and fervent hopes for good health, long life, and perfect weather. The king settled my indecision. Skipping the usual amenities, he launched into a denunciation of Syria as soon as I was seated. Syria was an ally of Egypt, a pawn in fact. The Syrians never made a move of importance without the concurrence—and even instigation—of Egypt. President Nasser had long wanted to bring Jordan into the tight circle of the UAR but Hussein had refused. "The United Arab Republic?" he sneered. "The Arabs have many talents, but doesn't Nasser know that the supreme Arab talent is to disagree on everything? Disunity has its disadvantages, but it also shows that our people are independent."

The king was speaking strongly in perfectly cultured English with the same directness one might expect from a Westerner. I realized again how much Hussein was a part of the West. He had grown up in England, where he went to school, and spent much of his time in Europe, generally at posh ski resorts and spas. Known as an international playboy, he was charismatic, charming, and beloved by the ladies, many of whom he loved in return. Still, he never forgot his dedication to Jordan or his mission in life as an Arab. In Jordan he was usually dressed, as now, in an Arab *kaffiyeh* and an army uniform with several rows of impressive medals on his chest.

"Yes, your Majesty," I said, "The State Department understands your point of view—in fact, applauds it. We see no contribution that the UAR can make to the welfare and peace of the Middle East. I know your provocation—we all had the highest respect and affection for Hazza Pasha, and we understand your emotional reaction. But in this case, we would caution you not to increase tensions by taking precipitate action that we may all regret later."

As I mentioned the name of Majali, I noticed tears in Hussein's eyes. This was no Arab charade of pretense but the outpouring of a man deeply affected by the death of a cherished colleague.

The king's normally strong voice turned tremulous: "Hazza Pasha was one of my closest friends, a man I could trust, beloved by all who knew him—Now we must find his murderer—tear him apart just as he tore Hazza Pasha apart. This is the only revenge we can accept!"

Revenge. The same word used in the desert by the sheikh. The same concept. Was the king merely echoing the demands of his supporters or did he too believe in bloody retribution? It became clear the king had temporarily put aside his Western clothes and culture and reverted to the code of his ancestors. The gnawing need for retribution would strangle him unless it was set free by revenge.

"I appreciate the concern of your government," the king said, once more in control of himself. "But let Washington understand my thoughts, my honor."

"Will you keep your armies mobilized on the border with Syria?"

"Until we have the murderer," he said.

"But you don't know for sure that Syria is responsible," I said.

"We are following the clues. We know the bomb was placed by Syrians. But in whose employ are they? Surely not for their own sake. They have nothing to gain. Are they employed by President Nasser of Egypt, or the Syrian government, or Israel? One cannot discount the possibility this is an act of the Israeli government intended to sow discord and confusion among their Arab enemies. The Israelis would have much to gain if Jordan went to war with Syria."

"Not if the war spread until it enveloped the whole Middle East. Surely everyone would lose. But let us return to the present crisis. Your Majesty, is there no danger of war in two armies both fully mobilized and bristling at each other across a thin boundary? One misstep—a chance shot?"

"There is that danger," the king admitted. "But our troops are under orders not to respond to any provocation unless specific orders to fire come to them from their commanding officers. You can assure Washington we will act with restraint, at least until we trace the origin of the assassination."

Then he stood up. "I thank you for coming." He went to the huge door and opened it for me. "Oh yes—," he said as we were shaking hands, "Your elections next month. Who do you think will win? Nixon or Kennedy?"

I was amazed. At a time of deepest personal political crisis and threat of war, Jordan was interested in the American elections? Then I understood the king's concern. Jordan depended heavily on American money for economic development and military hardware. Both American candidates would issue policy statements, one of them about economic and military aid. Would aid to Jordan be recommended by both Nixon and Kennedy, or only one, or by neither?

A few days later I received a cable from the secretary of State. It was, as usual, a NIACT, one requiring night action and an immediate reply. Sam Spiegel, the movie producer, was making a film called *Lawrence of Arabia,* and was even now in the Middle East scouting for a suitable location. He wanted to visit Jordan and talk with the highest authorities to negotiate terms for the film. Similarly *Holiday on Ice* was scheduled to give several performances in Amman two weeks hence. Both Spiegel and the *Holiday on Ice* entrepreneurs had read of a possible war between Jordan and Syria. Both wanted to visit Amman, but because of the present unrest they were unsure if they should come. What was my estimate of the situation? Did I think war would break out between Jordan and Syria?

I sat down and started methodically whipping out a cable in reply, then suddenly stopped and tore it up. I was indulging in the most unimaginative cliches, taking refuge behind portentous words and shameless gobbledygook. What did I *really* think about the prospects for war or peace? Did I know? Could I know? Should I guess?

Dismayed and a little frantic, I called a staff meeting and for an hour I tossed around the question with embassy officers. Each officer knew a part of the complete picture, but only a small part. What could they really tell me? Why should I expect them to know—or to guess—better than I could? What I was really doing was asking for support in an impossible decision. All they could do was contribute the small incomplete part of the picture they knew. The

economics officer could only tell me that the economy of
Jordan was in lousy shape—Amman would be crazy to
start a war with anyone, but who isn't crazy these days?
The military attaché gave me an assessment of the military
capabilities of both sides: the Jordanians had superior
equipment, much of it British and American, and were
probably better trained than the Syrians. The Syrians had
more troops to begin with and, when these were deci-
mated, Nasser probably would supply more manpower
from the Egyptian stockpile. None of this information was
really helpful. I was still miles away from the wise decision
expected of me in Washington.

Well, I thought, why not throw it back where it
started?

"Dorothy," I said to my secretary. "Call the palace and
ask for an urgent meeting with Hussein."

Two hours later I was sipping another cup of Arabic
coffee with the king, again dressed in his *kaffiyeh* and army
uniform. I told him of our predicament. When I mentioned
Sam Spiegel and *Lawrence of Arabia* the king nodded. "Yes,
we have been corresponding.—"

I was amazed and disturbed. An Arab king in touch
with an American Jew? The last known Arab-Jewish contact was between Golda Meir and King Abdullah, the
grandfather of Hussein, who was assassinated by his own
people for his contacts with Israel. To be sure, Spiegel was
not an Israeli, but to most Arabs a prominent American
Jew was the same thing. Surely Hussein must know the
danger he was in.

"What do you think of Spiegel making a film here?" I
asked.

The King smiled in a small pained way. "The money is
good."

"The visit of a prominent Jew to Jordan will not affect
you?"

"There will be no publicity." Jordan's policy was to
allow no Jews in the country. Clearly Spiegel was to be an
exception.

"The money he pays you is for what?"

"He wants to rent a thousand camels and riders for many weeks. It will be most helpful for our treasury which as your government knows is almost empty. Besides, he will want hundreds of thousands of gallons of water transported from Aquaba to Wadi Rum where the picture will be made—each gallon we sell him also adds many *dinars* to our slim treasury. How much do you think he might pay for the camels?"

"He can't make this picture without them—and he's certainly not going to import them from Hollywood."

"He has much money?"

"He made *Bridge on the River Kwai*—it made millions."

"Then four *dinars* a day for a camel with rider is not an exorbitant amount?"

"I wouldn't think so."

Hussein smiled boyishly. "A new role for a chargé—mediating between the Jordan government and Hollywood."

"More interesting than many of my other chores," I admitted cheerfully. "And what about *Holiday on Ice*?"

"They will also pay us many *dinars*. The rent of the Roman amphitheatre, the lighting, a tax on admissions—all of this for three days." His slow smile made me wonder if he was forgetting the spirit of revenge. "Besides," he said, "I understand some of the women skaters are very beautiful indeed."

The king's penchant for beautiful women was well known. "Very beautiful," I agreed. "So what shall I advise the State Department?"

"Let them come. *Tfaddal,*" he said with a sweep of his small hand. "We will make them comfortable."

"But can you offer them safety?"

"What is safety? Who can be guaranteed anything? Even in America."

"Especially in America," I said. "But that isn't the point. We're talking about Jordan—now in 1960. Will there be peace or war?"

I fell silent as Hussein pondered the question. His

head was turned slightly away from me. A light film appeared in his eyes as if he wanted to distance himself from the room where we were sitting. "Tell Mr. Spiegel and *Holiday on Ice*," he finally said, "There will be no war until at least they leave the country."

I stiffled a guffaw, "Spiegel will be in Jordan many weeks, maybe many months—"

"He will be in the desert—many miles from the Gulf of Aquaba—if there is any war, it will certainly not spread to the wilderness."

I felt like asking Hussein if he could guarantee that the Syrians, outraged by the potential threat of the Jordanian army standing on their border, might not let loose with a barrage of gunfire. Then I thought: Don't push it. You've got an answer. Perhaps it's not the most complete. But good enough.

Dutifully, I reported to the Department of State what the King had said. The next day I received a cable from Sam Spiegel saying that his yacht had already left the French Riviera and would be arriving in the Gulf of Aquaba in the next three days. He would call me immediately upon arrival to arrange a visit to Amman.

A few hours later, the embassy cultural officer told me he had received a wire from *Holiday on Ice* confirming its engagement for three performances in Amman the following week.

During the next two days I worked with the embassy cultural officer on both the Spiegel and *Holiday on Ice* visits. Appointments had to be made. Schedules worked out. Briefings prepared. All at a time when the stability of Jordan and the Middle East was threatened. I needed to spend all my time keeping abreast of the progress made by the Jordanians in tracking down the Majali killer. I should be busy sensing the mood of the palace and the bazaar regarding imminent war, and informing the Department of my findings and estimates. I resented the time I would have to take away from these pressing matters to spend on Spiegel and *Holiday on Ice*, but the truth was I was enjoying my participation in the world of film and entertainment.

During the following days no progress was made by
Jordan in determining responsibility for the Majali murder. The curfew was lifted, but tensions remained. Most of
the population of Amman remained indoors. When people
did venture out, they would walk swiftly to the market and
hurriedly make their purchases, skipping the usual savor-
ing of wares and spices.

When Spiegel arrived in Amman, he and his director,
David Lean, and the latter's new and very lovely Indian
wife, lunched with Peggy and me at the Residence. Over
coffee and liqueurs, I gave them a short briefing on Jordan,
its problems with Israel and other Arab countries, the assassination of Majali and how it might affect the filming.

Sam puffed on a small cigar. "Doesn't seem like the
best of times to ask the government for assistance in making a movie."

"On the other hand," I said, "it may be the best of
times." I told him of the king's interest in amassing more
dinars and dollars in his treasury. "How far along are you
in negotiations about camels and drivers?"

"Just about to start. What do you think is the lowest
price I can pay to get all those lousy goddam camels and
drivers?"

"Who knows? All I can say is that Jordan dearly needs
the business—and you need the camels. If you can afford
four or five dinars a camel—"

"High, very high. I should pay that?"

"You might be able to do better, but if you don't pay
the price they want, you may get the camels—but find that
the water you order from the government will arrive late.
The Arabs often demonstrate their dissatisfaction not directly in connection with the cause of their unhappiness. A
kind of indirect revenge for injury. Perhaps four *dinars*
might be a fair price."

"Four *dinars* then," Sam said with a grimace. He was
known to be a pennysaver on his pictures even though the
results never betrayed it.

Before he left, Sam invited Peggy and me down to
Wadi Rum for a day to watch the initial shooting of the

film. Peter O'Toole was expected in Jordan shortly, and we would be able to meet him. A company plane would come for us in Amman and take us to Aquaba. We would visit Sam's yacht in the harbor, then a jeep would get us to Wadi Rum. It seemed a splendid idea and I accepted with the proviso that if the political situation heated up we might have to postpone the trip at short notice.

Negotiations went rapidly, for the very next week Sam called to say the camels and drivers were already in Wadi Rum. Tomorrow would be a good day for a visit—would it be good for me? I was due to attend the opening performance of *Holiday on Ice* that night and told Sam that my wife and I would be delighted to come for a visit if we could be back before dark. Before hanging up, Sam said that the Jordanian Queen Mother would also be visiting Aquaba tomorrow. She had been invited on board his yacht at noon and he hoped we would be there at the same time. His voice seemed uneasy, as if he might not be sure how to entertain royalty.

The next morning the plane picked us up at the airport. Peg and I were the only passengers. After an hour of luxurious flying, with two stewards proffering us unlimited drinks and hors d'oeuvres, we set down at Aquaba. There in the harbor was a gleaming white yacht. It was not only a home but an office for Spiegel.

Seen from afar, the yacht was graceful and slim; at close hand it looked as if it was several blocks long, although I was later told it measured less than two hundred feet. Sam showed us around the various decks. I had heard of gold handles in palaces but not on yachts. Sam had several staterooms with a gold handle, behind which, he said, the cabins were plush, elegant and sybaritic. I asked Sam if we could go inside and look at one of the cabins. Somewhat sheepishly and a bit hurriedly he told me they were occupied. Then, giving me a slow glance as if testing my trustworthiness, he said two of his girls from the French Riviera were on board. He had ordered them to stay in their cabins during the Queen Mother's visit and had locked the doors. Not only would they not be able to leave but no unsuspecting guest might invade their privacy.

The Queen Mother was all charm and good will. She knew no English, Sam knew no Arabic, and Peg and I, with our modest knowledge of the language, made one small gaffe after another. Perhaps we even exaggerated our gaffes to increase the excuses for laughter and thereby ease the tension.

Once the Queen Mother put her hand on one of the golden handles but Sam put his finger to his lips and whispered "asleep." The Queen looked questioningly at me, and when I translated, she responded with a knowing smile but what she actually understood is still not certain. Sam thought it must be a royal expression on occasions of uncertainty. I, on the other hand, thought it was an awareness of the contents of the cabin.

After lunch, the Queen Mother returned to Amman on one of the palace planes and we headed for Wadi Rum. The shooting that day involved a long shot of hundreds of camels on the horizon framed by a reddish sun behind them. It is one of the best known shots in the film and certainly the most beautiful. How the director, David Lean, managed to get his camels and drivers in perfect formation on the exact edge of the hill, to give him the shot he desired, is still a thing of wonder.

Our admiration for Lean was shared by neither Sam nor Peter O'Toole. Sam fretted about the behavior of the drivers—they seemed unable to make the camels perform stunts that horses did easily. He also accused Lean of being impervious to budget restrictions. Lean, according to Sam, was so wrapped up in the poetry of the scene that he kept on taking shot after shot of the camels on the horizon every few minutes just to compare the differing quality of beauty as the light changed. "Who the hell pays to see quality of light," Sam stormed.

Peter O'Toole, hardly known for a cool head, stood restlessly on the sidelines all afternoon. Increasingly infuriated at the attention paid to camels, he finally blew up at Sam, causing a scene infinitely more dramatic than anything else that was shot that day, and demanding that the company plane take him back to Amman, from where he would get a flight to London to spend the weekend.

After a hurried conversation between Lean and Spiegel, O'Toole was given leave for the weekend, but he was still fuming when he boarded the plane with Peggy and me later that afternoon. During the trip he kept on cursing Spiegel and Lean, the latter for keeping him overtime, the former for wasting his time in Aquaba that day. His rage seemed somehow irrelevant as we flew over the glorious mountains of Moab, which in the setting sun were changing hue from rose to brick red to dark purple, then over spectacular Mt. Nebo from which Moses first viewed the Promised Land. All this magnificence was apparently lost on O'Toole, his thoughts fixed firmly on London.

The next time I saw Sam, he was still swearing he would never make another film with David Lean because he was a demented poet hypnotized by camels on the horizon. And, several weeks later, when Sam left Jordan before the picture was finished, the crew threatening to resign because of the intense heat and insufficiency of water, he also swore he would never make another film on location. As for Lean, seemingly immune to the temperament of his star and the tantrums of his producer, he went about his business making a landmark picture. It was a wonder that the picture was ever made or that it turned out so well.

That evening, on our return to Amman, I immediately checked on the military situation. No change. Jordanian and Syrian troops were still snarling at each other across the border.

The *Holiday on Ice* company had arrived. Though the Roman amphitheatre was in shape for the first performance that evening, the ice was not. It was still being manufactured. Influenced no doubt by the temperamental outbursts of our Hollywood friends all day, I began to seethe until I was told sternly by the manager that ice was always manufactured at the last moment. How in hell did I imagine it could withstand the pervasive heat of this crappy desert?

I arrived at the amphitheatre at eight with a group of
Jordanian officials as my guests. Excitement was running
high. The people of Amman had never seen any ice skating,
much less an ice extravaganza with music, lighting, and
scenery. We pushed our way through a crowd of Arabs
milling around the sole entrance which was also the sole
exit. Seats were all sold out. Those without tickets demanded to be admitted. As hands clutched at the Ticket
Takers' sleeves and coat, a group of young ruffians representing the extreme right wing of Islam pulled out knives
from their long caftans and attacked some of those entering the amphitheatre.

Soon we were embroiled in a first class brawl. The
police arrived and battled the religious fanatics who, as
nearly as I could understand, were shrieking, "Whores—
bitches inside—beat them—hit them—women in short
skirts—they show their legs—they want to dirty us, corrupt
us, make us impure so we cannot find peace with Allah!
Throw these evil women out of Jordan—beat them—hit
them!"

The screams of the attackers were mixed with the
screams of the attacked. When the police finally overcame
the fanatics, several dozen wounded were taken to a medical van parked close to the entrance.

When I finally got inside the amphitheatre, I saw immediately that the ribbons closing off the seats reserved for
high government officials had all been torn down. Apparently, the first Arabs to enter the amphitheatre had
promptly cut down the ribbons and stormed into the seats.
It is my guess that some of the fanatics who had shrieked
the loudest about whores and sex were among those taking
over the reserved section from where they could have a
close view of the luscious American legs.

I had eight officials with me including the acting prime
minister, the foreign minister and their wives. We waited in
the aisles several minutes while the ushers aided by armed
police cleared out the first row of reserved seats.

Given this melodrama, it was not surprising that the
show started an hour and a half late. Howls mixed with

cheers, and a few jeers punctuated the performance. Throughout, a serene full moon hung over the ice, lending an eerie light to the performance below. Despite the emotional tumult, the show was an enormous success.

The next night I returned to politics. Weeks before the assassination of Majali our press attache had received a film of the Nixon-Kennedy presidential debates in the States. The attache suggested I might want to invite key government officials to see the film. Remembering Hussein's interest in our elections, I agreed immediately and asked the attache to draw up a list of officials to invite.

Twenty officials came to the showing, all without their wives. The logic seemed to be that presidential debates fell under the category of politics, from which Arabic women were known to disassociate themselves.

Looking around at the all-male group, I thought once again of the inferior role assigned to women in the Arab world. Unfortunately, they were seldom allowed to participate in affairs of state or in the military, perhaps one explanation for Arab weakness compared to Israel.

There was much interest in the film. Afterwards I suggested we hold a secret vote. "If you were an American, for whom would you vote? Nixon or Kennedy?"

I passed out slips of paper and pencils and asked them to write the name of their choice. I suspected how the results would turn out: weren't all Arabs sympathetic to the Republicans because Harry Truman, a Democrat, was the first head of government to recognize the state of Israel? I was not surprised at the results: Nixon received one hundred percent of the vote and John Kennedy zero. Fortunately for Kennedy, the vote in America was the only one that counted.

It was the last relaxing evening I would spend for some time. Even before *Holiday on Ice* arrived in town, we were receiving hints from the prime ministry that clues to the Majali murder were pointing to Syria. The day after the presidential debate film, Talhouni, the acting prime minister, told me that two murderers had been clearly identified: the Syrian cleaning woman, plus an accomplice, a technician. Both were employed by the Syrian government, and were even now in Damascus where they had been secreted by the Syrian Intelligence Agency.

What effect would this knowledge have on Hussein? War or peace? When I asked Talhouni how he thought the King would react, he twisted the palm of his right hand up and down to show his uncertainty. *Holiday on Ice* was leaving Jordan the next day. They would probably be out of the danger zone before any war might break out with Syria. But *Lawrence of Arabia* was quite another matter. Lean was still shooting camels on the horizon, and a lot more footage remained to be filmed on location before returning to London for the interior scenes. Would the king honor his promise—start no war, at least until Spiegel was out of the country?

I reported my talk with Talhouni to the State Department. Within hours a frantic cable from the Department was placed on my desk. Again I was instructed to see the king and express, in the strongest terms, the United States government concern that he should refrain from starting a war with Syria, which could only lead to a major Middle East conflagration.

As I read the cable, I tried to visualize the king's reaction, now that he had the facts about the murder. He had publicly pledged revenge to the Majali family, to the Bedouins in the desert, to all of Jordan in speeches and official announcements. But now that he was faced with the certainty of a Syrian connection, how would he respond? He could maintain his honor with a costly bloody fight, but would it be worth it to decimate his troops and open the country to sabotage from the United Arab Republic and Nasser?

I tried to gauge the progress of Hussein's emotions since the assassination. In the heat of the moment, he had felt the need for revenge. Now that weeks had passed and emotions presumably cooled, might he be less rigid on the question of revenge? He might even now be looking for a compromise, a way to keep his honor intact—his country intact—yet still satisfy the Majali family and Bedouin tribes that were demanding revenge in the bloodiest terms. How could I help the king find a compromise acceptable to all, assuming he was looking for a way out?

I called my team together—the small group of officers who headed up the various sections of the embassy. We had met almost every day in the last few weeks, and they had been an enormous support to me. I would bounce ideas to them and each member of the team—the political officer, the economic officer, the military attache, the head of the Point 4 Economic Aid Program—would bounce back his impressions. Today would be the ultimate test of their imagination. Could they come up with a suggestion that would save the king's honor without weakening him in the eyes of his people?

I posed the question to the team. Sandy thought revenge to the Arabs meant revenge in its purist form, that it could not be watered down by time. If the king had promised his people revenge, he would have to deliver it to them in the bloodiest form possible. The administrative officer agreed the situation was quite hopeless. I should urgently cable the Department to reserve a Pan Am plane to evacuate embassy families if and when war broke out. In any case, his wife was already making preparations to return to the States immediately, assuming the airport was still open.

The economic officer wondered if a trade war—perhaps an embargo on the import of Syrian products—might fulfill the definition of revenge. I briefly considered his suggestion, then cast it aside. This might hurt the Jordanians more than the Syrians. For one thing, Jordan was not a major trading partner for Syria. Syrian products would go elsewhere, and the Jordanians would end up buying them through another country—perhaps Lebanon—at a higher price than before.

"How does this sound?" I said drily. "There's an organization called the United Nations. It's supposed to be a peace-keeping organization. Doesn't the king's problem fit squarely within the purview of the United Nations ?"

"Where's the revenge?" Sandy asked.

"Depends on what the United Nations does," I said.

"Does the United Nations ever do anything?" someone else wanted to know.

"Not often, and not much," I had to admit. "But what do you say; shall we give it a whirl?"

As no other suggestions were forthcoming, I decided to test the idea out on the king.

Later that day, I gained an emergency audience with Hussein. He seemed pale as if he might have spent a sleepless night pondering what action to take in light of the recent findings of Syrian involvement. If he had truly been agonizing over the problem, my suggestion might be timely.

"Your Majesty," I began. "I've just received the most urgent instructions from my government. We're concerned that in light of the recent findings of Syrian involvement in the murder of Hazza Pasha you will be pressured into military action against Syria—"

At this point Hussein interrupted with a dry smile. "A king pressured into doing something he does not want?"

I raised my voice slightly hoping to gain assurance. "We very much fear the results of a conflict between Jordan and Syria. The first casualty may well be the destruction of the East Ghor canal, which as you know was financed by Point 4 money from the United States. It is very close to the border, and, therefore, extremely vulnerable to Syrian attack. The economy and agriculture of your country depend a great deal on this canal for necessary irrigation. We can also see other disastrous results of a conflict with Syria. The involvement of Egypt. Nasser will see a conflict as an opportunity to support Syria with his own troops or perhaps even act as peacekeeper. In either case, he may emerge stronger than before and become an even greater threat to Jordan."

"What does your country suggest?" Hussein said impatiently. "That I forego action against Syria—that I let the memory of Hazza Pasha wither and decay because of inertia? What do you suggest?"

"The United Nations, your Majesty," I offered, and paused, waiting for a brusque turndown.

Instead, the eyes of the king clouded for several seconds. "It is not what I intended," he said simply and without force.

"Who can judge the wisdom of intentions?" I said. I knew I was beginning to talk like an Arab and wondered if it would help or hurt my case. The king shot me a quick glance and looked out the window at the royal park.

"People play down the United Nations," I said. "But its potential has seldom been tested. If you brought a complaint against Syria it would be handled by the General Assembly which is just now in session. That means your representatives can hurl all the insults and accusations at the Syrians you want."

"And is that going to demolish Syria—even punish it?"

"In the eyes of the world it will. Syria has much to lose if it gains a reputation for terrorism."

"A war of words then?" I could sense he was evaluating the United Nations approach. Would the Majali clan be sufficiently placated? And the Bedouins in the desert?

I kept silent, desperately hoping that the early emotions of the Bedouins and the Majali family might have softened by now and that they too might be considering a way out.

"Words are a cowardly and useless substitute for revenge," he said, but there was little conviction in the way he avoided my eyes.

I pressed my point, while trying to avoid the appearance of paternalism. The aim of the United States over the years had been to strengthen the economy, with the East Ghor canal, and the various programs of education, agriculture, health. Were all of these to be sacrificed to the need for an act of primal revenge that would benefit neither the people nor the country of Jordan? Jordan might save its honor but in the process return itself economically to where it had been twenty years before. Would the United States be able or willing, then, to help again? It was not certain how Congress might respond. Would it appropriate enough money to rebuild the East Ghor canal once it was destroyed? There were certainly enough anti-aid Congressmen around who criticized the United States for ignoring its own poor in favor of foreign countries.

I ended with a pep talk: "Try the United Nations approach, Majesty. Give it a chance. If, after a while, you see it's not giving Jordan the satisfaction you need, you can throw the idea out the window."

Hussein seemed about to speak several times, but hesitated at each occasion. He either was undecided, or else he wanted to give me the impression of an internal struggle. Probably the latter. After all, his honor would not allow him to be swayed by a foreign power, even a friendly one.

Finally he said, "Well, let us see."

I left hurriedly, certain that the king would take the problem to the United Nations. The first thing I did on returning to my office was to cancel the Pan Am plane that had just been reserved for possible evacuation of embassy staff members and their families.

A few days later, Jordan took its case to the United Nations. By the time the United Nations got around to considering it, tempers had cooled still further. There were days of discussion, accusations, counteraccusations, mountains of paper that filled several file cabinets and tumbled eventually into monumental piles in the corridor. The threat of war had come and gone. Not a shot was fired.

Near the end of my tour of duty in Jordan, the Jordanian driver of an embassy car was taking Peggy and me to a military reception in a neighboring town. Buzzing along a narrow twisting road at sixty or seventy miles an hour, he approached a curve. With reckless bravado, he was driving on the wrong side of the road. Just as he rounded the curve, another car, driving on the right side, came zooming toward us. Both cars crashed and overturned. The occupant of the other car was taken to a hospital. Peg and I scrambled out of our car, testing various limbs to see if everything worked properly. We had bruises, but seemed otherwise to be intact. Meanwhile, our driver was lying in the dirt, eyeing us carefully and moaning.

When he saw us walking, he miraculously recovered; the groaning stopped, and he jumped to his feet.

A few days later I found out I had fared less well than I previously thought. I began to experience severe pains in my back and leg, along the sciatic nerve. These kept on at intervals until one night, weeks later, in Cairo where I had come to give a presentation on Jordan to our embassy, I woke up at two in the morning in a sweat and with stunning pains running down my back and legs. Unable to walk, I crawled to the bathroom and later to the living room, where sometime later in the morning I was greeted by the American ambassador. He fitted me out with a cane so I could give his staff the presentation he had promised. Somehow I got through the speech that morning by leaning on the podium and my cane and by hoping I was making sense, as my mind barely functioned. Later, at the hospital in Beirut, I was diagnosed as having a herniated disk, the fifth lumbar. Apparently the car accident had cracked the disk and all it took was the enormously soft and mushy mattress in Cairo to complete the job. Instead of surgery, I chose bed rest.

I was soon out of the hospital, perhaps too soon for my back troubles returned later. In the meantime, I finished my tour of duty in Jordan and returned to the States.

A foreign service officer often leaves a country for another assignment experiencing a feeling of incompletion: things planned, but never implemented, projects started, but not yet completed.

This was particularly true for Peg and I in Jordan.

For a year and a half I had seen hordes of children scrambling in the dirt and rubble outside of their huts. There were no playgrounds anywhere in Jordan: no play equipment, no jungle gyms, no swings. I had managed, after a year and a half, to persuade the Jordanian government to set aside an area for a playground. Then I set about obtaining the necessary equipment for America, hunting down equipment manufacturers and seeking contributions for a playground. The equipment had not yet arrived as we folded our tents like Arabs. Only years later would I learn that the equipment had arrived and been assembled, amid the laughter and joy of countless children.

Peg also was leaving with a sense of incompletion. As Chairperson of the Board of the American School, she had been working constantly to improve its curriculum and obtain a full time principal. It would be years before she would learn that the School had increased to a full twelve years, and that a full time principal was now in place.

After home leave, I was assigned to Belgrade, Yugoslavia. I was delighted. George Kennan was the ambassador there, and I would be his deputy. As number two man in the embassy, I hoped to learn a great deal from this seasoned expert who had made an international reputation in Soviet affairs.

THIRTEEN

Communists Never Laugh
(Yugoslavia)

I had no great hope of success as I trudged along the dark corridor of the Yugoslav Foreign Ministry to the office of Petric, officer in charge of American affairs. I hoped, impossibly, that Petric had made a dramatic and miraculous change from an automaton into a human being.

In the early 1960's, I knew I was crazy to nurture such a hope. After all, I had been seeing him regularly for the last six months regarding Yugoslav-American problems. Each time, I'd found the same frozen exterior.

Petric's secretary greeted me tersely and, without getting up, pointed to the door of his office. As I entered, he was sitting, as usual, behind his desk, slumped over a sheaf of folders neatly piled before him. A short, rotund man, with a reddened complexion, he always seemed slightly out of breath. With an abrupt, but familiar, gesture—as if he had been surprised in a compromising situation—he jerked up his head and looked at my face as if he had never before seen it. Brusquely, he pointed toward the couch, his hand remaining outstretched for a moment before dropping to his side. I particularly disliked, even hated, that gesture. There was never a civilized handshake, just that ritual gesture of distaste—as if I was a capitalist virus invading a sacred Communist enclave. Actually, that was exactly what I was. When George Kennan has retired a year after I arrived in Belgrade, he had left me as Chargè, with a large post and a vastly talented staff.

After a few basic amenities, painful because of their strained artificiality, I posed the same question I had posed to his colleague Avramov just a half hour earlier.

"*Gospodin* Petric," I tried to appear concerned. "My government has just heard a rumor that Yugoslavia is considering joining the Warsaw Pact. Can you confirm it?"

Washington's concern about the rumor was understandable. If Yugoslavia joined the Pact, all the Communist military forces in Eastern Europe would be unified against the NATO forces in the West. It was hard to believe, however, that the rumor was correct. The Yugoslavs had broken from Moscow only a few years before and were as suspicious of Russia as they were of America.

Petric looked at me a long time before replying.

"*Gospodin* Chargé." As he paused, I heard in my mind the same words from Avramov: "*Gospodin* Chargé."

I had memorized Avramov's reply and was prepared to compare each of his words with what I was going to hear from Petric. I was not excited at the prospect. What's the fun of hearing clichés repeated?

"The Warsaw Pact," Petric continued, "is a military pact of all the Socialist countries in Europe."

Again I heard the echo of Avramov's voice. "The Warsaw Pact is a military pact of all the Socialist countries in Europe."

I mentally switched back to Petric.

"Russia is the leader of the Pact," he went on solemnly, then again he slowed down. He seemed to like to tease me with these short pauses, perhaps to prolong the effect of his words. Hurry along, for Christ's sake, I thought. Otherwise I'll tell you what you're going to say even before you say it.

Avramov's voice rang in my ears: "Russia is the leader of the Pact."

Petric was again talking.

"We do not trust the Russians—"

Then an echo from Avramov. "We do not trust the Russians—"

Then Petric, "Have you forgotten?"

Then Avramov, "Have you forgotten?"

Then Petric, "Yugoslavia had to fight the Russians at the end of the war to get them out of Yugoslavia."

Now Avramov, "Yugoslavia had to fight the Russians at the end of the war to get them out of Yugoslavia."

One hundred percent consistency so far. I was already mentally reviewing Avramov's last sentence: "Therefore it is not likely we would accept the invitation of the Russians to join the Warsaw Pact."

Please, Petric, I begged soundlessly; be different.

I listened longingly as Petric began, "Therefore it is—" Suddenly he slowed down and I bent forward to hear him better. . . . "unlikely . . ." Then he came to a full stop. This time it was not a teasing pause like the others, but a pause of insecurity. Startled, I sat up straight. A terrible look of uncertainty had come over his face. He's stumbled, I thought. He's forgotten the next word.

Petric looked at me, panic in his eyes. Wildly he searched my face as if it would give him an answer. Slowly I bent my head and looked at the floor. I heard him clear his throat. He was beginning again, this time in a small tentative voice.

"Therefore it is *not* likely—" He accented the word *not* and continued triumphantly, "We would accept the Russian invitation to join the Warsaw Pact."

I groaned. Right back to square one. Grudgingly, I gave the Communists perfect marks for memorization. Avramov. Now Petric. Perhaps all the Yugoslav officials in the Foreign Ministry. They must all have been briefed that morning, then memorized the exact wording of the Party line.

I stirred restlessly. Damn the Department of State anyway. What was the point of instructing me to get several replies to the same question? Didn't they know in a Communist country there was only one reply? No Communist official would dare depart from the Party line.

I knew I had to do something about Petric. Then immediately I found myself smiling. Petric looked embarrassed, an expression that somehow revived his face, as if it no longer wished to remain dead.

"What I said is not humorous," he warned. Again his face reverted back to its original grim expression.

"Of course not. It's utterly serious."

I thought perhaps my sarcasm might trigger a response, maybe not the one I wanted, but at least it would be something. But no, I was wrong.

My frustration was building. I wondered why I was taking the party line of one Communist so seriously. Recently, I seemed to be taking everything too seriously. No wonder. My wife was in the States having a hysterectomy, and I sorely missed her. I had just lived through several weeks of professional stress resulting from a major earthquake in Skopje, during which the embassy had worked around the clock with Washington and the American forces in Germany gathering blankets, food and medical supplies for thousands of destitute Yugoslavs. Next week, we were scheduled to receive the visitation of eighteen Congressmen, senators and spouses for meetings of the Inter Parliamentary Union. At this point, I badly needed a major breakthrough, some warmth and lightness, any sign of camaraderie.

Petric droned on.

Was there no human quality behind his stupid mask? Where was the sadness, the humor, the vitality that marked the difference between a machine and a human being? In all my dealings with him over the past six months I had never once seen Petric smile. Certainly, I had never heard him laugh, neither at the numerous receptions or dinners we attended, nor in his office. Perhaps he laughed unrestrained at home or at parties with his comrades, but never in front of a capitalist. It would be like allowing me to see him naked, a kind of intimacy no Communist could risk.

As I left his office, I pondered my predicament: how to make the automaton come alive? I wondered then if a live Petric might be thrown out of his job. After all, at the United Nations, Molotov repeated "Niet" regularly and dourly and Khruschev loved to bang his shoe angrily on the table. But, no, none of the great Communists were great laughers. It was definitely a challenge.

I continued pondering it. I even thought about Greta Garbo in the film *"Ninotchka."* Americans tend to get most of their great ideas from films. As a Soviet commissar in Paris, she was stiff and unapproachable until, finally, armed with champagne and some asinine jokes, a romantically-inclined Melvyn Douglas transformed her into a laughing flirt. The trouble was I was not romantically-inclined, certainly not toward Petric. No, Garbo was not going to be of any help here.

The following evening I attended a reception at the Italian embassy, a carbon copy of every embassy reception: same guest list, same food, same conversation. The thick hum of voices rumbled increasingly through the huge rooms, giving it the appearance of an immense beehive in which millions of mandibles never stop moving.

I clutched my glass of scotch and drifted for one group to another. I had begun to feel as if every time I had a drink in my hand, I was automatically on duty. And so I was. But tonight my duty would be different. Instead of searching for points of view about the United States-Cuban missile crisis just then beginning to break, I was after a far more subtle quarry: an insight into the Communist mind and personality.

I joined a small group composed of the British chargé, the French ambassador and the Greek ambassador. I said I'd just heard from a good source that Tito had decided to join the Warsaw Pact. The Greek ambassador asked for the name of my source. With a practiced smile, I reminded him that it was hardly ethical to divulge confidential information. The British chargé emphatically denied the truth of the rumor. The French ambassador was puzzled. I tried to play it cool. I said I would ordinarily disbelieve the rumor myself, but, this time, with such a reliable source, who could be sure? Besides, I added as I was leaving the group, Communist unity would be solidified by bringing Tito into the Warsaw Pact. In these Cold War days the Communists needed strength in their dealings with the capitalist West.

Several yards away, I turned and saw the British
chargé and the French and Greek ambassadors break up
their group, fan out and head precipitately toward other
groups of diplomats. The decibel level in the huge room
suddenly seemed to be rising, and I relaxed for five minutes on the sidelines before joining another group. Immediately I was grabbed by the Moroccan ambassador and
asked if I had heard that the Yugoslavs were joining the
Warsaw Pact. No, I said. I hadn't heard any such nonsense.
And yet—here I tried to appear puzzled—Yugoslavia was a
strange country: Tito, though usually stolid, had his volatile moments, so anything was possible. Later, I joined a
third group and learned from the Belgian ambassador that
Tito had just gone to the airport on a secret trip to Russia
and would come back a full-fledged member of the Warsaw
Pact. I nodded solemnly and thanked him for sharing this
important information with me.

At the end of the evening I searched for Petric and
found him edging toward the door. Hurriedly I cornered
him and asked if he had heard that Tito was about to join
the Warsaw Pact. He gave me a dirty look, said nothing and
hurried past me out of the room. I definitely had not
achieved my goal. Petric was not smiling, and far from
laughing.

I was on my way out when the Russian ambassador
and his wife rushed up to me.

"Mr. Chargé," he said breathlessly. "Did you know—
Yugoslavia today joins the Warsaw Pact? A magnificent day
for the Communist world. We are stronger than ever. Is
that not so, Masha?"

He threw his arm around his wife and squeezed her
shoulder tightly. She detached herself, laughed, and began
to fan herself. The movement seemed so compulsive I supposed it must be an outlet for nervousness. Whenever I saw
her, Masha always reacted with an artificial cocktail laugh,
no matter what remark was addressed to her. Before it
completely dwindled off, the high-pitched laugh would be
quickly reignited by another remark, so that the whole effect resembled a laughing puppet. I was convinced that

Masha could not tell the difference between comedy and tragedy, and had somewhere along the way decided to keep laughing, a long, drawn-out marathon that never ended.

I scratched my head thoughtfully. Communist laughter was apparently not a simple physical expression of joy. Petric did not laugh because he was afraid to reveal himself. And Masha laughed perpetually in a ridiculous way because she too did not want to reveal herself. On one hand no laughter, on the other hand, a steady stream. Were they the same after all? Was this a clue as to how to attack the cold unemotional fortress in which the real Petric resided?

Two evenings later I was invited for dinner at the Indonesian embassy. Petric was to be there. And the Russian ambassador was the guest of honor. With Masha, of course.

That evening, I felt like an *enfant terrible,* exhilarated but more than a little nervous. Whether or not I succeeded in making Petric laugh, I guessed it would be a long time before I would be invited to any more diplomatic dinners.

So be it. I deliberately set about picking a fight with the guest of honor, Zaroubin, the Russian ambassador. The attack would be verbal, not physical, but I knew I was taking a risk. The Department of State would undoubtedly reprimand me if it heard I had deliberately provoked a foreign diplomat. But as I was the only American at the dinner it was unlikely that State would hear about my naughty behavior.

During cocktails I edged closer to Zaroubin. I asked him about Mr. Khruschev. How was he these days? Zaroubin looked at me uncertainly. "You are interested in Mr. Khruschev? You think I see him every day?"

"Doing a noble job, isn't he—but quite impossible." I raised my voice. "Trying to change the whole Communist system—attacking Stalin. Now really. Your people won't stand for that." I looked him bluntly in the face. "Now will they?"

Zaroubin took refuge. "In what newspaper do you read such nonsense?"

"No newspaper," I said with pronounced volume and

emphasis, "my own personal point of view. Do you disagree?"

That was all Zaroubin needed. He quickly took the
bait and launched into a fiery defense of the whole Communist system.

"Why, Mr. Ambassador—" I interrupted him after he'd
gone through the whole litany of Communist philosophy in
which he was taking the part of both Politburo and peas-
ant. "How can you defend a system that destroys the proletariat, disgusts the few intellects that still survive, and dispatches half the population to *gulags*. I—"

Zaroubin interrupted me with a shout. His cheeks
were red, his eyes blazing.

"And your American system! That capitalism—exploiting the proletariat—bleeding the poor! That is a system?"

I saw Petric edging closer. Masha, too. In fact, all the
other guests had stopped talking and were silently gathering around us in small clusters.

Petric was eyeing me strangely. Not harshly. Maybe
even with approval. There was something unfamiliar about
the set of his facial muscles that seemed dangerously close
to a smile. I rejoiced.

Our host, the Indonesian Chargè, was becoming visibly and increasingly distressed. With his soft voice and
gentle manners he tried admirably, but unsuccessfully, to
defuse the tension. His face paled, and he backed off. I felt
sorry for him and a little guilty as well. (When he originally invited me to dinner, he said he hoped the Russians
and Americans would end the evening with a greater understanding of each other.) Even during my tirade I kept
thinking I'd have to call him in the morning and apologize.
I'd say I'd been drinking too much.

I softened my tone from blatant attack to sarcasm.

"Did you hear," I said to Zaroubin, "the latest joke
from Moscow?"

"How you hear what jokes in Moscow? You are in Belgrade."

I smiled gently, maybe even a little smugly, for I
wanted a big response from Zaroubin. "You know, we all

know America is a free country. If I don't like what our
President is doing I can go to the White House and tell him
right to his face, 'President Kennedy, you are doing a lousy
job.' Can you do that in Russia?"

"Oh?" Zaroubin was bellowing triumphantly. "Of
course. I can go to comrade Khruschev and tell him President Kennedy is doing a lousy job, same as you. Ha-ha-ha!"

I could see Petric's small eyes twinkle. Then everybody
heard a series of hoarse, deep, rumbling laughs, that
erupted again and again. When I looked, it was Masha; at
least her mouth was wide open. I wondered what possible
craziness was possessing her. Zaroubin glowered at her,
and she promptly put a hand over her mouth.

"How about another joke," I said, "right out of Moscow." Then I turned reflective. "Odd, isn't it, how I get these
stories. I've never been in Russia."

Most of the guests smiled. Now they seemed to be with
me.

I cleared my throat. "It seems comrade Khruschev was
taking a trip on his yacht in the Black Sea. All the members
of the Politburo were with him. Alas—a big storm came
up." Here I puffed up my cheeks and blew out the air. "Despite all their collective wisdom, the boat began to sink.
There was much yelling and screaming. Khruschev and all
the leaders of the Communist Party are thrown into the
water. No one can swim. Can you guess who is saved?" I
paused for several long moments to increase the dramatic
impact. "Is anyone saved?"

A slight murmur came from the French ambassador.
It was hardly a laugh, but a reaction of vague amusement.
A few twitches of the mouth from a couple of the other
guests. But no laughs. They all knew the dangers of taking
sides in a Cold War confrontation.

"O.K.," I said. "I'll tell you who is saved. The Russian
people."

A very sour look passed across Zaroubin's face. One or
two guests laughed out loud. Several others tittered. As for
Petric, a twitch had formed on his lips. He quickly used his
tongue to lick it away, and the fetus of his smile was

quickly aborted. But almost immediately another twitch appeared. This time the lips parted, and a strange bubbling sound came forth, as if a volcano was about to erupt. Then it happened. Spontaneous. Full-bodied. A laugh of pure delight.

Even while the guests were still laughing, a look of horror suddenly overcame Petric. I could see how exposed he felt. His absolute terror made his jaws clamp shut. The old sullen face returned. Then, from next to him, the high-pitched laugh rang out. It was Masha, of course. Now everything was back to normal. I flashed Petric a glance of approval, but as soon as I caught his eyes he turned away. I had won. I had made Petric laugh. Unfortunately I never saw him do it again.

FOURTEEN

When Is Intelligence Intelligent? (Belgium, Malaya and Singapore, Jordan and Yugoslavia)

The State Department, the Central Intelligence Agency (CIA) and the Defense Department all have their own intelligence apparatus. Sometimes they agree; sometimes they disagree. In Vietnam and the Middle East, two areas of crucial interest to the United States in the last thirty years, their assessments have varied 180 degrees.

In my four posts overseas—Belgium, Malaya, Jordan and Yugoslavia—I found many occasions when intelligence was considerably less than intelligent.

Belgium (Secret Affairs)

In Brussels, Peg unwittingly blew the cover of Brad when her article about new arrivals was printed in the *Foreign Service Journal*. Probably the article was never read by the Belgians. Even if it had been, I doubt if they would have had Brad recalled. Belgium would have had to scrutinize each new addition to the American Embassy staff in an attempt to identify a CIA replacement who would probably be hidden in some other Section of the Embassy under a new innocuous title. Once Brad was known, his operations could be followed and his activities neutralized if necessary.

What Brad did was puzzling. What he accomplished

was nothing. In a highly democratic country such as Belgium, the functions of a secret agent are severely limited. Political and economic activities and plans are well publicized by the government; each Deputy in Parliament is available to Embassy officials; the Belgian military are available to the Embassy Military Attaché; there is no labor matter that could not be discussed with the Belgian labor people, both in Parliament and in the trade unions. On top of it all, the United States felt no threat from the two major political parties, the Socialists and the Christians. There was no gap in which Brad could operate. Every aspect of Belgian life, politics, economics, military, and labor was covered. What then was left for an agent who thrives on the hidden and illicit?

In my work as Labor Attaché I established close connections with the Socialist and Christian Trade Unions, visited their offices frequently, and attended their Conventions. I had enough drinks with most of them at home to know them on a first name basis. Still, there *was* one I didn't. I didn't feel I was doing my job unless I had made contact with Communist Secretary General M. Detré of the mine workers.

I wasn't at all sure he would even see me. He might have the same fear of the capitalists as we had of Communists.

First I talked with Brad. Did he have any information about the Mine Workers Union? Brad said he had never heard of it. I wondered if he might be playing games to conceal information he might not want to share with me. But then he began questioning me "How big is it?", "What's the name of the Secretary General?" and other primitive questions that showed a sad lack of knowledge. I said I was going to try for an appointment and would keep him posted.

I had my secretary phone Detré. From her agitation I could see she was running up against some hard questions. She covered the mouthpiece of the phone and said M. Detré needed to know the purpose of my visit. I told her it was to introduce myself. Of course I'd be glad to answer any questions M. Detré might have about the AFL-CIO in America. With some hesitation he gave me an appointment for the following week.

His office was located in a dark alley off the Rue de Boucher, an ancient neighborhood of cobblestones and small winding streets. The gutters were overflowing with waste water pouring out of pipes from buildings on both sides of the alley, and I had to step around a few deep puddles to keep my feet dry.

I walked up two flights of squeaky stairs, dimly lit by a small ceiling bulb. I felt a bit squeamish—not fear exactly but potential danger. It was both a stimulant and depressant. I was eager to meet a Communist who in those days was usually depicted as sub-human and vicious. I had not cleared my visit with the State Department and the thought came to me as I slowly climbed the stairs that perhaps Washington would not approve of any government employee, even a Labor Attaché, cultivating a Communist.

When I pressed the small white button in the sagging door a small woman with messy black hair and sallow skin opened it. She was barely civil. She knew who I was and seemed programmed to be nasty. Curtly she told me to stand and wait. She would let me know when it was convenient for M. Detré to be disturbed. "M. le Secretaire-General is so very very beezy," she said flatly.

I looked around for a chair. There was none. I kept shifting my weight from one foot to the other. Three minutes. Six minutes. Twelve minutes. After fifteen minutes she returned, waved her hand, and said "Open the closed door ahead and enter." Inside a small man was sitting bent over a table. He pushed aside a few papers in front of him and stood up. Awkwardly we shook hands. I suspected he was as uneasy as I was. His voice was high pitched, coming out in fits and starts. His small eyes wandered over the room but never lit on my face.

Fortunately, there was another chair next to his table and he told me in fast nervous words to sit down. I offered him a cigarette which he looked at suspiciously, then took murmuring "with pleasure." Then he sat staring silently at me. I took the initiative, "I am a Labor Attaché, a new post in our government. I'm assigned to Belgium and Luxembourg to try to understand their trade union movements." His eyes opened wider and looked at a spot on the ceiling studying it intently for a moment. I could see he disbelieved me. What I was saying was not as explosive as he expected. Still he mistrusted me.

I told him about our unions, about the marriage of the conservative AFL and the more militant CIO, of the fight for union recognition during the 1930's. He nodded reflectively murmuring a few unrecognizable syllables in apparent appreciation. Toward the end I said "My reports to Washington are in the form of cables and Airgrams." All at once he turned quite pale. I took a deep breath. He must have feared I would be telling Washington too much about his precious Mine Workers. The atmosphere seemed as fragile as glass. One hard laugh, one misplaced word or gesture might crack the structure of our meeting.

But the idiocy of our conversation suddenly struck me and I tried to suppress my amusement. "I have gotten a few flyers from the Socialist and Christian unions of Belgium. I am sending them to Washington to inform the government of their activities," I said trying to cultivate a serious tone. "Could you give me something similar for the Communist unions? My people would be most interested in learning more about the important Mine Workers." He shook his head with a swift nervous movement.

"Nothing—*rien—rien—rien du tout—rien,*" he kept repeating. I knew I was making him walk through a mine field.

"Monsieur—Monsieur—Monsieur Kocher—." He launched into a short history of the Communist movement in Belgium. He said the Mine Workers was the strongest, best organized union in the country. When I asked him for membership figures, he just shook his head and went on with banalities. There was nothing in the least new, nothing that could interest Washington except that his words were describing Belgian Communism the way he wanted a capitalist country to know it.

All the time I could see him eying the open door. I wondered if his secretary was making notes of our conversation. Our talk was so innocuous, recording it would be a waste of time and paper. On the other hand, he might be protecting himself so that he could prove he had not given away secrets to a probing foreigner and perhaps he could even claim that he was gaining some inside knowledge of capitalist unions.

The only question he asked was about the American Miners Union. "Who is your Secretary General?"

"We have a President, John L. Lewis."

Detré's face brightened. "He is Communist then?"

"Not really. He's having problems with Communists."

I hoped I had not gone too far by telling the truth. I smiled and tried to lighten the atmosphere. His face darkened.

We were going nowhere and changed the subject. "My wife and I are having a few trade unionists for drinks next week. Would you and your wife join us?" He looked straight at the open door and said loudly, as if he were dictating, "I never drink with capitalists, I never eat with capitalists. Now I am busy with these papers."

I got up intending to shake hands but he stayed in his chair as if I had already gone, and began to ruffle the papers on his table. Without another word I went out the door, expecting to find his secretary busily taking down every word. She was so busy writing in fact that she did not even lift her head to say goodbye. With only the murmur of a goodbye addressed to no one in particular, I left.

When I told Brad about my visit with Detré, he was fascinated. He took copious notes. He even made a plan of Detré's office as I described it.

Two weeks later, in the Communist weekly paper, I saw a small item. Detré had been fired. No reason was given. I puzzled over it, trying to relate it to my visit. Had I really been his nemesis? Were there details in our conversation that damned him with the Party? And if so, why hadn't I picked them up?

Later I received a commendation from the Departments of State and Labor for my "perceptive" report detailing my visit with Detré. The same day I learned Brad took credit for getting Detré fired. At first I was annoyed. I was about to ask Brad by what magic rites he had gotten a Communist fired. Then I realized he was playing the old Foreign Service game—piggy-backing—climb on somebody's, anybody's, shoulders to reach your goal. After struggling fruitlessly to find a place in the political, economic, social, cultural fabric of Belgium that he could make his own, Brad had finally been able to justify his presence in Brussels.

Malaya and Singapore (Game Playing)

In my second overseas post, Malaya, we had no CIA representative. In the years, from 1953–55, the country was still a colony of Britain and the United States had a Consulate. An Embassy only came later with independence.

The British would have had little patience with intelligence operations from Americans or for that matter from any other country. Wisely we kept the CIA out of Malaya— at least for a time.

I ran up against the extreme sensitivity of the British against outside interference in a small but illuminating incident. Because of my labor background in Brussels, I often played host to trade unionists from various countries. One day a British trade unionist, on business of the International Confederation of Free Trade Unions, appeared at my office, having gotten my name from ICFTU headquarters in Brussels. The purpose of his visit was to bring greetings from many of the ICFTU staff and to request aid. He had forgotten to bring typewriting paper and pads. Might he have whatever paper I could spare? I invited him to lunch and left him at the end of the afternoon with several reams of paper and three or four yellow pads.

I forgot the incident but was reminded of it unpleasantly a few days later when Sir Gerald Templer, High Commissioner of Malaya, was hosting a dinner at Government

House. When I came in, Sir Gerald barely greeted me. His cheeks were flushed, his face seemed carved out of stone. A few minutes later he abandoned the reception line and came directly towards me as I was talking to Lady Templer. When she saw him approaching, she left me abruptly. I was astonished. She had always been the perfect hostess, charming and gracious at all times.

"Consul," Sir Gerald said brusquely, "You had a visit from a British trade unionist last week. You've got no business helping that bastard!" His tone became more icy and the flush on his cheeks was getting brighter. I started explaining that the help amounted to some pads of paper, but before I could get through, Sir Gerald turned to leave, then stopped and whirled again to face me.

"Keep your goddam hands off any trade unionists that come to Malaya!"

As he headed back to the reception line, I wondered what he would say if he knew I was not only talking to a British trade unionist but was also deeply involved in helping Tengku Abdul Rahman, a leading political figure, in his plans for an independent Malaysia.

The Tengku had come to me privately asking for information on the United States Constitution and laws, as well as on AFL-CIO practices and regulations. Even then, a year or two before independence, he was drafting a proposed Constitution for the new Malaysia. His requests sent me running to the library, and in the process I experienced enormous satisfaction. In Belgium I could only observe and analyze. But here in Malaya I felt I was an active participant in the building of a new country.

Toward the end of my assignment in Malaya, I was also assigned as Consul General to Singapore. I was to cover both posts and to share my time between the two countries.

In Singapore I came up against the rigidities of our classification of documents, a system supposed to insure that the material in any official document will not be available except to those entitled to read it. The lowest classifica-

tion is marked *Restricted,* meaning that the material can be
made available to most Department and Embassy officers,
but is not for publication. There are higher classifications:
Confidential (available to many officers); *Secret* (available
to a smaller group); *Top Secret* (available to a very few);
and *Eyes Only* (for one or two named individuals). The
names and categories have been changed somewhat since
my years of service (1947–69), but are roughly the same.

All documents labeled *Restricted* and above were required to be locked up in a safe or file cabinet overnight.
One evening before closing my office, I picked up all the
classified documents on top of my desk and locked them in
my filing cabinet. I was about to leave when I thought of an
Airgram written by my Press Officer which I intended to
read the next morning. I examined the Airgram and saw it
was marked *Restricted* but confirmed that it contained
nothing but quotes from the Malayan papers. Surely it
would make no difference if it fell into enemy hands. Alas
—the next morning I saw a pink slip on my desk made out
by the Security guard of the Consulate. I was charged with
a breach of security and was fined one day's salary.

Documents were often over classified. Cables and Airgrams with quite innocuous contents often carried the label *Confidential* or even *Secret.* The writer decided the classification of his material and was seldom challenged.

The temptation to put the highest possible classification on a document was often irresistible. Sometimes it
came from an excessive zeal for security. More often it
came from game playing. A high classification was the single most effective way of drawing attention to the document—and to the writer, who, like most employees in the
world, is hungry for promotion. Anything labeled *Confidential* was considered without significance. *Secret* would
be glanced at by top officials, and *Top Secret* virtually assured careful attention from the relatively few high level
officers authorized to read the document.

John Foster Dulles, Secretary of State in the 1950's,
had his doubts about the classification system. He once la-

mented that most secret matters discussed in his daily staff meetings found their way into the next day's *New York Times* or *Washington Post.* By perusing American newspapers, foreign agents are often able to gather more intelligence than by clandestine methods.

Problems of a CIA presence in Malaya only developed after I had been transferred to Washington. As Deputy Director of Southeast Asian Affairs, I was asked to meet with three intelligence officers representing the CIA, the Department of State, and the Department of Defense. I wondered why the top intelligence people from these agencies were so interested? Were they going to propose an intelligence operation in Malaya? How ridiculous can you get? A CIA presence in Malaya would be like adding one more hunter to an area where there was hardly enough game to go around.

When I arrived at the conference room the next day, Hugh Cummings, Director of Intelligence at State, was whispering to his colleagues from CIA and Defense. As soon as they saw me, they stopped talking. The swift transition from intimate whispering to silence put me on my guard.

Very pleasantly Cummings asked me, "How have you enjoyed your two and a half years in Malaya?" I gave the usual superficial answer; "wonderful country, exotic culture, the importance of tin and rubber for a sound economic base, political leaders well trained by the British. Local police forces and an efficient civil service system were also in place ready to take over from the British. As far as I could see, it all bodes well for a healthy independence. More importantly," I added, "The British have made only one misstep. After a small controversy, they had thrown Tengku Abdul Rahman, leader of the largest political party, United Malays Nationalist Organization, into jail." Finally, I said, "the United States needs a friend in South East Asia and Malaya is the obvious choice. They trust us—and we can trust them."

Again Cummings nodded his agreement, "Yes,

Malaya's future seems bright." His two colleagues nodded approval. All this agreement, I sensed, was to create a friendly atmosphere in which to get my support for whatever they had in mind.

"I take it you agree with us?" Cummings said. "Tengku trusts us enough not to negate or neutralize any CIA representation in Malaya." He smiled at me jovially while his two colleagues continued nodding.

"Neutralize—negate—?" I expressed appropriate astonishment without being in the least astonished.

"You know—make a fuss." This from the CIA man.

"First things first," I said. "I don't think I've yet heard the case for putting an operator in Malaya."

"There now," Cummings said smoothly. "It's obvious, isn't it? We have someone in almost every country."

"Let's stay with Malaya. What would we gain by having someone there?"

"To know their plans," the CIA man said solemnly.

I tried to contain my impatience. "I had access as Consul General to Malayan Government plans. As a matter of fact, the Tengku asked me questions about the United States Constitution that sent me running to the library. He wanted to know what provisions in our Constitution might be used in the Malayan Constitution. The Malayans also needed help in organizing their own trade unions."

Without a pause Cummings came back to the question of trust. "Very good. They trust us already. Surely there'd be no objection if we put one or two of our people in Kuala Lumpur."

The Malayans may have trusted us, but I mistrusted these Americans. Hugh Cummings, agitated, filling the room with glib nonsense, made my head ache. The CIA man, slightly pugnacious, unpleasantly assured, as if every word he spoke came directly from some deity, and the Defense Intelligence man who echoed the thoughts of the other two without having any of his own.

"You haven't yet said—Why would you want a man in K.L.?" I asked.

All three looked at me as if I lacked common sense.

"To know what the Malays are doing," Cummings said. "What else?"

"We already know what they're doing," I said.

"That was before independence," the CIA man said impatiently. "We're thinking of afterwards."

I could see they were beginning to bristle. They must have expected an easy pushover and I was sorry I couldn't oblige.

"There's a reasonable chance they will continue to trust us," I said,,"if we don't do a lot of dirty tricks behind their backs."

Cummings sighed again as if he was dealing with a stubborn child. He had been in intelligence work in the Department for many years. No wonder he sounded patronizing.

"There now," he said. "Every government has its secrets. The Malayans are no different. They'll have subtle things we can't know—"

"Secrets? Subtle things?" I felt like laughing. "You mean—information like when the Tengku is going on vacation?"

"That—and also where he goes."

"Like Bangkok—Bali?" I couldn't believe my ears.

He nodded sagely.

"I can't believe it. Why do you want an agent to dig up all this trivia?" I asked.

"Don't make light of it. Nothing is as it seems on the surface. The Tengku may be hatching plans on his vacation."

I started laughing. "The only plans the Tengku hatches on vacation is for picking up women. Do you want one of your people to follow him and bring back the names of all his pick-ups?"

"There now—" Cummings was always saying "there now" as if he was an old English biddy trying to soothe some wild eyed maniac. "Put your mind on it. Can't we make some capital out of the Tengku in jail?"

"What capital?"

"The Tengku must harbor a grudge against the British
—I know I would if anyone threw me in jail without provocation."

"I doubt there's any grudge. After all, it was only overnight. Why do you want him to have a grudge?"

"It will help us overcome the British lead—maybe we
can even replace them."

"Why do we want to replace the British? What's the
point? We can work with the British to help the Malays
after independence. The Malays don't have to choose one
of us over the other."

"It would be good to be number one," he said a little
wistfully.

"Number one nincompoop," I muttered to myself.

Regardless of my protests, Malaysia (Malaya's name
after independence) was saddled with a CIA operative attached to the Embassy. Heaven knows what he did. Perhaps our CIA man found out once that the Tengku was
going on holiday before it was announced in the paper.
That and other big deals. The fact that we haven't heard
any more from our man in Kuala Lumpur may be a good
sign. All his plots may have worked and still kept the cloak
of secrecy. Or more likely, they didn't work at all and no
one cared.

Jordan (King Hussein and the CIA)

In Jordan we had another curious CIA relationship,
this time with King Hussein.

The Embassy had four CIA employees attached to it.
Three male officers and a female secretary. The function of
two of the officers was never clear. The CIA has its own
coding system for sending out cables and its own code
clerk to transmit its messages. It also had a radio transmit-
ter for its communications. As a result, its work was effectively concealed from Embassy officers, even those cleared
for Top Secret information. The CIA station chief would
sometimes inform the Ambassador of some of its activities,

or in his absence, me as Chargé. But at that time in 1961 there was no requirement to inform either of us.

Frustrated at times by lack of knowledge of CIA activities, I ultimately was just as happy not to know. Without control over the Agency, I had no desire to be responsible in the eyes of the Jordanians for CIA misdeeds if they should come to light.

After a series of embarrassing incidents in various countries, President Ford in 1976 set up a policy requiring the CIA in each country to inform the United States Ambassador of that country of its activities.

One only wonders if all United States Ambassadors were delighted with this policy which brought them into a temporary partnership with the CIA and made them appear responsible for the Agency's activities.

The third CIA officer in Jordan was assigned as companion to King Hussein. Bill was especially chosen for this assignment. Hussein was twenty-four at the time and Bill, not much older, was friendly, witty, and low key. He was flexible enough to fit into the King's moods, whether playful or serious, and was welcomed by Hussein, who was surrounded by elder statesmen with no interest in his hobbies. Hussein was a great lover of car races and he and Bill went to the races every Friday. Bill also attended the weekly Saturday night party at the King's second palace near the Dead Sea for daughters and sons of diplomats and British military. There was no doubt in Hussein's mind about the connection of his new young friend to the CIA.

The close connection between the CIA and Hussein seemed to guarantee that the United States would know of any plans the King might have politically or otherwise. Included was the question of a new wife. Hussein had been married to an Egyptian woman from whom he was divorced. In the preceding year there had been rumors of a new marriage. It was presumed that an Arab girl with a distinguished ancestry would be his choice.

He was known to be seeing a great deal of a British colonel's daughter, Toni Gardiner. But it was foolish to imagine the King would marry a British girl. His throne would be threatened. The Bedouins on the East Bank on whom the King counted for support were political and religious conservatives. It was highly unlikely they would accept a Queen who was neither Arab nor Muslim.

The United States was not the only country with a close link to the King. The British had their own link: the chauffeur of the King seemed to have established as intimate a relationship with the young monarch as Bill had. In any case, it was the chauffeur who first found out the King intended to marry the British girl. The chauffeur told the British Ambassador and the British Ambassador told me. He swore me to secrecy, however. I could let my people in Washington know, but not my CIA staff in Amman or CIA Headquarters back home.

Perhaps it was foolish of me to agree not to divulge this information to my CIA people, but the Agency seldom seemed part of the American Embassy. They had a secluded corner of the building and, apart from attending the regular Embassy staff meetings, were seldom seen. I also must confess I felt a certain glee in beating the CIA at its own game.

I reported to the Department what the British Ambassador had told me in confidence. Despite my warning not to let the information out, the Department lost no time before telling CIA Headquarters in Langley, Virginia. CIA headquarters, of course, promptly cabled its people in Jordan for confirmation. To the great surprise of most of the diplomatic set, the marriage of the King and the British girl caused hardly a ripple, much less rock the throne. Hussein married Toni Gardiner and placated his Bedouin supporters by withholding the title of Queen, calling her Her Royal Highness Princess Muna al Hussein ("beloved of Hussein"). The Arabic name was given her to make her more acceptable to the Jordanians. Since the CIA in Jordan found out about the King's marital intentions, not through Bill, but through his supervisors back home, needless to say, this incident created a temporary strain in my relations with the CIA people in Amman.

Yugoslavia (Medical Espionage)

In Yugoslavia, two CIA representatives were stationed in the Embassy. One was the Embassy doctor. In addition to treating American Embassy personnel, he also tended some members of the Yugoslavian military. Fortunately he was clever enough to satisfy both groups. At first I wondered why the Yugoslavians would consult him at all. After all, a capitalist doctor? Wouldn't he poison the lot of them? Still, our doctor was amiable, talented, and brought the latest pills and techniques from America. Accordingly, the Yugoslavians forgave him his capitalist connections.

Soon after his arrival in Belgrade, a Yugoslavian general fell seriously ill. The Embassy offered to let our doctor take a look at him. After that, the doctor was in great demand. The Yugoslavians learned to respect his diagnostic talents and especially his connections with American hospitals. Not only were generals occasionally sent to the military hospital in Frankfurt, but also in one instance to Walter Reed Hospital in Washington.

The doctor certainly brought to the CIA and military Attaché insight into the health of Yugoslavian military officers. He may also have learned a bit about their military tactics. In any case, his reputation grew. During the years he was in Belgrade the relations between the Embassy and the government improved.

The other agent, Claude, was a small, somewhat frightened, man who saw a spy around every corner. He took his instructions from Washington.

Unlike Belgium, Malaya, and Jordan, our Embassy in Belgrade had access to relatively few non-military officials. Claude had two functions. One was to establish contacts with a few additional Communist officials not on the authorized list. I doubt he was successful. He hardly seemed imaginative enough. His other function was probably research. Although television and Hollywood would have us believe that the CIA exists solely for exploits of daring and skullduggery, the actual Agency's agenda is more tepid than that. A large part of its work is analyzing newspaper reports and unearthing episodes, unsavory and otherwise, in the lives of Yugoslav officials—a role that well suited Claude.

Claude would never talk to me in any room of his house or in my residence or at the office. He was sure bugs and listening devices were hidden in every United States building. Whenever he wanted to talk to me, he would whisper to me outdoors. Since he lived in the house next door, we would hang over the wooden fence and talk away, as if we were two housewives who had just hung up a load of wash.

Claude was right to be suspicious. When an inspection team from Washington arrived, it found considerable bugging in the Embassy—in the walls, behind pictures, in the ceiling. As a result, the CIA and the security people of State devised a scheme. They would build a soundproof chamber big enough for a conference table and twelve chairs and suspend it from the ceiling on cables. It would therefore touch no wall, ceiling, or floor.

By raising the soundproof chamber so that it would float in space, it seemed the ultimate answer to Communist attempts to plug into our conversations. No device can jump from a wall through space and into another wall. In the unending game of oneupmanship in security we surely had won the final battle. Our triumph was only temporary, however. In recent years, the Communists have penetrated our defenses and we in turn have tried to construct a whole new system of security that is sure to be foolproof.

An incident in Belgrade illustrates the futility of trying to preserve secrecy in a world populated by news-hungry journalists. While I was Chargé, the Embassy hosted a large American delegation attending a meeting of the Inter Parliamentary Union. Senator Ted Kennedy was one of the delegates.

Several days into the conference I received an *Eyes Only* cable from President Kennedy instructing me to talk to his brother Ted on a personal matter. I caught the Senator as he was about to enter the conference room in the morning.

"Senator," I said, "I've just gotten a special message for you from the President."

"Yes?" Ted said quietly.

"Let's walk around the block," I said. "Secrecy is much better assured outside. Inside you can't be sure if a conversation is bugged. Is this a good time for you?"

He nodded affably, "The meeting today isn't that important. And even if it were—." He stopped without having to go further. The Kennedys were known to have close family ties. Suggestions and instructions from the President were almost always followed.

We went out the front door of the Embassy and strolled to the right. I looked casually behind to make sure no one was following us. The cable was short and I had memorized it.

"The message says," I began, "Please advise Senator Kennedy that the Washington papers have carried stories about his private lunches and dinners with Mme. Nhu, the delegate of South Vietnam to the conference."

I glanced at Ted a moment before continuing. He had no visible reaction. His face was placid, almost stolid.

"The President goes on to say—These newspaper reports are embarrassing to me. I hope the Senator will not see Mme. Nhu again outside conference hours."

I glanced at Ted again. His head was bent and he was looking at the sidewalk. I wondered if he was thinking of his wife Joan who was with him in Belgrade. Did she know of his interest in Mme. Nhu? If the papers back home carried stories about their lunches and dinners, Joan probably did know.

I had had several talks with Joan at receptions and I found her a lovely person, graceful, blonde, even beautiful. She struck me as highly sensitive, rather shy, and particularly interested in music and art. We never talked of politics, but I had the impression she was trying to promote her husband's career without in the least enjoying it.

We had almost returned to the Embassy. The Senator was still silent.

"The cable was marked Eyes Only," I said. "The only ones who have seen it are the code clerk and myself."

The Senator seemed distracted but thanked me.

As far as I know he had no more private lunches or dinners with Mme. Nhu.

As might be expected, the day after my talk with Ted, the *Washington Post* carried a short item reporting quite accurately the President's warning to his brother. Is it possible to reconstruct the leak and guess what happened? I talked to no reporter about the cable. Might the code clerk have leaked it? Unlikely. He had been investigated thoroughly and never leaked anything before. Nor would it have been in his interest to do so. The leak must have taken place in Washington. At the White House, perhaps right in the President's office. Or perhaps in the State Department where several officials and code clerks were probably involved in sending the cable to Belgrade.

PART THREE

THE UNMAKING OF A
FOREIGN SERVICE OFFICER

FIFTEEN

Apples and Oranges
(Home Leave—Virginia
and Florida)

A Foreign Service career offers many opportunities for exotic vacations. No matter where my family and I were posted, there were always exciting places nearby for holidays. Italy, Greece, the Adriatic, Bali, Bangkok, Angkor Wat, Cairo, Cyprus, Beirut.

However, after two years at the American embassy in Belgrade, I came back to the States on home leave in 1964 thoroughly depleted. I feared that whatever sanity I had left was slipping away from me through nervous exhaustion. As *chargé d'affaires*, I had taken on the responsibility of a large embassy, complicated by having to deal with a Yugoslavia under Tito that was as suspicious of America as it was of Russia. Both powers, in Yugoslavian eyes, were trying to dominate it. As a result, Yugoslavian officials, though correct in their relations with both Americans and Russians, were genuinely friendly to neither. In every other post, my wife Peggy and I made many close friends whom we retained over the years. Today we are in touch with no one from Yugoslavia.

Oddly enough, the most wearying part of the job in Belgrade was not the drudgery and pressures during the day, but the parties at night. On almost every evening we found ourselves at a diplomatic reception or dinner, and frequently two receptions and a dinner in the same evening. There had also been an onslaught of visiting congressmen and senators, all of whom needed to be briefed and entertained.

During the time I was chargé, I had two encounters with Tito, then dictator of Yugoslavia. The first was a confrontation during the Cuban missile crisis, the other an emotional visit to the embassy after the assassination of President Kennedy.

The confrontation took place late at night in Tito's palace. I had received instructions from the Department of State to arrange an urgent meeting with Tito to explain United States actions in connection with the missile crisis. The appointment I received was for midnight. Tito trusted Kruschev no more than he trusted the United States, but he was incensed when he heard my presentation. "Why the hell doesn't the United States take the Cuban problem to the United Nations instead of acting unilaterally?" he growled. A good question, but one whose answer demanded a recital of the many instances of United States disillusion with the United Nations as a source of action.

Following Kennedy's assassination, Tito visited the embassy to sign the book of condolences. He had met Kennedy and, reputedly, had established a father/son relationship with him. Tito was moved to tears as he shook my hand and expressed his sorrow, one of the few human moments I experienced with this tough, hard-bitten man.

Not long afterwards, the disastrous Skopje earthquake occurred, and preparations for the American airlift took a toll on my mental and physical resources. The Yugoslavs were preparing a ceremony at the airport to greet the plane and I was expected to be there, but, exhausted, I found myself refusing the invitation and asking Larry Eagleburger to represent the embassy. It was only after an appeal from the administrative officer that I grudgingly agreed to go to the airport. He was right, of course. The ambassador or chargé should be there to highlight the importance of the American gift to the people of Skopje. Throughout the ceremony, however, I could not help resenting the earthquake, the Yugoslavians, the Americans.

Home leave, at a particularly propitious moment,

came to me as an escape. Peggy suggested I have a complete rest or undertake some manual work. Either would give me welcome relief from diplomacy.

I've never been the resting type, so it was logical I'd gravitate toward manual labor. I do not remember how migrant work actually occurred to me. Perhaps the idea surfaced because I had suffered with the Okies years before as I read *The Grapes of Wrath,* and because I had started my Foreign Service career as a labor attaché in Belgium. Regardless, fruit picking now promised refreshment and renewal. Physical work versus desk work. The country instead of the city. Off with coats and tuxedos, on with flannel shirts and jeans.

Peg and I agreed that she would care for the children during my absence, and when I returned she would visit her brother in Denver for a week, leaving the kids with me. Though generally ardent believers in togetherness, we felt we had both exceeded its desirable limits in our twenty-four-hour-a-day habit of sharing the personal and professional life demanded by the Foreign Service.

We had rented a house for two months in the Boston area and it was there that I began making plans. First I thought of picking citrus fruit in Florida, but that season started in November, and it was now only October. Since the fall season meant apples, I was told that Winchester, Virginia was the center of large scale apple picking operations.

The evening before I left Boston, I was reading the children a simple book of comparative religions, one that dramatized for young people stories of Islam, Buddhism, Judaism, Hinduism, and Christianity. In Jordan we had lived in an Islamic atmosphere, next to the sacred roots of Christians and Jews. In Malaya we were surrounded by Buddhists, Muslims, and Hindus. Both countries provided admirable background for understanding these varied religions. We had visited a mosque and Buddhist and

Hindu temples. We had seen the wailing wall in Jerusalem, had attended midnight mass at the Church of the Nativity in Bethlehem and partaken of the Shepherds' supper, traditionally served in a nearby open field. And I used to tell the boys stories of Buddha and Mohammed. But that last night before my departure, I read a page or two, then put the book down uneasily. I was thinking of what I would have to tell them. They were already yawning.

"Read something else," said Chris. "Like *Charlotte's Web*. "Did you bring our copy from Belgrade?"

"Sorry," I said. "When I get back from my trip, I'll buy you another copy." Then I told them I'd be leaving in the morning for several weeks.

The children were used to prolonged absences. Several times I'd been sent from Brussels to Washington for consultation and from Washington around the world on briefing trips and conferences. So the evening should have gone smoothly, but it went miserably. For the first time, I could not blame my absence on the Foreign Service.

"I've been losing touch with America." I gestured with my hands in an attempt to be more persuasive to them—and perhaps to myself. "In Belgrade when I read about America, thousands of miles away, nothing sounded real. It was like reading something out of fiction."

Taking her cue from the magic word "read," Debra, a precocious five-year-old, tugged at my pants and pushed a book in front of me.

"Read me a story," she demanded.

"Later," I said, pulling away.

The eyes of all four children were looking longingly at the television. I knew I was about to lose them, so I quickly changed tack.

"I'm going to work with some exciting guys—I'll get their stories, write them down. Fantastic stories to tell you when I get back."

"Yeah—like what?" There was a faint stirring of interest from Terry.

"Like everything."

My trip was to be a big adventure, I rhapsodized. It

would open up a whole new life, a necessary change after too much partying and desk work.

At the first mention of adventure, Eric Glenn, now sixteen, promptly said, "I'll go too."

I had hardly persuaded him to stay in Boston to take care of Mom when Terry, now fifteen, said, "Me too."

"What do you mean 'me too'?" I yelled back, even though we were in the small den and had no problem hearing each other. "Your work is at school. You have to pass your exams."

Terry sulked a bit, then must have thought he had me, for a lovely smile spread over his face.

"I need a rest, too," he said. "Something outdoors. Who wants inside work all year long?"

I tried to conceal a slight tremor in my voice. "Your vacation starts in June."

"Too late." Again that knowing smile. "How can I pick apples in June?"

"O.K. Then you can pick strawberries and cherries!" Again I was yelling to kill that stupid tremor in my voice.

Meanwhile Chris, now thirteen, impervious as usual to family bickering, had plopped on the floor with a book and was reading. Debra was puzzling over a choice of blocks to crown a tower she was constructing.

I would be leaving early in the morning before they were up. Without really saying goodbye, I hurried out of the den.

The next morning I said goodbye to Peg. It was as emotional as the night before. Leaving the family seemed more and more like setting myself adrift in uncharted waters.

As I headed for the bus depot, I felt sadness, exhilaration, and a slight terror. Ahead of me were new experiences, a new environment, new people. Why couldn't I convince myself I was in for a glorious adventure? After all, didn't I believe my own words the night before with the kids? Then the terror came back. Migrant workers were known as a rough bunch with a whole different set of values. Would we get along? I remembered how as a kid I was once pursued by a group of toughs who wanted to beat me up. Of course I ran. As hard and as fast as I could. I had never learned to stand up and face my fears as a child. How would I measure up now, in an apple orchard?

Arriving in Winchester in the middle of the day, I walked around the street of this quiet, empty town half an hour or more until I gathered enough courage to talk to two men whom I took to be apple pickers. At least they fit the stereotype: stubbles of beard, rough craggy hands, holes in the elbows of sweaters. My guess was right. They were migrants, and they told me of the desperate need for workers in their orchard.

During the course of the afternoon I walked the five miles out of town to the place where they worked. It was old and overgrown, but two spidery, sunken-eyed children were playing happily in the weeds. In the kitchen I smelled the good aromas of hot coffee and cooking apples. The manager of the orchard looked at me skeptically.

"You a fruit picker?"

"I want to be," I answered, eyeing the heavy, 24-foot ladders that each picker carried on his shoulder from one tree to another.

Again, that half reflective somber glance. "You don't look boisterous," he said.

"Oh, I can be boisterous all right," I smiled, realizing how ridiculous the whole conversation sounded. The manager subsided into a raucous laugh.

"Time we had the quiet kind. I'll try you out."

I offered to give him my Social Security number, and I remember how pleasantly surprised he seemed. Years later I understood why. When it came time for my retirement, Social Security had no record of my work in the orchard. The manager had deducted Social Security taxes from my paycheck and kept them instead of sending them to Washington. Fortunately for the men with which I worked, they had no Social Security cards. If they had, some of their wages would also have been stolen.

The manager motioned to the wooden barracks where twenty-six pickers slept, and I went in to find a bunk. Most of the men were lying down smoking and relaxing on their day off. No one got up to shake hands, nor did I put out my hand. I said a perfunctory "hi," as I looked around for an empty bunk. The men eyed me silently with vague and uncertain looks. I was dressed in my oldest clothes, but felt preposterously overdressed in the barracks atmosphere.

I located a bunk near the door, a stroke of luck, I thought, as I listened to the racking cigarette coughs of the men and smelled the assorted human aromas of the large room. In my corner I would hopefully not be surrounded by a bunch of potentially hostile men. At least I'd be near fresh air. Soon I learned just how fresh the air could be in Virginia on an autumn night. That night I slept with my heavy jacket over my clothes, under the wisp of a thin, torn blanket and a stretch of dirty gunny sack. I still felt frozen. To insure the freshness of the air, every half hour or so someone would stumble through the cabin's darkness, open the door, and bang it closed on his way outside. Moments later, after relieving himself, he would come back in, again banging the door and sending a fresh chill over my bunk.

Somewhere outside a cat screamed at intervals. The screams were so piercing they made me think of the night in Belgrade when Terry and Chris Kennan, son of Ambassador George Kennan, were camping out in a tent in our garden. As the two boys were reading a comic book by flashlight, our son Chris tossed through the opening of the tent two of our cats, which, shocked and frightened, let out piercing screams just like the ones I was hearing in the apple orchard. The kids' camping party came to an abrupt end. Chris Kennan departed for home, and Terry went back to his room. Unfortunately, my camping in the apple orchard was only beginning. Towards morning, I seriously wondered, "What the hell am I doing here?" and fell into a restless sleep, shivering and muttering to myself, "Dummy, dummy."

The next morning I started sizing up the men. I first noticed Jerry and Terry, twins in their late teens, gangly, good-natured country boys, obviously not long from the farm or the hills. Otherwise, most of the men were in their thirties and forties. At fifty-three I was probably the oldest of the group except for Bobby, small and wizened, who looked to be in his sixties.

In the washroom that first morning, standing next to me, was a huge grizzled hulk of a picker. He looked at me in the cracked and cloudy mirror and muttered, "Hey, you ain't a revenooer, are you?"

"Who, me?" I said, startled and amused. "Why would I be a revenooer?"

"You look like one." He spat in the sink and moved toward the dining room.

"Well, I'm not," I yelled after him.

I realized only later the threat a "revenooer" might pose to these migrants. Their names appeared on no federal government records. Officially, they really didn't exist, and that's the way they wanted it. As I heard more than one of them say, "What the hell is government? Fucking crooks out to screw people—that's what."

After washing up, I followed the workers through the kitchen of the small farm house into a dining room with two long wooden tables, each with benches on both sides. As we sat down, I looked around in anticipation. Here I was in the same room with twenty-six other pickers. All of them must have lived remarkable lives. And under my prodding all might divulge their stories. I would store them away carefully in my notebook until I recounted them to my kids. I could already envision their looks of astonishment and rapture.

How would I begin? I was sitting between one of the young twins and a fattish, bloated individual who might have been the sheriff in some Western movie. He was even wearing a ten-gallon hat.

A huge batch of pancakes had just been set in the center of both tables. Here was the opener I needed.

I turned to the ten-gallon hat. "Hi. Wonderful pancakes."

No reply. Not even a turn of the head to show he had heard me.

After a few seconds I turned to the youngster on my other side.

"Hi. Wonderful pancakes."

This time the twin, Terry or Jerry I wasn't sure which, abandoning his good-natured expression, shot me a nasty glance as if I had trespassed on his land and turned back to the steaming cakes on his plate.

I looked across the table to see if anyone was aware of my desultory attempt at conversation. The six men on the other side had all stopped eating just long enough to register their extreme annoyance before going back to their pancakes.

I soon figured out the rules. Food and talk were incompatible, an unbreakable code of silence. I shut my mouth and opened it only to push another pancake inside. Before the end of the meal, I was laughing to myself. The silence was strange, but it was tremendously refreshing after so many years of observing the opposite ethic at parties and dinners where the only rule was, "It doesn't matter what you say, just keep the jaws moving."

As soon as the last pancake was eaten, and the last cup of coffee drained from the huge cauldron, we piled into an open truck that took us to the orchard. It was about 7:30.

I forget whether the huge ladders were with us on the truck or if they were stored in the orchard. I remember, however, the ease with which the pickers handled them, while I was clumsily learning to keep mine balanced on one shoulder without breaking my back. Both my shoulders were bruised and scarred after a few days. In view of my recent back trouble, it seemed a small miracle that after carrying the heavy ladder from one apple tree to another, my back seemed better at the end of the day than before.

In addition to a ladder, each worker picked up a large canvas sack which he slung over his shoulder. As apples were picked, they were put into the sack, and the sack, when full, was dumped into a huge bin. When the trees in the immediate area were bare, we piled into the truck and moved on to another part of the orchard.

Lunch was from 12:00 to 12:30, afternoon work until 5:00, then a return to the barracks for supper and a free evening. Dinner was boringly consistent. Whole loaves of bread with some sort of grease to smear over the slices, accompanied by two white and brownish kinds of beans that I prefer not to dwell upon and are better relegated to oblivion. Each time I took a helping of beans I thought of Peggy and imagined her smile. I who had scorned all but green beans over our many years together.

Wages depended on the weight of the apples picked. The diligent cleared over a hundred dollars a week. My take was seldom more than half of that. Wages, though relatively good in those days, were paid for with scarred hands, muscle strains, bent backs. Even so, workers performed the job gracefully. Several times I stopped my own fumbling among the branches of a Red Rome to watch how the picker in the next tree deftly snapped the stems and slipped a handful of apples into his sack. The sound was like a muted typewriter in the trees.

Every day was the same except for Saturday afternoon and Sunday when we were free. Some men went into Winchester to bum around. Some lazed on their bunks listening to the radio. Some took a jug of cheap wine to the orchard, sat under a tree, and drank themselves unconscious.

My kids will love this, I thought, as I wrote about George, who during the week would bury gallon jugs of apple wine in the orchard the way a dog buries bones, then dig them up Saturday noon. After polishing off each jug, he would fold up in the meadow, legs up to his chin, a childlike peace spread over his face.

Little by little, I gathered their stories. I wrote them down, and soon a notebook was full. Their background of restless movement and homelessness was similar. In the summer they would pick strawberries and cherries in the north; in the winter they would move south into the citrus area. All would have fled the threat of a permanent job.

Most of them had been picked up by the police as vagrants in one city or another. All had long since divested themselves of the faintest responsibility. Jimmy, for example, was divorced nine years before and never paid a penny in alimony.

"How did you get away with that?" I asked.

"Easy, so easy," he said proudly. "Just made a deal with my wife. Promised never to see my kids no more."

How the hell could he abandon his kids, I wondered. I know I couldn't. Or could I? Wasn't that what I was doing? Was I any better than Jimmy? It didn't really help to tell myself I was only doing it temporarily.

And with the thought came an image of Eric Glenn, Terry, Chris, Debra. What were they doing now? It was about nine in the evening. The kids were preparing—or being prepared—for bed, at just the time I usually read a book to Deb or helped one of the boys with his homework. Who was doing all that now? Anyone? After that, I avoided Jimmy. He reminded me of obligations I had difficulty handling.

From the beginning I noticed a spirit that held the men together. That first Sunday afternoon, after securing my bunk, I said I was returning to town to collect my suitcase at the bus depot. Since I had walked to the orchard from town, the pickers assumed I was broke and would have to walk back. Within seconds one of them thrust a dollar in my hand and collected another fifty cents from several of the others to pay for a taxi. Even though I had more than sufficient money in my pocket, the loan was raised so swiftly and was so warmly offered that I did not have the heart to refuse it.

Again and again I witnessed the solidarity among the pickers, a type of "male bonding" that offered them companionship and emotional support. At times they were generous and caring, at others brutally competitive. I particularly remember one incident where one of the workers put his ladder against a tree and started climbing toward the apples, when another worker, who considered this particular tree part of his private domain, toppled the ladder in a rage.

Outside the orchard, the world seemed shadowy and

vague. Wives, relatives, children (if any) had no impact on their lives. Neither did local and national events, in which there was almost no interest. Two of the men did not even know that Lyndon Johnson was their President.

Although essentially loners, almost every picker had a special buddy. Together they travelled from job to job, got drunk on weekends (and sometimes during the week as well) and shared money and clothes.

I entered as fully as I could into the spirit of "buddyhood," but I must confess to serious lapses. If I did have a buddy, I suppose it was Randy. He arrived in the orchard a few days after me and took a bunk next to mine. He owned only the ragged clothes on his back, and they smelled of sour dried sweat. I gave him a pair of socks, a sport shirt, a towel and an old pair of slippers. "Thanks, buddy," he said. The next day he asked if he could wear my flannel shirt. Since it was my only shirt in reserve, I was a little sharp. "No buddy," I said. "That's mine." I'm sure he never understood why I let him down. Nevertheless, we continued as buddies of sorts.

Giving these clothes to Randy made me think of the Skopje earthquake and the supplies we had handed over to the Yugoslavians at midnight. I had felt no emotion for the homeless people of Skopje then, even though I had intellectually understood the devastation they suffered. But as I handed the clothes over to Randy, I felt a warm glow. These were my clothes; they were being given to an individual. I personally got to see the pleasure in a human's face as I satisfied a need. A gift to a whole town loses its human proportions.

The men's brand of loyalty and friendship was unique and enlightening. One night during a poker game Eddie, the loser, attacked Willy, the winner, in a fury. The two rolled on the cement floor of the barracks, attempting to bash in each other's head. I expected this to be the end of their long "friendship", but the next day Willie, who lost the fight but won the money, loaned his only spare shirt to his attacker.

On another occasion a picker fled the orchard with ten

dollars he had just stolen from the pocket of his buddy, who had passed out in the barn. The next day I asked the victim, now that he was sober, what he would do if he came upon the thief again. I feared a vendetta. Instead he sighed philosophically, and explained to me that the other picker had just "borrowed the money. If I see him again he'll give that ten bucks back, and probably ten bucks interest as well. We're buddies."

From the first, however, I was at a disadvantage in pursuing the illusion of "buddyhood" and at least partial acceptance by the workers. I was the only Yankee in the crowd, and my accent was just as confusing to them as theirs to me. During my first week the Virginia, West Virginia, and Tennessee dialects fell on my ears like a foreign language with a familiar ring.

I had entered the camp without explanation and tried to be accepted as one more drifter. To reinforce the illusion during the first week, I read comic books only, completely neglected the newspapers, listened to soap operas and country music on the radio, and dusted off some of my favorite but little-used four letter words. This last tactic was not unimportant, as the vocabulary of the average migrant worker is pure primitive, as realistic, colorful and uninhibited as the men who used it.

I was successful for a time. I seemed to be accepted by my colleagues, and the proof was that they began to call me "buddy." Now I thought I was in. But the inevitable moment of truth came only a week after my arrival. A picker —I remember him by his eyes, sharp and glinting like a snake—gave me an accusing look as I was combing my hair in front of the broken mirror over the communal wash basin.

"You gone to college, ain't yer?" It must have been my use of words and my accent that gave me away. With sinking heart I admitted to the sin of higher education. Hamming it up a little, I said I hoped he would not hold it against me.

"What the hell yer doing here anyway?" he flung at me.

I knew it would be difficult to explain why I was really there, so I let myself gently off the hook.

"I'm a writer," I explained. "I do articles and stories—I bum around looking for material."

From that time on my relationship with the men underwent a subtle change. Some of them were impressed and began pouring out their life histories to me, hoping I would write them up, make them famous. Others regarded me suspiciously, although with more respect. A writer was strange and foreign territory; he inhabited another world. But could he be trusted?

I began to be treated as a rarity, a curious bird with a special vocabulary and an elegant handwriting. I thought of Peggy and smiled. She would be fascinated to hear about the elegance of my writing. After all, she had once given me a typewriter so she could decipher my scrawl.

I had a vision of her sitting at her own typewriter. What would she be writing? How was she doing by herself? Were the kids being hellions? With a pang I knew I was missing her.

I was consulted from time to time as an expert on words. One day Woody looked up from a comic book.

"What's erysipelas?" he shouted. He was always shouting, even if he was only discussing apples.

"It says here—ery—sip—elas." His voice dropped slightly as he savored the word. I wasn't at all sure what it meant but I made a wild guess.

"The god-damnedest thing." He shouted at me. "I know all about sipelas but I sure never heard nothing of this erysipelas!"

Again, I thought of Peggy. She was a Scrabble and crossword puzzle whiz. She should be here to enlighten Woody.

I eventually found a better and more encompassing way of establishing myself with the group by buying a couple of jugs of apple wine for everyone.

Conversation came in the evening. After supper we would sit on our bunks and wrap adhesive tape over the day's bruises. After ten hours in the orchard, our hands were scratched as if they had been sorting wildcats. Then, once we were in our bunks, tongues rapidly unstuck. It was the most promising time for a bull session, and I tried to stimulate one whenever I could.

But I ran up against one serious obstacle: Sex, liquor, and work represented, almost exclusively, the extent of their conversational repertoire, and I was getting bored with all three. I longed for an intelligent talk with Peggy and some of my friends. But here in Virginia I needed desperately to find a new subject. Why not foreign policy? Perhaps I could help the pickers—and myself—understand some of the successes and absurdities of United States activities abroad.

I tried various techniques and ruses to steer them away from their favorite subjects. In the barracks there was one transistor radio, owned by Jerry. It was his fetish and he carried it with him to the orchard, the washroom, the outhouse, a lock of hair invariably covering the dials as he bent his ear to the instrument. Occasionally, in his search for hillbilly music, Jerry would come up on the news. A puzzled expression would creep into his eyes as he was about to turn the dial.

"Jerry," I would yell out quickly. "Did you hear that? God Almighty!"

"What's that?" he would ask in a startled drawl.

"The news—what's happening. Did you hear that about Cuba?" I would try to fasten his attention on Castro, but usually there would be a "Naw" and an impatient turning of the dial.

After the first week I picked up a newspaper whenever I could find one and tried to use some of its articles as a springboard for discussion. This netted results of a sort, but generally what I got were fragmented and biased opinions. Then I bought Time Magazine in town one Sunday, and after reading it offered it around. Two pickers glanced over it, but only momentarily.

The same issue of Time ran an article on Vietnam and one night I said, "Poor old Vietnam." I mentioned the dangers threatening the regime in Saigon. The two men who had glanced at the magazine looked at me without expression.

"Getting worse every day," I smiled encouragingly and waited for a comment. Nothing. Two increasingly listless faces looked at me. After another moment I asked, "I wonder—what should we do in Vietnam?" Still no answer. In desperation I continued, "Send in the marines?" "Naw," said one. "Send them to Hawaii. They'll have a better time."

Somehow I got my buddy Randy to take an interest in Vietnam. He said he wanted to learn more about the war, but didn't want the other pickers to know of his interest. So I suggested we take a walk. It was a Saturday afternoon, one of those wonderfully clear autumn days with a warm sun and cool breeze. Our walk took us to the woods between two large apple orchards. As we walked, I talked of Vietnam, how the war started, its problems, the dangers for the United States.

Randy listened to me thoughtfully. When I told him about the role of the State Department in making policy in Vietnam, his head jerked up and I could tell I had lost him.

"In what state is this State Department?" He asked.

"It's part of the United States—it's responsible for all our doings with other countries."

"Oh . . ." He was getting more and more puzzled, his eyes narrowing and his brows working their way up on his forehead. "What business is it of this state? Why does it fuck around with foreign things anyway?"

Randy's attitude was typical of the other pickers. For days I felt frustrated and annoyed. I'd been spending much of my working life on what I considered of vital importance to all Americans, and now I was finding out there was zero interest in what I had spent all those years doing. I would have cherished disagreement, tolerated ignorance, but indifference was unendurable. Finally, I had to accept the sad fact that nothing grabbed these men, unless it had an immediately tangible and direct effect on them. Furthermore, and even more disillusioning—I began to see that not only these pickers but a majority of our population can and do get along beautifully without spending so much as a moment's thought on the subject of international affairs.

Although I grew to accept the basic fact of ignorance in the camp, I was continually interested in exactly which biases and misinformation their particular ignorances had led them. I learned, for example, that the Russians and Castro were sending "nigger agitators" from the North to kick up trouble in Virginia. I also learned that President Johnson's voice had been cut off the radio the other day in the South because it was discovered "he's from Maine."

It was equally fascinating to hear that Randy was against Johnson because "he's gonna cut out all this freeloading." When I questioned him further, Randy said there was a home in Michigan where able-bodied men could go, draw free room and board, pick up a relief check each month, and go to bed with a jug of wine.

There was a remarkable lack of interest in the presidential election even though Johnson and Goldwater were winding up their campaign. The only time I even remember the subject being raised was two days after the election. "Did yer find out yet who win?" was the unforgettable question.

Political misunderstandings, I found, spilled over into economic ones. Southern pickers were disturbed because, they said, there were 100,000 Cuban refugees in the Miami area, each of whom was "guaranteed a job by the government even if it meant firing Americans."

On international events, reactions were equally bizarre. Obviously, I was told that Socialism and Communism were the same. But I also learned it was useless for the United States to be in South Korea because all Koreans wanted to go Communist and there wasn't much the United States could do about it. On Cuba the administration was pitilessly attacked. It was President Kennedy who had made the first goof. We should have bombed Castro out of Cuba, sent in the Marines, sunk the Cuban navy. Now Castro has his missiles, and they're underground and can't be detected. As for Germany, it's crowded with nuclear weapons and cobalt bombs. Uncle Sam better be careful. We'd been stung before by the Germans, and it could happen again.

The only time anything remotely resembling a group discussion took place was at the end of a rainy day when the pickers were restless and edgy. Even Jerry was sated with hillbilly music. He was lying on his bunk, empty eyes pitched upward at the dirty patches of beaverboard ceiling, letting the transistor take its own course. The music faded into news, and Vietnam was mentioned. I began to listen and so did some of the pickers. This precipitated a brief exchange on Vietnam which went something like this.

Picker 1: "I don't like that fucking war in Vietnam. I never believed in it."

E.K.: "Why not?"

Picker 1: (Spitting Copenhagen into a tin can on the floor) "It's a put up war. Like all the phony wars in the past."

Picker 2: "There was that shooting offshore."

E.K.: "Tonkin Gulf?"

Picker 2: "Yeah, that were it. Someone goofed."

E.K.: "How did they goof?"

Picker 3: "By letting those goddam Communists get away. We shot and they got away. What's wrong with our shells? It ain't never used to be that way."

Picker 1: (A little triumphantly) "Yuh see. It's like I said. A fucking put up war."

Picker 3: "What'll happen when the Chinese Communists step in?"

E.K.: "Hopefully they won't step in. After all, we're not invading North Vietnam."

Picker 4: "That's what we should do. Invade North Vietnam."

E.K.: "And get the Chinese involved in the war? They've got an A-bomb now."

Picker 4: "But we've got more than them. And the H-bomb too."

Picker 3: "We should stop all this pussy-footing. Get in there and lick the pants off those dirty Communists."

Picker 1: "I still think it's a fucking put up war. Time

was when the U.S. could snap its fingers and see the rest of the world hop. (Sadly) Times ain't like that no more."

E.K.: "No, they sure ain't."

And so it went. I grew to like the men enormously, but I shuddered at much of their thinking. This split reaction disturbed me at first until I remembered a few people at home whose thoughts I found admirable but whom I thoroughly disliked.

T he apple picking season of three weeks ended with sore hands, but a strangely invigorated back. I had made plans to continue in Florida, where the oranges were waiting to be plucked beneath southern sunshine.

It was time for all of us to move on.

On my last day, we went around the barracks, shaking hands and saying good-bye. I asked for addresses, but there were none to give. The pickers had no homes, no relatives or friends who ever forwarded mail, no concrete plans for being at any place at any certain time. I gave Randy and a few others my address, but I knew they would never write. It was odd—and a little sad—liking the men, becoming intimate with them and knowing I would never see them or hear from them again. Even worse, I felt guilty. I could leave this life. They couldn't.

I was at the door with my suitcase when Randy yelled cheerfully.

"See you in Vietnam, Buddy."

"Yeah." I waved back. "Perhaps we can pick apples together."

In Florida it was more of the same. Only this time it was oranges instead of apples. But the people were as empty and likable as in Virginia, the ladders as backbreaking, the hands as raw, the fingers as bloody. But something happened to me in Virginia. One Sunday morning, after a particularly brutal week along the Indian River, I hitchhiked to the nearest town and phoned Peggy.

We had made no agreement when I would return.

When I went to the phone booth in that small town in Florida, there were still three weeks of home leave left.

There was no specific event that roused me or sent me rushing to the phone. Perhaps I'd had my fill of stories of empty lives. Perhaps I didn't really need another week as physically brutal as the last one. Perhaps the nervous fatigue that sent me fruit-picking in the first place had been washed out of me with the sweat of many weeks' physical work. Perhaps seeing the unstable lives of these migrant workers made me want to rejoin those whose lives were more stable. Perhaps there were just too many beans on the dining room table each day.

I wanted to go home.

It was more than a vague desire. I was amazed to find I was even anticipating a return to Belgrade with its dress clothes and endless parties. Once I thought only kids became homesick. Yet here I was, a middle-aged fifty-three, going into a crazy sweat as I picked up the phone and told the operator I wanted to make a collect call to Cambridge, Mass.

A moment later I was talking to Peg.

"Hello, love."

"My God, it's you." There was a strange breathy quality to her voice. "How are you?"

"Lonely. Rested. Ready."

"Ready for what?"

"Everything. You—the kids—Belgrade. The works. Everyone O.K. ?"

"Everyone's O.K."

"Hey", I said. "I hate to think of a woman abandoning her kids, but do you think your mother might take care of our four geniuses?"

"Why, are you thinking of declaring me incompetent?" There was a silly, joking quality in her voice I'd been missing for weeks. "I'm not going to be a migrant worker if that's on your mind. It's not one of my fondest dreams."

"What I mean—I miss you—"

"Didn't you say that before?"

"Not really—maybe I said I'm lonely. That's as far as I've gotten."

"If you've planned the whole conversation, what comes next?"

I took a big breath and stumbled forward.

"Come meet me in Miami. We'll have a few days together, then go back home together."

Within seconds she agreed to meet me in Miami for a long weekend. She arrived three days later.

On my return to Belgrade at the end of home leave, I shared my experiences with some of the embassy staff. The information was received at first with disbelief, then with some embarrassment. Most Foreign Service officers on home leave visit relatives and friends, go to the dentist and doctor, play golf. What I had done was as incredible to them as if I had gone to the moon. Maybe more. An embassy officer just wasn't supposed to act that way.

SIXTEEN

Diplomat in Residence—Most Foreign of All Posts (University of Texas)

A good record and swift promotion had taken me to the National War College, my first academic assignment in the Service. A car crash in Jordan eventually brought me to my second, the University of Texas in Austin.

Although I had a herniated disk when I left Jordan, I recuperated gradually until I was again mobile and productive. For several years in Yugoslavia, I almost convinced myself that back problems were behind me. At the end of my Yugoslav tour, however, I was bothered by sharp pains in the legs. My back was deteriorating again.

Because of it, the Department judged that I was not fit for overseas duty. I had to stay in the United States.

The chief of Personnel, Derek Roberts, and I sat discussing the matter in his office one afternoon. There was nothing unusual about Derek except for his precise little moustache, as manicured as a lawn in the Washington suburbs.

"The choice is between an assignment at the Department of State Headquarters," he said, brushing his moustache with his index finger, "or at a university."

"What do you mean, a university," I asked cautiously. "The anti-Vietnam and civil rights eras are upon us. Students are taking over buildings. Some campuses resemble battle grounds. What would my role be? Helping students burn down a building or two?"

There was no smile from Derek. He saw only the serious side of things.

"The Department has just started a new program—Diplomat in Residence. We are selecting a few senior Foreign Service officers to spend one year at an academic institution."

I found it hard to believe that this could be a legitimate Foreign Service assignment.

"What would I do?"

"You've been abroad continuously for six years. Haven't you lost touch with a lot of things in this country?"

"Just about everything."

"And you don't feel a need to catch up?"

"Of course I do."

At my last post in Belgrade, every time I read *TIME* Magazine, events in America—riots, racial tensions, murders, new buildings, trends—all of it had seemed so far away, another world, in fact. I missed my country and wanted to become part of it again.

"To be a good representative of America abroad you have to know America and its people," he said. "Not facts—you can read about them. I mean people—the "feel" of the country—"

I was impressed. I leaned towards him. "While I'm being Americanized—what does the University get out of me?"

"You've accumulated a lot of wisdom in international problems while you've been abroad." He looked me up and down as if he was trying to find the evidence of wisdom on my clothes.

"Share that wisdom with those less fortunate than you—those who have never been abroad." He drew a deep breath as if he was gearing up for a speech. "As a practicing political scientist you will interact with the theoretical political scientists of academia. Out of this contact hopefully will emerge more proficient individuals on both sides."

He was talking as if he was reading from a directive. It all sounded vaguely sexual. As if my contact with teachers would result in the birth of a new kind of individual. What kind of conversation does this guy have at home, I wondered? How can his wife tolerate him? He must have other virtues. But judging from his coldness and lack of communicative skill they must be deeply hidden.

The Personnel chief seemed unaware of my feelings. He kept on reciting, his face and voice expressionless, "The Department of State will enhance personally and professionally the desired interplay with those pockets of American life contributing to our national purpose". He stopped. "I'm about to write the brochure for the program. I hope I remember what I just told you."

I felt like telling him to forget all the gobbledygook. And just tell me how to apply for the job. What better dose of re-Americanization than a college campus? Remembering only too well my three and half years at Headquarters as Director of Southeast Asian Affairs, I had no desire to reexperience that heavy burden of bureaucracy.

"I'll take Diplomat in Residence", I said.

He was looking at a list of colleges in his hand. "Brown University? Columbia University? University of Illinois?" He paused.

"Keep on going". The colleges he named were all in the East or Midwest. I wanted an area I had never seen before. "Anything in the Southwest?"

"As a matter of fact—President Johnson just sent in a memo. In his own handwriting. He said he wants a diplomat in his University".

"I didn't know he owned a university".

A first suspicion of humor made Roberts' left eye crinkle. "Didn't you know that everything in Texas belongs to LBJ? Not only did he say "I want a diplomat at *my* University." He ended with "in *my* State."

"Characteristic anyway".

"Actually a lot of Texas does belong to him. TV stations, newspapers, real estate".

"Thanks. I'll take Texas", I said.

"One last thing", Roberts said. "You know United States policy. You will, of course, defend it—explain why we do what we do. You'll have no difficulty about explaining our policy in Europe and almost everywhere else. But there'll be problems in Asia—Vietnam, for example—"

As he paused, I began to think of United States responsibility for the Vietnam war—of contravening the Geneva accords and illegally sending American troops to South Vietnam. Did Personnel know of my negative feelings about our policy in that part of the world? Could they have found out that I was so negative that I left the Southeast Asia office of the Department to go to Jordan? How was I to explain United States policy in Vietnam to Texas students? If they were like students everywhere, they'd be dead set against our role in the War. Was I supposed to try to change them—make them see "the light of day" as the Department said, when I didn't see "the light of day" myself? It was with a great deal of uncertainty that I left Roberts' Office.

Early in the fall Peg and I arrived in Texas with just one child in tow, Debra the youngest, then about five. The three boys were all in school in the East. Eric Glenn in American University in Washington, D.C.; Terry at High Mowing in N.H.; Chris at Millbrook in N.Y.

For Peg, Texas was a windfall. During our Belgrade assignment she had taken an interest in linguistics and knew that the University in Austin had an excellent Linguistics Department. She intended to take courses there on her way toward an MA.

I had never before been in Texas. Many of the Texans I met both in and out of the University were impressed with the presence of a diplomat in their midst. I was assigned a corner office and was readily available to students and faculty for questions about the Foreign Service and United States foreign policy. Since the University was building up its international courses, I was often used for advice and information about the Foreign Service. I had two television interviews and gave speeches to classes and clubs inside the University and to clubs outside the University.

Despite the warm welcome I received, there were

some who considered me an intruder from Washington, bringing unpleasant memories of bureaucrats and regulations that threatened the rugged individualism of Texans, many of whom considered Washington an impediment to their schemes and ambitions. As a representative of Washington, I was occasionally looked at with suspicion. At those times I felt that Texas was the most foreign of all my posts. Peg and I were sometimes tempted to raise the American flag over our small cottage in the suburbs of Austin as if we were envoys from a foreign country.

The same feeling of being suspect that I had when I was working as a migrant laborer permeated the air. The apple orchards suspicions centered around my possible connections with the IRS; in Texas, bureaucracy and regulations were the villains.

Texans have a special reason for disliking Washington. After all, Texas has a history of living under six flags. At one time or another the flags of France, Spain, Mexico, the Confederacy, and the United States waved over the Capitol. The sixth flag, that of the independent country of Texas, is the most revered, giving us the impression that many Texans would welcome a return to their nine years of independence.

A few weeks after my arrival I was invited to the home of a wealthy Texan rancher, Billy Joe. If his intention was to impress me, he succeeded beautifully. He was dressed in an elegant cowboy tie with a dazzling diamond pin bursting out of his shirt, shining black leather boots and a broad brimmed hat, even though we were sitting in the living room having a long cool drink of tequila and lime. The room itself was a weird combination of palatial log cabin and rustic palace. Pictures of spouting oil wells, cattle, cowboys, and endless open ranges looked down on us from gaudy gilt frames. Before we went outside to take a "looksee" as he called it, he pointed proudly from his throne-like chair into the distance— "From here you can't see where my land ends". And after we had returned forty minutes later from our "look-see", we still hadn't reached a point from where we could see the end of his land.

He had another three tequilas and lime before lunch. Unequal to his seemingly bottomless thirst I stopped after the first. Taking the last gulp of his third drink, he hurled the glass into the fireplace, laughing as it crashed.

"All that property crud. Forget it. Who cares for land? I've got something real precious to show you. Here come."

I followed him to a large glass covered case next to the huge fireplace. Pieces of glass were lying bunched up on the hearth. In the case was an old tattered flag. His fingers lovingly almost reverently traced the outlines of the flag on the cover of the case.

"Ever seen anything like it before"?

"Very special", I replied, careful to be vague.

"Hell, you ain't seen nothing like it before", he snapped. "That's why I asked you to come here today. A Texas flag, my friend—the only true flag you will see in Texas. Our flag for nine years before 1845 when Texas had the big misfortune to become part of the United States."

I looked at the flag. On the left was a broad vertical bar of blue, in the center a single white star, and on the right, horizontal bars of white and red.

"My Daddy gave it to me and he got it from his Grand-daddy", Billy Joe continued. "Texas would be the greatest country in the world if it weren't for Washington. We should have kept this flag. Pretty, ain't it?"

"Very pretty," I said.

"If we still had this flag, we could tell Washington to stay the hell out of our way." His intensity melted and he smiled. "Even if we don't have the flag, we can still tell Washington to stay the hell out of our way." He shook his head violently. "Laws, regulations—we don't like those things in Texas. That Lyndon Johnson—he sure got spoiled when he got to be President—"

"He's passed some great social programs." I said, trying to be positive.

"Who cares about social programs?" he said scornfully. "Oil—cattle—that's what counts. LBJ taxes land—controls drilling—can't turn this way or that without permission from Washington. Anyway, that is why I invited you here today," he said, appropriately forgetting he had just said he had invited me to see his flag. "Who's your boss?"

"In Washington? Dean Rusk, Secretary of State."

"I know Rusk. From Georgia—not all bad, but not all good like Texas. You go back and tell your Mr. Rusk—'Mr. Secretary, Texas wants you to stay out of its way.' We want progress in Texas—not rules—too much government is a mean thing—nasty thing—we don't want government here."

"Who is we?" I said.

"Everyone—everybody," he snapped back. Then a pause and a drunken yawn. "Well, half of Texas anyway." Again that sudden disarming smile.

I was tempted to get into a debate with Billy Joe about Washington, but figured he was more than half drunk already and would probably not remember what I said— much less, be impressed with my arguments.

Some weeks later I was asked by a student club to debate with Dwight MacDonald—on a subject I dreaded talking about: Vietnam. MacDonald was a noted critic, also at the University for a year. He had lectured and written extensively against United States involvement in the Vietnam War. He had the reputation of being a formidable speaker and a seasoned debater. He, if anyone, would be speaking out of fervor. Without equal fervor on the other side of the question I wouldn't stand a chance. And that fervor I lacked.

Until then Vietnam had not been a primary concern of the students. Compared to students in California and the East, Texans were conservative. They had not taken over school buildings or trashed the administration. But every time Washington increased its involvement in the war, I could sense a rise in tension on the Austin campus. As each month went by I found more questions—and more embarrassing questions—asked at the end of my speeches. I tried to explain both sides of the case, generally satisfying neither the questioner nor myself.

One day I was asked: "Do you really think a Communist Vietnam would be a threat to the security of the US?" I dodged that one too. I said perhaps there might be no immediate danger, but there was always the possibility of the domino theory being activated. This theory was then very popular in Washington. If Vietnam fell to the Communists, it wouldn't be long before Cambodia fell, then Laos, then probably Burma and Thailand. To help my case, I tried to think of the worst possible scenario. If all of Southeast Asia fell to the Communists, wouldn't there be danger to the US? The answer was not persuasive. Did we really expect an attack from these agricultural countries with their small industrial base? The closer I got to examine objectively United States rationale for involvement in Vietnam, the nearer to madness it seemed. Yet I couldn't say it.

I had dodged the Vietnam problem—and myself—as long as I could. I had run out of gas.

At the beginning of the second semester the president of the student body, Mark, was finally standing in my office. He was asking me to do the one thing I feared most: publicly take the pro-government side of the Vietnam question. I had come to a brick wall, I could not get around it or through it. I was stuck with my pro-government position even though I had as many reasons for hating the war as MacDonald had. I could see disaster ahead. Instead of defending State Department policy, I was going to have to agree with MacDonald and create the amazing spectacle of the pro-side in the debate coming over to the anti-side before the debate ever began.

Mark was visibly excited at the prospect of the debate. It would be the show of the year—two well known guests debating what was fast becoming the number one question on campus. The whole school would turn out. In his excitement, his hands were never still, sometimes gesturing to emphasize a point, sometimes passing his fingers through his hair, wiping the spittle off the corner of his lips, or scratching some itch behind his right knee. Words gushed out of his mouth.

"What date do you have in mind?" I asked cautiously.

Regardless of the date he set, I intended to look sad and say I was scheduled to speak that day in El Paso.

"What date do you prefer?"

"I have no preference," I said nervously. "It's up to you to fix a date."

"You fix whatever date you want," he said. "We want to be sure to get you."

I paused, beautifully stymied. He had already gotten me.

"O.K.," I said. "I can't set a date right now. I have a commitment to visit El Paso for a couple of speeches. After they fix the dates of my visit I'll let you know. Probably in a month or so."

"Just think," Mark continued exuberantly. "If we could have the debate the last few days of the semester—just before final exams—wow!"

"That would be a wonderful time," I said, trying to hide my misery.

Several weeks later, on my trip to Texas Western College in El Paso, I carried the Vietnam problem with me. Debate or no debate? If yes, what could I say that would not shame me? If no, could I get out of the whole thing gracefully?

After a couple of speeches in El Paso, Peg and I returned to Austin for a day or two, then went on to Tuskegee College in Alabama for two days. I gave a lecture on international affairs and was pleased to see the interest and knowledge the students brought to the questions on Vietnam. In the evening I had dinner with a couple of the faculty from the Political Science Department and we talked a great deal about the Foreign Service as a career. Tuskegee was founded as a college for blacks in the 1880s, yet very few blacks were taking the exams. I tried to find out why. The answer was not encouraging. Many used to take the exam but without exception failed. Several of the professors said the exam was slanted toward whites; therefore blacks could not effectively compete. The next day I met with several students interested in an international career who also affirmed that they had tried the exam but could not pass. "Questions only for whitey," one said angrily.

When I got back to Austin I wrote those in Washington who administered the Foreign Service exam and shared my findings with them. I knew the Department was eager to get more blacks into the Service. Had they checked all exam questions to be sure they were not slanted in favor of any one group? If any bias existed, I suggested, add questions that blacks would be more likely to know than whites. This would redress the balance. Recognizing that the exam should eventually be the same for all applicants, a further possibility should be explored. For a limited number of years, admit blacks without a written exam but with an interview, similar to the system directly after World War II, when I was admitted with an oral exam. Subsequently, I found that the Department began to experiment in various ways to get more blacks to apply. Today there are increasing numbers of blacks, women, and other minorities in the Service.

When I returned from Tuskegee to Austin, I had not yet worked my way out of the Vietnam debate mess. It had haunted me through much of my trip but I was no closer to a solution. Mark was still waiting for me to call him, and I was still reluctant to do so.

Oddly enough, about the same time I began to experience a whole new set of emotions unrelated to anything in Vietnam. Everytime I had a counseling session in which I clarified a career problem or helped a student I rode on high for several hours.

I was delighted yet concerned at the emotional lift I was getting. I had seldom felt anything like it before. Perhaps working for UNRRA or with the DPs, but rarely in the Foreign Service. Here in Texas I would start talking with students about the Foreign Service as a career, describe the exam, then, following their questions, get into other international careers: business, banking, foundations, the United Nations, non-profit organizations, publishing, journalism, teaching, law, in fact almost every profession.

I felt my way through these discussions. But many

times I was beyond my depth. What did I really know about these international careers? Only that they existed. I had no information on qualifications needed to apply, the nature of the work, the availability of jobs. For that matter, what did I know about counseling students? Was I approaching the problem of advice in the way most helpful to them? Further, what did I know about counseling itself? The only experience I had was counseling displaced persons in Austria, but that counseling, unrelated to jobs, was to help DPs resume life after the Holocaust and adjust to the post war world.

More troublesome yet were my inner feelings the work I was doing with the students felt more rewarding than a lot of my Foreign Service work had. Was I heading toward another change of careers? I approached this question reluctantly. I was in my mid-fifties. As much as I loved counseling, I felt I was getting too old to make a career change.

I couldn't help remembering my formative years when I drifted from one job to another without any sense of direction. This memory depressed me. Then a new thought entered my mind. Perhaps all my indecision and searching could be put to use with students who were now as confused as I had been. I would be able to use all the information I had accumulated over the years to help young people clarify career problems. Everything I learned could now be put at the service of those uncertainly stumbling along.

Toward the close of my year at Texas, after many talks with Peggy, I decided to risk a change. Before I could start my new counseling career, I needed two things. One was an academic degree. I could go to George Washington University just a few blocks from the State Department building. I would take counseling courses at night. After two or three years I would have my MA in Education and Counseling. Then it would be time to make my move.

In addition to a degree, I needed more experience in counseling. I would have to request some assignment in the Department which had access to a nearby academic facility. Fortunately the Department had recently started an

Outplacement Service to help retiring and resigning Foreign Service Officers find jobs in the cold outside world.
Even more fortunately, the present Director was retiring
and the position would soon be vacant. The work would
not be counseling students but it would give me experience
in the basics of counseling. I applied for the job and got it.

I don't think my decision to change my career directly
arose because of my predicament about the Vietnam debate. Yet I had to admit it seemed nonsense to work in an
organization wedded to policies some of which embarrassed and tormented me.

I had promised Mark to get back to him in a month's
time. It was now five weeks since I had made that promise.
And just two weeks before final exams. The night before I
called him I had a restless night. I dreamed that Secretary
of State Rusk, accompanied by a walking mustache which
could only have been Roberts of Personnel, came at me
with razor-sharp iron attached to his fingers and tried to
nail me down to a board on the floor marked TREASON.

The next morning I got Mark on the phone.

"Mark," I said. "About the Vietnam debate—I've got a
new idea."

"I knew you'd do it," Mark yelled. Wow! When?"

"There've been a lot of discussions on campus about
Vietnam in the last couple of months. Every day in the
college paper I read about another lecture or seminar."

"Sure enough. Your debate will be a terrific climax.
Terrific!"

"One thing worries me," I said. "By now everyone interested in Vietnam must have heard all the pros and cons
about American involvement."

Mark wouldn't swallow this. "But they haven't heard
you and MacDonald together."

"After all, there are only so many arguments pro and
con," I said. "They'll all know what we're going to say."

"But when you say it—boy, oh boy—," Mark said in his usual manic voice.

"That's what I'm wondering—a new approach—something new—a novelty—maybe that's what they need—" I sounded a little breathless. I'd already faulted Mark for not being precise. As I listened to myself I wondered if I was learning from him.

"Why not change the debate?" I suddenly said.

I could sense even over the phone what must be running through his mind. This guy is trying to get out of debating. He's letting the student body down.

Slowly and tentatively in a quiet voice Mark replied "What do you want instead of Vietnam?"

"Don't misunderstand. I still want Vietnam. Very much. But I just want to change it a bit."

"How?" Mark seemed to be hanging on a limb.

"Suppose MacDonald and I change roles—He argues the pro-government side—I argue on the anti-government side. Get it?"

"Oh, I see," he said. Then after a moment. "No, I don't really see."

"Give the students a novelty. They expect me to support involvement. Won't they be damned surprised—and pleased—to have me tell them what a shit hole we've gotten into. They expect MacDonald to shoot holes in our policy— then suddenly he comes out in praise of American imperialism. Think of the screams and applause that night! The headlines the next day!"

"Are you kidding—?" Mark suddenly began to laugh, a wild delighted laugh.

"It is funny."

I tried to laugh, "That's the beauty of the suggestion. In one hour you overturn conventions—preconceptions—everything the students believe in—and what do you substitute? Astonishment—You tell everyone it's a surrealist entertainment—and you know everyone loves surrealism."

"What date did you say?" His voice was calm but there was a shadow of surprise and pleasure in it.

"Two weeks from tonight—just before final exams. That's your time table."

"What will we do if MacDonald doesn't think the format is as funny as we do?"

"He will. He will. He's a wit. It's a great occasion for a wit to bemuse and dazzle an audience. And he'll do it. He has style."

A bit of a pause. Then Mark spoke. "Let me take it up with my board. But they won't like it."

"They will—if you present it as a challenge. A historical event that can go down in the history of the University. After all, you have a reputation for scheduling bizarre events—the more bizarre the more popular."

"It sure will be an entertainment," he admitted.

"At exactly the right moment. Just before finals and the terrible pre-exam depression. We'll snap the students out of it."

Mark presented the proposal to his board. I heard later the reception was mixed. The discussion was prolonged into a second meeting. It took a few more hours to douse the hesitations of the last hold outs.

Then MacDonald had to be approached. He had said he could make the debate at any time. Mark took him at his word. But when MacDonald heard the new proposal he stalled. He said he would have his answer the next day. When Mark phoned him the next day, MacDonald withdrew from the debate with a plea of illness and the need to return to New York. I blessed him for it—yet I was a little put out too. I would have loved to have debated Vietnam on the side of the hippies.

Texas then was a transitional year for me. I left Austin with a clear conscience and clear view of where I was going. I called it my three year plan. The Russians and others had their five year plans. I could do mine in three.

On our return to Washington, I wondered what Roberts would think of a Foreign Service Officer offering to take the anti-government side of a Vietnam debate. Would I have to tell him?

When I saw him in the Department, he inevitably asked if the students had many questions about Vietnam.

"All the time," I said truthfully.

"Most college students are violently opposed to our policy in Vietnam. How did you find them in Texas?"

"Oh, about 50-50," I hedged.

"That's good."

"I even had a debate on Vietnam."

He jerked his moustache, "How did it go?"

"I won," I embroidered my little white lie and plunged forward, "The students said I taught them things about our involvement they hadn't heard before—not even from me."

"Good boy!" Roberts boomed, patting me on the back.

SEVENTEEN

All's Still Well That Ends Badly (Washington, D.C.)

When I left the University of Texas, I was in the best possible position to wind up my Foreign Service career and move into the field of counseling students in international affairs.

I had no compunctions about leaving the Department. After twenty years I had reached the highest career level in the Service, FSO-1. The next and final step would be an Ambassadorship. Ambassadors are often political appointees, friends of the President or big donors to the Party in power. ($100,000 at the time would generally "buy" a large Embassy in Western Europe and considerably less an Embassy in the Middle East or Africa.) If not a political appointee, an Ambassador then comes from the career Foreign Service. The proportion of political to career appointments varies from one administration to another.

It was unlikely I would get an Embassy either way. I was not rich and had no political clout. Nor was I good at the art of making influential friends in the Department.

Some years earlier I had tried lobbying for myself with pitiful results. In the early 1960's I collected letters of recommendation from Congressmen and Ambassadors who knew of my work in Belgium, Malaya and Jordan, then set about "cultivating" the Assistant Secretary and Deputy Assistant Secretary of African Affairs. An increasing number of African countries were getting their independence and the United States was planning to set up Embassies in several spots. My hope was that one of these might come my way.

I ended up exactly nowhere. Short appointments with the Assistant Secretary and his Deputy were followed by fruitless promises of serious consideration. My esteem was at a very low level. I felt I was playing poorly a bad role in a third rate play. I am sure I would have been more effective if I had been lobbying for someone else, but I found it hard to sell myself. Perhaps the Secretaries estimated my qualifications and found them wanting. Perhaps they researched my record in the Bureau of Far Eastern Affairs and found that I was less than enthusiastic about the Vietnam War. Or, in addition to the many efficiency reports and letters of commendation in my file, they may have found a letter of outrage from the wife of the Director of the US foreign aid program and close friend of President Eisenhower. She was incensed because I had sent my Deputy to the Singapore airport to meet her while I was attending a national day celebration given by the British High Commissioner. I still feel that the United States Government profited more from my attendance at an official diplomatic function than by greeting an American at the airport.

In any case, when I returned to Washington from my Texas assignment, I was told that my plans for the next three years were okayed. I would counsel retirees as Director of Outplacement Services in the Department and be able to take counseling courses at night at George Washington University. Of course, seeing my family would be problematic at best, but everything was proceeding according to my plan when something occurred that made me tear up my time table and move considerably faster than I intended toward a new career outside the Department.

The incident might appropriately be titled How to Achieve Exile in the Fastest Possible Time.

I was doing well at my new job—helping retirees and resignees and those "selected out," a crude euphemism for being fired. I worked with them to identify their career aims, analyze their qualifications, and help with appropriate job openings. I had even uncovered a record number of job leads requiring an international background. My supervisor, John Steeves, Director General of the Foreign Service, commended me several times for my performance. He was particularly pleased with my success in persuading those "selected out" that life had its pleasures even without the Foreign Service. This was no easy task. From the beginning, Foreign Service Officers were programmed to make the Service their whole career, until retirement or until they dropped dead, whichever came first. The question used to be debated in the old days, "Is there Life After the Foreign Service?"

Each time my small staff—a deputy director, an assistant administrator, and a secretary—got news of a retiree landing a job, it celebrated. Our files of letters of appreciation kept growing.

After I had been in the outplacement job for about a year, Steeves asked me to take on an added function, planning and organizing the first annual Foreign Service Day for all former officers. Until then, there had been no occasion to bring together all alumni.

I accepted the new assignment reluctantly. It was a purely administrative job of logistics, space and invitations. Moreover, I was working full time on developing new job leads for retirees. All the hours spent on planning and implementing Foreign Service Day would mean fewer job leads and fewer hours for those working toward a new career.

To make life even more complicated, I was now in a wheel chair. My back had been deteriorating for some time. When exercises and rest no longer made the pain tolerable, I had had an operation on the fifth lumbar disk. The operation was a success—all the broken crablike pieces of cartilage were removed from the spine—but, in the healing process, I became a paraplegic. I was unable to take more than a few steps without considerable pain. Every day I drove my car from home, parked it in the State Department garage, and transferred to a wheel chair waiting for me. It was hoped the scars around the nerves and muscles controlling walking would be stretched through exercises so that I would be able to abandon the wheel chair and eventually walk normally.

In my wheelchair I organized Foreign Service Day with the help of a Committee of retired officers and Department representatives. The schedule caused little discussion. A State of the World presentation by the Secretary of State as well as seminars on various parts of the world were obvious choices.

Finally we came to the obligatory reception at the end of the day. It was seemingly a simple event but turned out to be one filled with traps and egos. We drew up an invitation list—not only of the retirees and resignees, but also of Department Assistant Secretaries and others whom the retirees would like to see and hear. Then we came to a further breakdown of the reception. Who were to be included in the reception line? We reached a list of names with little discussion. The obvious ones were Assistant Secretaries and Deputy Under Secretaries. But who was to head up the reception line? This is a highly sensitive choice in diplomatic circles, because it represents to the guests the one individual among a group of hosts who is actually giving the party and who represents the theme of the occasion.

An obvious choice was John Steeves, Director General of the Foreign Service, in whose name the invitations went out and who was the official host. A slightly less logical choice was Idar Rimestad, the Deputy Under Secretary for Administration, who was Steeves' boss. Another possibility would be to ask both of them to stand on the reception line. But there was one snag and a nasty one at that. Those who knew Steeves and Rimestad thought they were quite hostile to each other. Two of our Committee members judged they would not stand next to each other. And even in the unlikely event they should be agreeable to stand in the same line, the major problem still remained: which one should stand first? A choice had to be made, and, as the Chairman of the Planning Committee, I had the privilege to walk into a mine field.

Rimestad had shown no interest in Foreign Service Day. I thought he might view it as Steeves' baby and would perhaps have none of it. Besides, Steeves had been in the Service many years and in his present job was a symbol of the Service. He was much better known to retirees and resignees attending the Day's festivities than Rimestad who had come into the Service as a salary and wage specialist. Finally, I liked Steeves personally and could work with him more easily.

My choice then was Steeves, who accepted with pleasure my request to head up the reception line. Rimestad, of course, was on the invitation list along with the top brass of the Department.

It was the first time I had to choose between two of the highest ranking officers of the State Department. I didn't like being in the middle of a squabble and I had an uneasy feeling that in making my choice I had little armor to protect myself in case of an unwise choice.

Foreign Service Day was a success. It brought together old friends who had not seen each other in many years. Through its seminars and discussion groups it updated their knowledge of foreign policy and international problems. Most of all, it re-established and strengthened the close bond of retirees with the Foreign Service and Department of State.

Dean Rusk, Secretary of State, gave a lucid and comprehensive State of the World address without a note in his hand—although his speech went on for an hour. The reception too went off well. All the in-house conversation bottled up for years by officers came pouring out. Everyone enjoyed everyone else.

Rimestad, however, did not attend the reception; he declined the invitation. Two days later, still in my wheel chair, I met him in the hall. I greeted him only to have him walk by without acknowledging me. I knew then I was in for trouble.

A week later I received a formal notice that the Office of Outplacement Services would be inspected. In all my years in the Department, inspection was usually used only for overseas Embassies, which were visited every two years by an inspection team from Washington.

I had no objection to an inspection—in fact, I was proud of our work and knew that a fair inspection could only conclude that the office was doing an outstanding job.

I had a meeting with my staff and instructed them to collect the various lists, dossiers and files requested by the inspector. During the next few days, my secretary, Natalie, and my deputy dropped their work on retirees and concentrated on collecting the desired material. They not only brought our records together, but made out statistical summaries that had not even been requested.

One week later, the inspector arrived, a small woman in a light blue dress. Polite on the surface, she had a manner as searching as a ferret.

At first I was pleased to see the care with which she proceeded. She scrutinized everything closely: records, lists, names. I concealed nothing. I probably gave her more than she wanted, because I wished to be sure she knew the good results we had been achieving. She was curt in her dealings with me. She seemed not to want to hear what I had to say, but, instead, preferred to pore over papers and files.

The inspector spent a week with us, every day wearing the same blue dress. I began to have increasing anxiety about her report.

"Will you show me a copy?"

"You will see it soon enough," she replied. Her goodbye was cold.

Two weeks later, arriving at work on a Monday, I saw the contents of my desk dumped into a couple of boxes strewn in the hallway outside my old office. The sight of the empty office enraged me. As I stood, staring, the phone rang. It was one of Steeves' assistants, informing me that I had been replaced as Director by another officer.

The whole scenario appeared sickeningly clear to me:

the inspection had been a setup with a pre-determined result.

Natalie was distraught, almost in shock. I told her to
get me an urgent appointment with Steeves. A half an hour
later, I propelled my wheel chair into his office. Usually
direct in his dealings, he looked embarrassed to see me.

"Your dismissal has not come from my office," he said.
"I've been extremely pleased with your work, particularly
with the appreciation I've received from many officers
about the help obtained from the Outplacement office. But
orders have come from on high," he said. I was furious.
Why wouldn't he face up to Rimestad? Then I realized I
was unrealistic. No one in the Service ever fights an order.
It was like defying foreign policy set by the Secretary of
State and substituting a policy of your own. Numbly I
heard Steeves say there were two other assignments he
could offer me. One was as State Department representative at the Job Corps—the other, lecturer at the Defense
Intelligence Agency. Neither pleased me in the least and I
said I'd have to think it over.

On returning to my office I asked Natalie to get me an
appointment with Rimestad. She called and the secretary
on the other end, probably expecting my call, promptly
said that Mr. Rimestad would not be able to see visitors
until the following week or two and then she hung up. Natalie looked at me helplessly. I asked her to call again and
say I'd like to talk to Rimestad on the phone. I listened in
on another line and heard his secretary say he was extremely busy and was not receiving phone calls for several
days. I told Natalie to keep trying. I finally ended up getting
an appointment with him two weeks later.

I picked up the boxes with the contents of my desk
drawers, put them on my lap, and steered my wheel chair
to the garage. I spent the next two weeks at home seeing
more of my kids than I had in many months.

Peggy shared my rage. More constructively, she
turned my thoughts to the future. Together we planned the
strategy for my showdown with Rimestad.

The memory of my previous visit to Loy Henderson's

office did little to reassure me as I faced my meeting with his successor.

I had never thought of Rimestad as repulsive, small minded perhaps, mean, and hardly the caliber for the position he held. But when I left my wheel chair outside his door and walked painfully into his office, I saw him as if for the first time. He was a small man, with a small round head, watery eyes, quite nondescript and unhealthy looking. My first thought was he needed exercise; my second was that he probably had bad breath. One of his aides was also present, an officer I had worked with before and one whom I liked immensely. Today he was singularly quiet. He kept shifting uncomfortably as he sat in a chair next to Rimestad.

After a routine shaking of hands, I told Rimestad I'd come to ask why he had replaced me.

"I don't have to answer that" he said quietly but defensively. I waited two beats before speaking. I wanted to be sure he had no reasonable answer for my dismissal.

"My job's been well done," I said. "I have a lot of letters from satisfied Foreign Service Officers who found new careers through my office."

"*Not* well done." Defiance crept into his voice.

"What evidence do you have?" I asked.

"The inspection report."

"The results weren't by any chance pre-arranged?"

"Pre-arranged? You're paranoid," he said.

"I'm sure I am," I replied.

He looked at me as if I were mad. I relished the look and kept it with me a few moments before I went on. "If you're not paranoid in the Service, you must be crazy."

I was glad I hadn't lost my equilibrium. There was a chuckle from the aide, but nothing from Rimestad. Perhaps a tightening of the lips, but I would have needed a microscope to be sure.

"Might I see a copy of the report," I asked as lightly as I could.

"It's confidential."

"I have a right to see it," I insisted.

"Oh, have you?" His voice was cold. I didn't need a microscope now to be sure his lips had tightened.

"Yes. So I can answer those parts of it I judge unfair."

"You have no rights. I make the decisions here," Rimestad said quietly, decisively. So far no voice was raised. Anyone listening to the conversation from the outside would hardly consider it a confrontation. And of course Rimestad was right. In those days Foreign Service officers had responsibilities, but no rights. The idea of confronting a superior was unthinkable. The only reason it was thinkable to me was that I had nothing to lose except my self respect.

I tried to keep my voice under control. "You shouldn't do things like that," I said.

"I do what I want the way I want." He tittered nervously, his cheeks flushed.

"You have a responsible position. You should not take actions that demean your position—and yourself—and let's not forget the State Department." I knew I sounded presumptuous. I meant to sound presumptuous.

"I think you should go now," he snapped.

I flashed a glance at my friend sitting next to Rimestad. His face was pale. He looked away. Then I looked at Rimestad. His cheeks were brighter than before.

I controlled my rage and walked out the door, collapsing into my wheel chair.

As soon as I returned to what used to be my office, I asked Natalie if she would take a memo from me to the Under Secretary of State, the number two man in the Department, with a copy to Rimestad. Even though Natalie was no longer working for me she was eager to help. The words poured out of me. The memo that went out later that morning presented my case simply and forcefully and requested that I be reinstated to my old position.

I never received a reply.

A week later I inquired at the Under Secretary's office. His usually polite secretary at first stammered she knew nothing of the matter. When I persisted, she admitted that my memo had reached her office but insisted the Under

Secretary had not had time to read it. He was too busy these days.

I should have anticipated this result. Even had the Under Secretary sympathized with me, he would never have overturned Rimestad's decision. In the Service, as in the medical profession, not only did you not criticize your colleagues but you protected them from outside criticism.

There were no grievance procedures in the Department when I ran up against Rimestad. Yet this kind of action was surely the stuff of which grievances are made.

I thought of writing to my Congressman but did not know him. Then I realized the futility of my situation. No Congressman was going to attack the whole Establishment for one unknown constituent.

The lesson of foreign servicehood was clear and painful. When forced to choose between two sources of power, choose the person with most power. Not the person you like the most, not the one who would do the best job. Just superior power. I wondered why I learned this only at the peak of my career. Even if I had known the consequences, I still might not have chosen Rimestad to head up the reception line at Foreign Service Day. He was graceless, without charm and would have done a lousy job as host. It would have cast a pall over the whole affair. Even more ironic: if I had chosen Rimestad over Steeves, Steeves might have been the one to reach for my jugular.

A year or two after my conflict with Rimestad, a group of officers from Turkey became aware of an increasing number of decisions in the Department and Embassies abroad that were high handed. They cried for examination by an outside body. Yet the organization of the State Department permitted no complaints. The growing awareness of human and civil rights spilling over the country in the 1960's finally reached the sacred precincts of the Department, and before the end of the decade, a grievance procedure was established. Today any employee who feels injured or unjustly treated can appeal to an objective Grievance Board. Both sides are heard and, as often as not, if the Board finds in the employee's favor, the Department then has to redress the damage either financially or in terms of the officer's record or assignment.

I tried to remind myself of my theme when counseling retirees and those "selected out": there is still Life after the Foreign Service. Didn't I believe my own counseling? For one bleak week I wasn't sure. The Service had such a tenacious hold on me, it seemed there really wasn't much worthwhile life outside. Yet hadn't I planned to leave the Foreign Service and start a new career at a university?

I told myself only my timetable had been moved up. Perhaps I was just frustrated at not being able to complete the job I had started. There were long lists of employers I still had to contact about job openings and many retirees who were in the middle of their career counseling. Or perhaps it was the humiliation I had experienced from an organization where I had worked for most of my life.

But as I write this, I experience a flash of the same anger I felt then and have to remind myself that twenty-two years have passed.

For a while I wavered between burning down the State Department or going into a monastery. Of course I did neither. Someone had told me if I couldn't walk perhaps I should try bicycling. It sounded silly but I tried it and was delighted. Within a few months, as I rode along the canal path near the Potomac River, the leg and back exercise stretched the scars of the operation. I was able to get out of the wheel chair. Daily doses of fresh air cleansed my mind of the past and opened it to future plans.

I concentrated on choosing my next and last assignment. The Job Corps and the Defense Intelligence Agency had been offered me. I had little interest in the latter, so I selected the Job Corps. I thought my background as Labor Attaché in Belgium might be of use to the Corps.

I was already taking counseling courses toward a degree. If my new job at the Job Corps was not demanding, as I felt it would not be, I could double up on my courses—

take twice as many in the next semester and perhaps get my degree in one year instead of two.

A short time after my run-in with Rimestad, the Medical Division of the Department tried to persuade me to retire. Perhaps the suggestion came at the instigation of Rimestad. Perhaps it came from the sight, unseemly to some, of a wheel chair rolling along the corridors of the Department. In any case, the promise of a disability, tax-free pension either immediately or after my next assignment was dangled before me by the Chief Medical Officer. I was tempted to take the money and run. Instead, I thanked him but refused. I would act on my own timing, perhaps in a year or two. I was thinking of the counseling degree I needed before I could move into a new career.

Job Corps (Austin, Texas)

When I accepted my one year assignment as State Department representative at the Job Corps, I had a certain curiosity about the assignment. It was going to be my first non-international job since the end of World War II and I thought I might welcome it while working toward my counseling degree. Alas—not only had I little to do but what I did did not interest me.

At that time, the Job Corps was a new agency started by President Johnson to help provide the underprivileged and unemployed with technical skills to make them employable.

In my first interview with David, my potential supervisor in the Corps, I asked what contribution someone with only international experience could bring to his organization. He laughed good-naturedly and promised to keep me busy.

In fact, David laughed good-naturedly with everyone. If there had been a contest for the Most Charming, Most Good Natured employee of the Corps, David would have won hands down. As any ambitious civil servant would do, he exploited his looks and intelligence to get his own way.

However, my job and the organization were without international content. I had hoped that my background as Labor Attaché in Belgium could be of use to the Corps, but what I had not anticipated was that the Corps had no idea how to use it. David may well have encouraged me to work with him with the misguided hope that the presence of a State Department Foreign Service Officer might elevate the influence of the Corps in Washington.

After several weeks of office changing, I was assigned to be head of an Inspection Team to a regional Job Corps office in Austin, Texas. Just the word "Inspection" made me uneasy, with its images of Rimestad and the little lady in blue.

David and the head of the Regional Office in Austin were good friends and it was soon apparent that the main purpose of the inspection was to enhance the status of the regional chief. This meant giving the Office the highest possible rating. Meanwhile, I was noticing the general laziness of the headquarters staff in Washington. Employees went out for two and three hour lunches that included considerable shopping. They had long coffee breaks morning and afternoon and still had little to do at their desks during the few hours spent in the office. I began to wonder if the Inspection Team would not serve the organization better by inspecting Headquarters.

Before the Team left Washington for Texas, David called me in and went over the list of inspection items on which a rating was based. In glowing terms he described the performance and personality of the Regional Office chief— "He should get an A for efficiency, A for morale of staff—and there's no rating high enough to describe his dedication—" Then his fingers hurriedly traced the remaining items—" In fact, A on everything."

I asked what the purpose of the inspection could be when the results were already known. Without hesitation, he said "For the record. The record is all important. Bear that in mind."

I also asked how he expected the four other members of the Team to fall in line.

"You're the leader of the Team, aren't you?" he said.

I nodded numbly, then mentioned that each member of the Team would be grading different parts of the rating sheet.

"Don't worry," he said a trifle annoyed. "I have already talked to the individual members of the Team."

"What did they say?"

"They agreed."

"About what?"

"The rating." Now he sounded belligerent. Over reaction, I thought.

"They want to keep their jobs, don't they?" he added sharply.

It was impossible not to think back to the inspection that had unmade me at the Department. There, too, the results were predetermined. I visualized Rimestad giving the little lady in blue instructions how to rate me. "On efficiency he gets a D; or even a D−." Now I was the Inspection Officer with the same pre-arranged instructions and the same god-like powers. I gagged at the assignment.

I considered resigning and returning to the State Department, but I could see no future there. A Career Counseling Convention was scheduled for Las Vegas the week after the inspection in Texas. If I attended the Convention, I could make useful contacts for my job hunt the following fall.

"OK, David," I said, "I'll go to Austin and give the regional director the rating he deserves."

"He deserves the highest possible rating."

"I'll give him the rating he deserves," I repeated.

David looked at me aggressively for several long moments, then suddenly relaxed and nodded.

"After the inspection," I added, "I'd like to take five days of annual leave and go to Las Vegas. If that is all right with you?"

"Gambling . . . ?" He seemed surprised and strangely pleased.

I told him about the convention. He chortled a bit and said my travel orders would include a stopover in Nevada.

At first I was tempted to insist on paying for the Las Vegas trip, then figured I had established my independence. If he wanted to bribe me, he knew I was not about to repay him with "the highest possible rating."

The team went to Austin and I was pleasantly surprised to find that the performance of the regional chief was almost as outstanding as David wanted it to be. We gave him a very high rating.

On the way back, I stopped over in Las Vegas. I met representatives of the State University of New York at Albany, the University of North Carolina and Antioch, and was offered a counseling job in all three for the fall. I was tempted to take the SUNY job, but hesitated because I would be counseling students embarking only on domestic careers, without international interests. I didn't feel I had the experience to do that as effectively as counseling students interested in foreign service.

The next week, the School of International Affairs at Columbia University in New York offered me an Associate Deanship to start a Career Counseling Office. I was glad I had hesitated; I accepted with delight.

EPILOGUE

I was still standing in the sunlight outside the State Department building. In the last few minutes the light had not changed. It was brilliant and very hot. My retirement paper was still in my hand.

The journey I had covered—fifty-six years and many continents—achievements and failures, excitement and boredom, pleasure and ignominy, peaks and valleys—was over.

I was tempted to look back at the gloom of the Department lobby, but a new journey lay ahead—to the international capital of the world, New York, which Tennessee Williams once called "that wonderful horrible town."

I put my retirement paper in my pocket and went home to start my packing.

GLOSSARY

Foreign Service posts abroad are either at an embassy in the capital of the country or at a consulate or consulate general located in major cities.

Ambassador: Head of an embassy and highest ranking American in the country—may be a foreign service officer (FSO) or a political appointee.

Chargé: Officer in charge of an embassy when the Ambassador is out of the country.

Counselor of Embassy and/or Deputy Chief of Mission: Number 2 person in the embassy, usually the Chargé in the Ambassador's absence.

The embassy is composed of four divisions or sections, each headed by an FSO:

Political: Follows political events in the country and reports them to the Department of State in Washington with an analysis.

Economic: Follows economic problems in the country and sends analyses to the Department of State.

Administrative: Maintains files, vehicles, personnel records, real estate and buildings owned by the United States government.

Consular: Grants visas to foreigners and protects rights of Americans working in or visiting the country.